The Johannine Gospel's Concept of Community

african christian studies series (africs)

This series will make available significant works in the field of African Christian studies, taking into account the many forms of Christianity across the whole continent of Africa. African Christian studies is defined here as any scholarship that relates to themes and issues on the history, nature, identity, character, and place of African Christianity in world Christianity. It also refers to topics that address the continuing search for abundant life for Africans through multiple appeals to African religions and African Christianity in a challenging social context. The books in this series are expected to make significant contributions in historicizing trends in African Christian studies, while shifting the contemporary discourse in these areas from narrow theological concerns to a broader inter-disciplinary engagement with African religio-cultural traditions and Africa's challenging social context.

The series will cater to scholarly and educational texts in the areas of religious studies, theology, mission studies, biblical studies, philosophy, social justice, and other diverse issues current in African Christianity. We define these studies broadly and specifically as primarily focused on new voices, fresh perspectives, new approaches, and historical and cultural analyses that are emerging because of the significant place of African Christianity and African religio-cultural traditions in world Christianity. The series intends to continually fill a gap in African scholarship, especially in the areas of social analysis in African Christian studies, African philosophies, new biblical and narrative hermeneutical approaches to African theologies, and the challenges facing African women in today's Africa and within African Christianity. Other diverse themes in African Traditional Religions; African ecology; African ecclesiology; inter-cultural, inter-ethnic, and inter-religious dialogue; ecumenism; creative inculturation; African theologies of development, reconciliation, globalization, and poverty reduction will also be covered in this series.

SERIES EDITORS

Dr. Stan Chu Ilo (DePaul University, Chicago, USA)
Dr. Esther Acolatse (University of Toronto, Canada)

"Over and against modernist interpretations of Johannine theology and its ethos as being individualistic or sectarian, this fresh analysis of divine and human love in the Fourth Gospel demonstrates the inadequacy of these monological views. In applying the African values of collectivism, unity, love, and service within Akan Christianity to several key Johannine texts, Godibert Gharbin sheds new light on communality as the heart of John's concept of community. A much-needed corrective to one of John's key riddles, for sure!"

—PAUL N. ANDERSON, author of *The Christology of the Fourth Gospel*

"Drawing on intercultural exegesis as a frame of interpretation, Dr. Godibert Gharbin has provided an insightful theological reflection on the significance of community in the Johannine Gospel and its implication for Akan Christian converts. He has skillfully demonstrated how the incarnation of the divine Word challenges people of all cultures to read and interpret their lives from the perspective of the divine community. Gharbin's research brings freshness into African biblical hermeneutics."

—GEORGE OSSOM-BATSA, Department for the Study of Religions, University of Ghana, Legon

"This book is a precious gift in a contemporary situation characterized by fear of the 'other,' violence, and conflicts because it guides the readers to rediscover in communion the constitutive element of Christianity. God is relationship; the incarnation of the Word (John 1:14) introduced humans into the divine community and empowered them to transform their society in the kingdom of God. The call to action of the text, however, needs to be contextualized in a specific space and time. The author analyses, therefore, the concept of community of the Akan of Ghana to discover how the encounter with the 'divine community' can challenge the Akan who embrace Christianity to rediscover their traditional value, to accept the invitation to dwell in God's love (John 15:1–17) and to mold the world in an inclusive community."

—NICOLETTA GATTI, Associate Professor of Biblical Studies, University of Ghana

"Dr. Gharbin provides a very timely and visionary reflection on faith and community, offering to us a novel theological perspective which blends Johannine thought with African (Akin) tradition and philosophy. In so doing, he inspires cultural renewal and spiritual unity, highly relevant to our current period of fragmentation and conflict."

—Jacobus Kok, Professor of New Testament Studies,
  Evangelische Theologische Faculteit Leuven

The Johannine Gospel's Concept of Community

An Intercultural Reading

GODIBERT KELLY GHARBIN

Foreword by ERNEST VAN ECK

◆PICKWICK *Publications* · Eugene, Oregon

THE JOHANNINE GOSPEL'S CONCEPT OF COMMUNITY
An Intercultural Reading

African Christian Studies Series

Copyright © 2025 Godibert Kelly Gharbin. All rights reserved. Except for brief quotations in critical publications or reviews, no part of this book may be reproduced in any manner without prior written permission from the publisher. Write: Permissions, Wipf and Stock Publishers, 199 W. 8th Ave., Suite 3, Eugene, OR 97401.

Pickwick Publications
An Imprint of Wipf and Stock Publishers
199 W. 8th Ave., Suite 3
Eugene, OR 97401

www.wipfandstock.com

PAPERBACK ISBN: 979-8-3852-2008-3
HARDCOVER ISBN: 979-8-3852-2009-0
EBOOK ISBN: 979-8-3852-2010-6

Cataloguing-in-Publication data:

Names: Gharbin, Godibert Kelly. [author] | Van Eck, Ernest [foreword writer].

Title: The Johannine gospel's concept of community : an intercultural reading / Godibert Kelly Gharbin.

Description: Eugene, OR: Pickwick Publications, 2025 | Series: African Christian Studies Series | Includes bibliographical references.

Identifiers: ISBN 979-8-3852-2008-3 (paperback) | ISBN 979-8-3852-2009-0 (hardcover) | ISBN 979-8-3852-2010-6 (ebook)

Subjects: LCSH: Bible.—John—Criticism, interpretation, etc. | Church—Biblical teaching. | Christianity—Africa, Sub-Saharan. | Akan (African people)—Religion.

Classification: BS2615.2 G43 2025 (print) | BS2615.2 (ebook)

Dedicated to my dear wife,
Priscilla A. A. Gharbin, my greatest supporter.

Table of Contents

Foreword xi

Preface xv

Acknowledgement xvii

Abbreviations xix

1. Introduction 1
2. Analyses of Four Community-Centred Narratives 23
3. Narrative Development of the Community Theme 92
4. The Akan Concept of Community 158
5. Intercultural Reading 185
6. Summary, Conclusions, and Recommendations 228

Bibliography 239

Foreword

IN AN ERA MARKED by increasing individualism, social fragmentation, and cultural dislocation, the concept of community has never been more urgently needed—nor more difficult to achieve. It is within this context that Gharbin's book emerges as a beacon of hope and a profound scholarly contribution. This book is not merely an academic exploration; it is a heartfelt intercultural dialogue that bridges the ancient world of John's Gospel with the vibrant, communal traditions of the Akan people of West Africa. By weaving together biblical exegesis, cultural analysis, and practical theology, Gharbin offers a compelling vision of what it means to live in an authentic community, rooted in the divine example and responsive to the challenges of our time.

The book begins with a bold premise—the Johannine concept of community, deeply rooted in the eternal relationship between the Father, the Son, and the Spirit, provides a transformative framework for addressing the sociocultural crises faced by the Akan Christian community. The author skillfully employs Ossom-Batsa's communicative approach, which emphasizes the interplay between the biblical text, the interpreter's context, and the call to action. This methodological framework allows the book to move seamlessly between the ancient world of John's Gospel and the contemporary realities of Akan culture, creating a rich tapestry of insights that are both intellectually rigorous and deeply practical.

One of the most striking contributions of this book is its exploration of the eternal community as the foundation for all human communal life. The author meticulously traces the narrative development of the community theme in John's Gospel, beginning with the prologue's profound declaration of the Logos' eternal relationship with the Father. This relationship, characterized by intimacy, unity, and reciprocal love, serves as the paradigm for the believing community. Gharbin argues that the incarnation of the Logos is not merely a theological abstraction but a divine invitation to participate in the life of the eternal community. Through Jesus' life, teachings, and sacrificial death, the values of this divine community are revealed and made accessible to humanity.

Gharbin's analysis of key Johannine narratives—the healing at Bethesda, the vine metaphor in John 15, and Jesus' high priestly prayer in John 17—demonstrates how John's Gospel critiques and reimagines community life. These narratives are not merely historical accounts but living testimonies that speak directly to the struggles of the Akan Christian community. The failure of religious authorities and established communal structures in John serves as a call for renewal, one that resonates deeply with Akan Christians navigating the tensions between traditional communal values and contemporary socio-cultural realities.

Equally compelling is Gharbin's engagement with Akan culture. He delves deeply into Akan proverbs, communal values, and anthropological concepts, revealing both the strengths and challenges of Akan communalism. While the Akan tradition emphasizes collectivism and mutual responsibility, Gharbin identifies a tension between these ideals and the realities of modern life, particularly the influence of materialism and individualism. This tension is not unique to the Akan context but reflects a broader global struggle to incarnate communal values in a rapidly changing world.

A positive aspect of this book is its ability to speak prophetically to this struggle. Gharbin does not simply critique Akan culture but offers a constructive pathway forward rooted in the Johannine vision of community. By engaging with the Akan Christian's pre-understanding of unity, love, service, and reciprocity, the study challenges believers to evaluate their communal practices through the lens of Jesus' teachings. The call to embody the values of the divine community is not presented as an abstract ideal but as a tangible, achievable goal. Through the power of the gospel, Akan Christians are invited to transform their communal life, becoming agents of healing and reconciliation in their societies.

This book also makes a significant contribution to pastoral theology. It provides practical recommendations for Akan Christian leaders, urging them to embrace servant leadership, prioritize love over mutual benefit, and reimagine the church as a "community of God." These insights are not limited to the Akan context but have universal relevance for Christian communities seeking to live out the Gospel in their cultural settings.

While writing this foreword, I was reminded of the words of Jesus: "By this everyone will know that you are my disciples, if you love one another" (John 13:35). This book is a powerful reminder that love is the foundation of authentic community and the ultimate testimony of our faith. It challenges us to move beyond theoretical discussions of community and to incarnate its values in our daily lives.

Gharbin's book is a masterful synthesis of biblical scholarship, cultural analysis, and practical theology. It is a call to action for Akan Christians and a source of inspiration for all who seek to build communities that reflect the love, unity, and mission of the divine community. As you engage with the pages of this book, may you be challenged, encouraged, and transformed. May it inspire you to participate more fully in the life of the eternal community and to incarnate its values in your own context.

Ernest van Eck
Principal and New Testament Professor
Knox College, University of Toronto

Preface

THE COPIOUS AND MULTIFARIOUS academic writings on the Johannine corpus makes it a daunting task to explore any of the themes in the Johannine Gospel, as such works must legitimize their inclusion in Johannine scholarship by carving a niche for themselves. Some of the ways to accomplish this is by addressing specific issues that are of great importance to modern readership as a result of their sociocultural ramifications. Against this background, the work explores the Fourth Gospel's concept of community, through a narratological reading of relevant narratives. In the awareness that the contextualization of the biblical text completes the hermeneutical cycle, the study examines its significance for the Akan community of God through an intercultural reading, because of the emphasis on collectivism in their epistemology.

Given that the work employs an intercultural reading, it makes contributions in the ongoing discussions on the Akan concept of communitarianism and Johannine scholarship. Even though the Akan ideation of community has been explored copiously, the acquisitive elements in Akan proverbial lore, the compendium of inestimable information about Akan epistemology and philosophy, have been ignored, raising questions about the academic community's portrayal of Akan communitarianism. Therefore, the attention given to these factors in this work brings new insights to the discussion and invites scholars to reevaluate their positions on this subject.

Additionally, the book makes new contributions to the current scholarship on the concept of community in John in various ways. First, it reads the prologue as a hermeneutical key to the community theme. It also casts the lifestyle of the inhabitants of the microcosmic community at Bethesda as a reflection of the precarious relationship between individualism and collectivism in the Johannine community. Finally, it draws on scholarly literature in such a robust way that different voices in Johannine scholarship are interpreted as a whole to develop a theology of community and trace its narrative development in John. This is done in such a manner that the conclusions of the work remain the idiosyncratic contributions of the author.

Acknowledgements

THE WORK INCLUDES UPDATED versions of previously published articles and is reprinted with permission from the publishers. The author and publisher gratefully recognize the collaboration of these publishers.

Chapter 2, "Narrative Analysis of the Prologue," was first published as "The Johannine Prologue: A Hermeneutical Key to the Community Theme," in *Verbum et Ecclesia* 43 (2022) 1–8, coauthored by Ernest van Eck.

Chapter 2, "Narrative Analysis of John 5," was first published as "Solitude in the Multitude: A Christological Response to Loneliness in the Akan Community of God," in *Verbum et Ecclesia* 44 (2023) 1–8, coauthored by Ernest van Eck.

Chapter 2, "Narrative Analysis of John 15–16:3," was first published as "The True Vine and the Branches: Exploring the Community Ideation in John 15:1–16:3," in *Verbum et Ecclesia* 44 (2023) 1–9, coauthored by Ernest van Eck.

Chapter 5, "Loving as a Community of God," was first published as "Redefining Love: Engaging the Johannine and Akan Concepts of Love through Dialogic Hermeneutics," in *HTS Teologiese Studies/Theological Studies* 79 (2023) 1–6, coauthored by Ernest van Eck.

Chapter 5, "A Call to Godly Service and Care," was first published as "Service and Care in the Johannine and Akan Conceptual Schemas: Inculturation Hermeneutics," in *E-Journal of Religious and Theological Studies* 9 (2023) 1–9.

Chapter 5, "A United Community," was first published as "Building a United Community: Reading the Johannine Concept of Unity Through the Eyes of an Akan Christian," in *HTS Teologiese Studies/Theological Studies* 79 (2023) 1–7, coauthored by Ernest van Eck.

Abbreviations

AA	*American Anthropologist*
ABR	*Australian Biblical Review*
ASE	*Annali di storia dell'exegesis*
ATR	*Anglican Theological Review*
AusBR	*Australian Biblical Review*
CBQ	*Catholic Biblical Quarterly*
Cf.	Confer
Deut	Deuteronomy
ERATS	*E-Journal of Religious and Theological Studies*
Exod	Exodus
GBT	*Ghana Bulletin of Theology*
Gen	Genesis
HBTH	*Horizons in Biblical Theology*
HvTSt	*Hervormde Teologiese Studies*
Isa	Isaiah
JBL	*Journal of Biblical Literature*
JSNTSup	Journal for the Study of the New Testament Supplement Series
JTSA	*Journal of Theology for Southern Africa*
Lev	Leviticus
LumVie	*Lumière et Vie*
Matt	Matthew
n.d.	no date
Neh	Nehemiah
NER	*New England Review*
NovT	*Novum Testamentum*
NT	*Novum Testamentum*
NTS	*New Testament Studies*

Num	Numbers
Ps	Psalms
RB	*Revue Biblique*
RSR	*Recherches de Science Religieuse*
RTR	*Reformed Theological Review*
SBL	Society *of Biblical Literature*
Sir	Sirach
subBi	*Subsibia Biblica*
VE	*Verbum et Ecclesia*
WBC	Word Biblical Commentary
WTJ	Westminster Theological Journal
WUNT	Wissenschaftliche Untersuchungen Zum Neuen Testament

1

Introduction

Background of the Study[1]

THE ASCENDENCY OF AFRICAN biblical hermeneutics over foreign concepts of Bible interpretation in Africa became visible in the 1960s.[2] In his assessment of the diverse methods that have characterized African biblical hermeneutics, Ossom-Batsa affirms that biblical hermeneutics followed the Western cultural viewpoint until this period, when some African theologians initiated hermeneutical models that prioritize contextualizing the Bible.[3] The political milieu around this time made such endeavors conducive due to the wind of colonial liberation that was blowing across the African continent, with its concomitant disconnection from imperialism. The fact that the theological schools used Western paradigms of interpretation before this new era was enough for some African scholars to question the legitimacy and perpetuation of such methods after independence. The discipline's provenance from colonial

---

1. This book presents a reworked version of aspects of my PhD-dissertation, "The Concept of Community in the Johannine Gospel," submitted in the Department of New Testament and Related Literature, University of Pretoria, and supervised by Prof. Dr. Ernest van Eck.

2. Bediako, *Theology and Identity*, 1; Ossom-Batsa, "African Interpretation," 91–92; Maxey, *Orality to Orality*, 50.

3. Ossom-Batsa, "African Interpretation," 91–92. For further reading, see Mbiti, "Bible," 27–39; Ukpong, "Christology and Inculturation," 40–61; "Development in Biblical Interpretation," 11–28.

powers led some to view it with skepticism.⁴ It is pertinent to note that it was not a rejection of hermeneutics but a call to integrate Western methods with a hermeneutical approach that considers the African context, also known as inculturation.

Moreover, the introduction of inculturation was not solely aimed at enhancing the body of knowledge in the field of hermeneutics but rather primarily intended to address an issue of identity. The question of African Christian identity was one of the concerns of African theologians that necessitated the idea of contextualizing or enculturating the message of the Bible in this setting.⁵ Bediako, for instance, stresses that "the question of identity is a key to understanding the concerns of Christian theology in modern Africa and the second century AD."⁶ Christians in Africa encountered what their counterparts in the second century faced: a struggle for identity with dominant cultures.⁷ Consequently, the imperative to ascertain their identification as African Christians became evident. The aforementioned finding could solely be attainable through biblical erudition that accords weight to the interpreter's milieu, acknowledging that the African Christian's identity is indivisible from its cultural or contextual background.⁸ According to Adamo's exposition, culture serves as the environment where the interaction between God and humanity may occur.⁹ In order to facilitate the process of identity reformation, it was deemed necessary to establish a connection between Western scholarship and the Africanization of their faith.¹⁰ It involved the replacement of Western cultural incidents with African cultural elements.¹¹

This necessitated the promotion of inculturation as a tool to afford Africans the opportunity to discover and maintain their identity as African Christians.¹² Inculturation is the ongoing dialogue between faith and

---

4. Gatti, "Toward a Dialogic Hermeneutics," 46–47.

5. Maxey, *Orality to Orality*, 25–28.

6. Bediako, *Theology and Identity*, 1.

7. Bediako, *Christianity in Africa*, 256. See also Maluleke, "Identity and Integrity," 29; Maxey, *Orality to Orality*, 54–55.

8. For some examples of how scholars have incarnated the New Testament, see Getui et al., *Interpreting the New Testament*, 120–44.

9. Adamo, *Reading and Interpreting the Bible*, 43.

10. See Martey, *African Theology*, 55.

11. Martey, *African Theology*, 55.

12. Bediako, *Christianity in Africa*, 256.

culture.¹³ More fully, it is the creative and dynamic relationship between the Christian message and a culture or cultures. Ukpong concurs that inculturation "involves interactive engagement between the biblical text and a particular contemporary sociocultural issue where the gospel message serves as a critique of the culture or the cultural perspective enlarges and enriches the understanding of the text."¹⁴ Consequently, one needs a text and a present context since the "focus of [African] interpretation is on the theological meaning of the text within a contemporary context."¹⁵ Therefore, the African who reads the Bible will be interested in its significance in the African context.

Reading the Gospel of John from an African perspective allows readers to consider dimensions not fully explored by western-oriented exegesis. For example, one of these is the idea of community, a key concept in both contexts.¹⁶ The indigenous African concept of humanism emphasizes communalism above individualism, to the extent that the individual cannot exist alone except corporately.¹⁷ Mbiti affirms that from the moment a person comes out of the womb until he enters the tomb, it is the community that defines his identity. Whether in life or death, the African belongs to the community.¹⁸ Thus, Africans perform rites for children after birth as a means of incorporating them into society. The dead are also "ritually incorporated into the wider family of both the dead and the living."¹⁹ The concept of communal identity is the underlying reason for the prevalent practice of burying the deceased on their native land in many African societies, as noted by Smith.²⁰ As Kaunda confirms, one's Africanness has its roots in the soil of the African continent.²¹

Mbiti, like most African scholars, stresses that the cardinal point in the understanding of the African view of humans is their appreciation of collectivism: whatever happens to the individual happens to the whole

---

13. Shorter, *Theology of Inculturation*, 11.

14. Ukpong, "Reading the Bible," 6. See also West, "African Biblical Scholarship," 249.

15. Ukpong, "Reading the Bible," 6.

16. See Mbiti, *African Religions*; Gyekye, *African Cultural Values*; Watt, *Family of the King*.

17. Mbiti, *African Religions*, 106; Gyekye, *African Philosophical Thought*, 155.

18. Mbiti, *African Religions*, 106; cf. Opoku, *Akan Proverbs*, 28.

19. Mbiti, *African Religions*, 106.

20. Smith, "Burials, 569.

21. Kaunda, *Letter*, 17.

group, or vice versa.[22] So, one can only say, "I am because we are, and since we are, therefore I am."[23] This dictum expresses the "logic" of the standard for the indigenous African's authentication and validation of reality, that is, communalism.[24] Therefore, it is incumbent upon members to exhibit their cultural (communal) values. They include sharing not only the joys of life's experiences but also their sorrows and perplexities. These are evident in caring for others, solidarity, reciprocal obligation, and social harmony.[25]

Likewise, communal values hold significant importance in Akan society. As a child of Akan descent residing in an Akan community, I observed the manifestation of communalism both within households and the community at large, particularly during events such as funerals, naming ceremonies, weddings, and cultural celebrations.[26] According to Gyekye, society is viewed as natural to human beings in their philosophical framework, rather than solely serving as a prerequisite for survival.[27] Some of these concepts could be extrapolated from Akan aphorisms and proverbial lore. For instance, the maxim "When a person descends from heaven, he or she descends into a human society" affirms the above point.[28] Gyekye maintains that embedded in the idea of descending from heaven into human society is the belief that human beings are created by the Supreme Being to live in a community.[29]

The criticality of the origin of human beings in Akan humanism is evident in its inextricable connection to the concept of society. If the human being is believed to originate from God, it follows that one is defined by one's celestial lineage but not by one's biological ancestry. Thus, the origin of the concept of community and the need for communality stem from the idea that since all human beings are children of God, the individual belongs to God and humanity, not his or her parents alone. This explains the Akan proverb, "all human beings are children of God; no one is a child of the earth."[30]

22. Mbiti, *African Religions*, 106.
23. Mbiti, *African Religions*, 72.
24. Dogbe, "Concept of Community," 790.
25. Mbiti, *African Religions*, 72; Gyekye, *African Philosophical Thought*, 154–58.
26. See Dogbe, "Concept of Community," 792.
27. Gyekye, *African Philosophical Thought*, 155.
28. Appiah et al., *Proverbs*, 201; Gyekye, *African Cultural Values*, 36.
29. Gyekye, *African Philosophical Thought*, 155.
30. Gyekye, *African Cultural Values*, 23–24.

Further, these beliefs form the substratum of human relationships. The way people treat each other is based on this foundation. Gyekye notes:

> The insistent claim made in this maxim is based on the belief that there must be something intrinsically valuable in God: the human being, considered a child of God, presumably by reason of having been created by God and having in his or her nature some aspect of God, ought also to be held as of intrinsic value, worthy of dignity and respect.[31]

With this understanding, society recognizes the need to reflect its beliefs in communal living. These are embodied in Akan proverbs such as "*onipa hia mmoa* [A human being needs help]," "*onipa na ɛhia* [It is a human that is needed]," "*onipa na ɔma onipa yɛ yiye* [A human being must depend for his or her well-being on his or her fellow human being]," and many others. Explaining this concept, Gyekye's elucidation on one of the maxims [A human being needs help] is worthy of consideration. "The real meaning of the maxim, then," he asserts, "is that a human being deserves, and therefore ought, to be helped."[32] In summary, help for the human being in the Akan setting is an entitlement.

In addition to this entitlement, the individual has responsibilities. Community necessitates contributions from the individual members of the group. Therefore, there cannot be a "communal" devoid of the individual. Primarily, society is based more on obligations than individual rights; people assume their rights in the exercise of their obligations, which makes society a chain of interrelationships.[33] This warrants the expectation of individual contributions towards the realization of the collective goal. The following are some of the proverbs outlined by Opoku, Gyekye, and Ackah to that effect: "*Benkum guare nifa, na nifa guare benkum* [The left arm washes the right arm, and the right arm washes the left arm]"; "*Akyekyedie se nsa kɔ na nsa aba* [The tortoise says, the hand goes, and a hand comes]"; and "*Huw m'ani so ma me, nti na atwe abien nam* [The reason two deer walk together is that one must take the moth from the other's eyes]."[34]

---

31. Gyekye, *African Cultural Values*, 24.
32. Gyekye, *African Cultural Values*, 24.
33. Opoku, *Traditional Religion*, 11; Gyekye, *African Philosophical Thought*, 156–62.
34. Opoku, *Traditional Religion*, 17; Gyekye, *African Cultural Values*, 188–89; Ackah, *Akan Ethics*, 53.

Nonetheless, the depiction of a functional social or communal system that is inferred from these proverbs exhibits certain inadequacies that are frequently overlooked.[35] Commencing with the topic at hand, it is noteworthy to acknowledge the distinction between the theoretical and practical aspects of communalism as it pertains to Akan ideologies and communities.[36] Gyekye acknowledges that despite society's effective dissemination of diverse moral knowledge to its constituents, not all individuals are able to actualize it into conduct.[37] Moreover, culture is characterized by a dynamic nature, implying that over time, alterations in the attitudes and customs of individuals are both feasible and anticipated. Thus, this position appears to suggest that the representation of Akan culture is anachronistic. Furthermore, scholarly research suggests that the process of urbanization and its corresponding socio-economic challenges foster individualistic tendencies, rendering it impractical to universally apply these principles to all urban regions inhabited by the Akan people.[38] Finally, Akan and other African scholars commonly depict the Akan notion of community as predominantly communal. Consequently, proverbs that convey a strong sense of individualism do not receive the same emphasis as those that align with communal values.

Paradoxically, present in this milieu are other proverbs that seem to affirm that some of the portraits of the concept of community presented in the Akan setting by the academic community rest on questionable assumptions. For instance, a proverb like "Life is as you make it" can breed both self-reliance and selfishness.[39] If the outcome of a person's

---

35. Kissi interprets the Akan adage "No one points to his or her father's village with his or her left hand" as the consciousness of the Akans to speak well of their ethnic group. Kissi, *Social Identity*, 21. In this setting, using the left hand in public is a sign of impoliteness and disrespectfulness. Opoku, *Akan Proverbs*, 20. Thus, its place in the adage means that speaking ill of this group would be tantamount to disrespecting the Akans. Perhaps this is one of the reasons why most Akan scholars do not stress the negatives with the same intensity as the positives.

36. Great voices like Kwame Gyekye and Kwasi Wiredu are not oblivious to this; however, they give extraordinarily little attention to these proverbs in their analysis of the balance between communality and individuality.

37. Gyekye, *African Perspectives*, 212.

38. Gyekye, in the conclusion of his discussion of communal and individual values, anticipates that urbanization and cultural changes are most likely to cause society to tilt more in favor of individualism. Gyekye, *African Cultural Values*, 50–51. See also Howard-Hassmann, *Human Right*, 28; Abraham, "Crisis," 14.

39. It is significant to note that Gyekye interprets these proverbs in support of the idea of creating awareness to be self-reliant without considering the problem of

life is solely dependent on himself or herself, those who struggle to succeed would want others to follow that trajectory. Again, others would use every means possible to "make it," even if they had to step on people to get there. Hence, the Akans say, "*adwene di adwene a, na ɔdore* [If fish eats fish, then it grows fat]," that is, we climb by pushing down others.[40] These are signs of a precarious relationship between communalism and individualism in this model of society.

Recognizing this conundrum, Akans who embrace Christianity and thus consider communalism as a traditional, theological, and missiological value must find in their faith (i.e., in the Bible) a way of reinvigorating communalism in their tradition, challenged by urbanization and globalization. In the New Testament, the church is presented as a group with the calling to be the community of God (or God's people) in anticipation of the kingdom.[41] And hence, members must live in unity, love, peace, and harmony, in the awareness that the church as an ecclesiastical community, is the foretaste of the eschatological hope for the whole human community.[42] Consequently, as members of the universal church, Akan Christians have the responsibility to pursue this mission.

Reading the early accounts of the life and mission of Jesus and his community, John appears to offer a unique contribution to the identity and mission of the community of the disciples. The writer of the book of John addressed a community that was undergoing a period of difficulty, as evidenced by various scholarly sources.[43] The author's teachings emphasized the importance of unity, which was to be achieved by emulating the harmonious and loving relationship within the divine community, as exemplified in passages such as John 15:9–17 and 17:21. This teaching may be construed as either a lack of harmony and shared

---

a potential breeding of individualism in a context that boasts of communalism. He admits, however, that the maxim "The clan is [merely] a multitude" means that within a clan there are no specific and reliable persons to always turn to for the fulfillment of one's needs. Gyekye, *African Cultural Values*, 48.

40. Appiah et al., *Proverbs*, 104.

41. Grenz, *Community of God*, 22–24; cf. Harrison and Dvorak, *New Testament Church*, 1–225.

42. Aye-Addo, *Akan Christology*, 173. The author stresses that in Christian understanding, the church as a whole community is the inheritor of the mission and ministry of the church.

43. Quast, *Gospel of John*, 7; Brown, *Community*, 97–106; Watt, *Introduction*, 20–21; Dunn, *Evidence*, 41–42; Martyn, *History and Theology*, 18–19; Kruse, *Gospel According to John*, 36.

responsibility within the community or the manifestation of a variant of collectivism that deviates from the divine conception of an ideal society. Consequently, the author endeavored to address these social issues by incorporating teachings from the Johannine Jesus. Hence, the prescriptions provided by John can serve as a guiding principle for the Akan community of adherents in addressing their communal issues. This can facilitate a re-examination and re-adoption of their traditional practices from the perspective of their newfound religious beliefs.

A critical exegetical analysis of John points to the importance of the community theme for the evangelist. John is not only a gospel written for a specific society but also about the concept of community. It is important to note that the author writes a narrative, a story that has a perlocutionary effect: to guide his readers to understand the concept of *community* and build a *missionary* community. It is evident from the introduction of the theme in the prologue and its explication in the Gospel.[44]

The prologue commences with John's depiction of a divine community comprised of the Logos and God (John 1:1–2). The fundamental constituents of the term divine community are the ontological equality, coexistence, communion, intimacy, communication, and cooperation that are manifested in the act of creation as described in John 1:3–5.

Again, implied in the Johannine concept of the divine community is the connotation that the community concept goes back to eternity. John dates the relationship between God and the Logos to the beginning (John 1:1). Ἐν ἀρχῇ (ēn archē) refers to a period before creation.[45] The implication is that John is not suggesting "a definite localized point of time, but rather an indefinite eternity."[46]

Moreover, the community concept became incarnated in human history when the Word became flesh to incarnate and exegete it, making the incarnation of the Logos the manifestation of the quintessential community in human history (cf. John 1:14, 18). Jesus descends from the ideal community into the world (John 1:11, 14) to give us a model of society. For instance, the relationship between God and the Logos demonstrates the possibility and aesthetic value of "unity in diversity" (John

---

44. The idea that the narrative only reflects the themes in the prologue is accepted by many Johannine scholars. Köstenberger, *Encountering John*, 44; *Missions of Jesus*, 87; Moloney, *Belief in the Word*, 24; Robinson, "Prologue," 122; Morris, *John*, 63; Carson, *John*, 111.

45. Moloney, *Belief in the Word*, 35.

46. Tenney, *John*, 64.

1:1). Hence, replicating the coexistence of two eternal distinctions, Jesus promotes unity in diversity in the human community. Consequently, in John, the ideal community is the theological basis for the existence of human society.⁴⁷

The concept of society that God had was actualized in a human community through the incarnation. The act of embodying the everlasting community extends beyond the Logos' manifestation in human form, encompassing the dissemination of his comprehension of the Father and the bestowal of the Spirit (cf. John 1:14, 29–34; 5:17–47; 15:26). The process of incarnation began with the calling of the disciples. Two disciples of John the Baptist who decided to become Jesus' disciples questioned Jesus about where He lives (John 1:38). Their question did not only necessitate an answer, but also commenced the process of gathering members for this new community.⁴⁸ Andrew's discovery of a novel community prompted him to introduce his brother, Simon Peter (John 1:42). Jesus also invited Philip to become part of the community (1:43). Philip found Nathaniel and asked him to come and see Jesus (1:45–46). And they became a new family that attended functions together (2:2).⁴⁹

With this new community thriving, the author elucidates societal issues using individual encounters. Apart from the disciples who encountered Jesus, there are two encounters with individuals that give the reader some ideas about this community, namely Nicodemus and the Samaritan woman. Going to see Jesus at night, Nicodemus reminds the reader of the conflict between the light and the darkness anticipated in the prologue.⁵⁰ It makes Nicodemus's journey a movement from darkness towards the light, thereby indicating that the people of this society are those who have moved from darkness into the light.⁵¹ Their conversation also shows that membership in the community is not dependent on biological birth but on a spiritual birth: birth through the Spirit determines the Christian identity (John 3:3).⁵²

---

47. See Grenz, *Community of God*, 112; Kanagaraj, *John*, 2.
48. See Talbert, *Reading John*, 83.
49. See Talbert, *Reading John*, 83–90.
50. Moloney, *Belief in the Word*, 108.
51. Moloney, *Belief in the Word*, 108.
52. As customary of John, this is a furtherance of the thought on those who embrace Christ in the prologue. They are born not of blood, nor of the will of the flesh, nor of the will of a human being, but of God (John 1:12–13). See also Burge, *Anointed Community*, 171.

Additionally, the encounter with the Samaritan woman at the well further heightens the centrality of community in John. Jesus' words to the woman show that the novel community defies race and racial boundaries (it belongs to neither Jews nor Samaritans) and instead encompasses all individuals who partake of the water supplied by the Son (John 4:9–14). In Christ, "the well of salvation," people who "have no dealings with each other" (4:9) or are divided by ethnic and ideological disparities are united to worship the Father in truth and spirit (4:23–24).[53]

Statement of the Problem

Given the centrality of the concept of community in both realities and the challenges Akans who embrace Christianity face with the precarious relationship between communalism and individualism in their context, how can the Akan Christian reader develop an interpretation that is reverential towards the biblical text and relevant to the culture? This study proposes an intercultural reading of the concept of community in the Johannine gospel through the narrative analysis of selected texts. Furthermore, it examines how Akan Christians read and engage the theme of community in the Johannine gospel through an intercultural reading.

Research Questions

The main questions of the study are:

1. What is the concept of a community of God in John?
2. What is the contribution of the Logos to the exegesis and incarnation of the divine community?

The following are the sub-questions:

1. How can the prologue become a hermeneutical key to explore the concept of community in John?
2. How can John guide Akan Christians to revitalise their tradition of communalism, challenged by urbanisation and globalization?
3. What relationship exists between John's culture and that of the Akans?

---

53. Köstenberger, *John*, 149.

Objectives

The focus is to explore the narrative development of the concept of community in John through narrative analyses of relevant narratives and examine its significance for the Akan community in an intercultural reading, using the communicative approach as the theoretical framework.

Literature Review and Research Gap

Generally, there are two overarching categories associated with how scholars employ the term community: territorial and relational. Whereas the former encompasses the context of location, physical territory, and geographical continuity, the latter points to the quality of relationships.[54] The study concentrates on the narrative development of the theme through the analysis of relevant narratives and reflects on its missionary relevance for the Akan Christian. Following the definition means that the quality of relationships in both realities is the focus. In this regard, the research discusses the literature that explores the community in John and the general interpretations of relevant narratives on the topic.

Johannine Concept of Community: Works and Research Gap

The study aims to explore the narrative development of the community theme because, even though most Johannine scholars opine that John stresses community,[55] the existing literature does not give attention to the above. What exists are works that examine some aspects of the community in John, such as problems in the community and the stress on communality. There are two potential explanations for this phenomenon: firstly, the characteristics of the narratives that emphasize the significance of community in John, and secondly, the inclinations of scholars who specialize in the study of the Johannine literature. John is replete with "materials" reflecting a believing community's interests, concerns, and experiences.[56] However, scholars discuss the quality of relationships

---

54. Gusfield, *Community*, xv–xvi; Cohen, *Community*, 12; Klink, *Sheep of the Fold*, 52.

55. Wenham, "Paradigm," 8; Loader, *Jesus in John's Gospel*, 142; Koester, *Fourth Gospel*, 247.

56. Martyn, *History and Theology*, 145. See also Aune, *Early Christianity*, 73–84.

among members of the believing community and the world through the prism of individual interests.

Brown and Martyn deserve special mention for their contributions to Johannine scholarship and community.[57] Both scholars attempt to excavate the history of John using the same approach: reading John on several levels so that it tells the story of Jesus and the believing community. However, Brown, Kobel, and Culpepper agree that a thorough application of the method is Martyn's contribution.[58]

Furthermore, in reconstructing this history, Brown, Martyn, and others identify problems that militate against communalism, including both internal and external conflicts ("relationship problems").[59] Scholars have postulated three main views on the conflicting factions: Christians, Jews, and Jews-Christians. Scholars who agree with the first view include Dodd and Jonge.[60] Dodd's view stems from the commonalities he draws from his comparative and semantic analyses of οἱ Ἰουδαῖοι in Galatians and John.[61] Jonge, on the other hand, builds his argument on what he considers an authorial intention of John: a polemic targeted against Christians who refused to accept the christological understanding of the Johannine group (non-Johannine Christians).[62] Dunn and Boer, conversely, advocate for a reading of the conflict on *racial* grounds.[63] Thus, Boer emphasizes that the conflict is between "two groups of Jewish people (Johannine Jewish Christians and the Jews)."[64] Finally, the position of most scholars is that the conflict is between Jews ("the Jews") and Christians.[65]

Who constituted the group commonly referred to as the Jews? What was the rationale behind their opposition to the community of believers? Anderson's classification of the diverse methods aimed at identifying this

---

57. Brown, *Community*; Martyn, *History and Theology*.

58. Brown, *Community*; Kobel, *Dining with John*, 27; Culpepper, *John*, 43. See also Martyn, *History and Theology*.

59. Brown, *Community*; Martyn, *History and Theology*; cf. Brodie, *Quest for the Origin*, 10–14.

60. Dodd, "Johannine Dialogue," 41–57; Jonge, "Jews," 121–40.

61. Dodd, "Johannine Dialogue," 41–57.

62. Jonge, "Jews," 121.

63. Dunn, "John," 293–322; Boer, "Jews," 149.

64. Boer, "Jews," 149.

65. Martyn, *History and Theology*, 18–19; Culpepper, "Anti-Judaism," 63; Reinhartz, "Jews," 225.

demographic warrants particular recognition. Anderson outlines seven different approaches that have characterized the reading of οἱ Ἰουδαῖοι in John as follows: (a) Seeing John as theologically anti-Jewish; (b) reading "the Jews" as a reference to "the Judeans" within Palestine or the Levant in general; (c) taking the term to mean "particular Jewish authorities" who wanted to do away with Jesus; (d) considering the presentation of religious authorities in John as narrative characters who represent the ambivalent relationships with local Jewish authorities by Johannine Christians in a diaspora setting, as they sought to convince family and friends that Jesus was indeed the Jewish Messiah, sometimes to no avail; (e) viewing John's presentation of the Jews as archetypes of the unbelieving world: the world; (f) a sixth approach is to see John as pro-Jewish; and finally, (g) a proposal for an integrated approach that requires more than one of the above.[66]

However, out of the seven approaches that have characterized the reading of the term, the majority view is that John employs it generally for Jewish religious leaders.[67] However, scholars who rely on the application of double meanings in John opine that it includes the followers of the Jewish ecclesiastical authorities.[68]

Furthermore, two specific concerns served as the catalysts for the conflict between this group and Christians. One of the primary reasons was Jesus' assertion of his divinity. Another factor was the Christians' conviction in Jesus' messiahship.[69]

Additionally, there are community dissensions, which have received scholarly attention.[70] Based on the correlation between the epistles and the gospel,[71] the general interpretation extrapolated from juxtaposing the narratives on communalism in John to the ones on dissension in the

---

66. Anderson, "Anti-Semitism and Religious Violence."

67. See Brown, *Community*, 41; Martyn, *History and Theology*, 41; Köstenberger, *Encountering John*, 26; Dunn, *Evidence*, 41; Morris, *John*, 357; Moloney, *John*, 97.

68. Boer, "Jews," 148; Wheaton, *Jewish Feasts*, 41.

69. Dunn, "Embarrassment of History," 47; Brown, *Community*, 43–46; Martyn, *History and Theology*, 46–47; Ridderbos, *John*, 10; Culpepper, "Anti-Judaism," 62.

70. In determining the nature of internal issues, the scholarly discussions take into consideration the Johannine corpus (apart from the apocalypse of John), for in the epistles is the appearance of the problem. See Brown, *Community*, 56; *New Testament*, 133.

71. Both are parts of the Johannine corpus.

letters[72] is that the community had problems with schisms over divergent christological positions.[73]

Ironically, there are expectations in the gospel that indicate that the Johannine community was to demonstrate a form of communal living. In consequence, scholars have devised various methods to explore how the Gospel of John articulates God's ideal community to a group plagued by external and internal conflicts. One of these is, for instance, the attempt to establish the concept of ethnicity in John and its implications for the believing community or the church as a community of God.[74] Generally, these works focus on ethnic labeling or characterization in John to extrapolate a position on how the Johannine community handled ethnicity.

Despite the similarity of goals, the above scholars follow different trajectories. Arguing from a Johannine pneumatological standpoint, Estrada underscores the significance of the Holy Spirit in the formation of communal identity by examining how the community's theology of the Holy Spirit helped them to respond to the ethnic challenges of their times and exist as a community of God, constituted by members from different ethnic backgrounds.[75] Estrada's work is based on the Spirit's role or involvement in the conversion of members of the new (believing) community through the new birth into one body. Conversely, Penwell focuses on the ethnic characterization of Jesus in John ("Jesus the Jew" and "Jesus the Samaritan") to argue that the author used ethnic labeling to assert a trans-ethnic identity for Jesus' followers and augment the traditional Judean ethnic identity into one community: "children of God, who were born, not of blood or the will of the flesh or man, but God (John 1:12b–13)."[76] In contrast to Penwell's methodology, Lim concentrates on the ethnic characterisation of the mother of Jesus and John the Beloved.[77] His study establishes that the function of the ethnic portrayal of the mother of Jesus (a Galilean Jew) and John the beloved (a Judean Jew), vis-à-vis Jesus' command to adopt each as family members, is to

---

72. Some of the narratives in John that stress communality are John 15:1–17 and 17. In the Johannine letters, 1 John 2:18–22; 4:2–3; and 2 John 7 have the same focus.

73. Boer, *Johannine Perspectives*, 63; Brown, *New Testament*, 133; Skinner, "Virtue," 305; Harris and Harris, *1, 2, 3 John*, 21.

74. Penwell, *Jesus the Samaritan*; Estrada, *Gospel of John*; Lim, *Otherness*.

75. Estrada, *Gospel of John*, 4.

76. Penwell, *Jesus the Samaritan*, 1.

77. Lim, *Otherness*, 140–50.

show that in Christ, people from heterogeneous ethnic backgrounds become one family: children of God.[78]

Moreover, alternative methodologies are employed by some scholars, prioritizing the thematic categorization of communal narratives in the Gospel of John for their communal implications. However, a select few merit particular recognition for the all-encompassing scope of their literary contributions. Bauckham's study focuses on John's usage of the term "one" and its implications for the concept of "individualism" assessment as well as the unity between the divine and human community within the narrative.[79] Kobel employs a socio-rhetorical methodology to illustrate the significance of communal meals in fostering group cohesion, community establishment, and group identification.[80] Specifically, Kobel elucidates how communal experiences are intricately linked to meal scenes in the Gospel of John. Furthermore, drawing from the analysis of Kanagaraj and Kunene, it can be observed that John utilizes the concept of mutual indwelling to emphasize the importance of unity and community within the communal passages.[81] According to Kunene, the narratives emphasize communal holiness as their central theme.[82]

Moreover, some scholars investigate the concept of kinship in the Gospel of John in order to comprehend the nature of interpersonal connections, utilizing diverse analytical approaches. Campbell employs a social-science methodology to examine the concept of kinship in the Gospel of John.[83] Specifically, the study centers on the interplay between Jesus, his biological and fictive families, and the resulting effects on the nature of relationships depicted in the Gospel.

Furthermore, some individuals analyze narratives that explore John's use of familial terminology as a metaphor to reveal the Father-Son relationship and its significance for the disciples. Scholars such as Thompson, Moloney, and Watt have engaged in discourse regarding the concept of the "family relationship" within the context of the Gospel of John.[84] Despite Stovell's objections regarding certain aspects of Watt's

78. Lim, *Otherness*, 150.
79. Bauckham, *Gospel of Glory*, 1–34.
80. Kobel, *Dining with John*, 2–4.
81. Kanagaraj, *Mysticism*, 264–70; Kunene, *Communal Holiness*, 208–16.
82. Kunene, *Communal Holiness*, 208–16.
83. Campbell, *Kinship Relations*, 26–57.
84. Academic scholars do not overlook the familial connection that exists between the Father and the Son. Even academics who have not conducted exhaustive research

work, it provides a thorough examination of the subject.[85] Watt's analysis involves a critical examination of the family metaphor in the Gospel of John and its potential implications for the Johannine community as a family of God.[86] Thus, delving into the familial lexicon (e.g., father, son, brothers, house, birth, and life), he explores the Father-Son relationship and establishes its effects on the character of the relationship required of the disciples.[87]

From the above, John 15 and 17 are the most commonly discussed narratives concerning the church as a community of God. And, generally, these chapters are interpreted as stressing communal values such as unity and love for members of the believing community.[88]

Identifying the Research Gap

Despite the scholarly attempts to establish the character and quality of relationships in John, there are still gaps that the various approaches devised to explore communalism in John have not filled. To begin with, no author has read the Johannine prologue through the lens of community. Therefore, no work in the existing literature considers the prologue as a hermeneutical key to unearthing the concept of community in John (as established in the background of this study). The significance of community in John requires tracing the theme from the prologue to the Book of Glory. It helps to discover its perlocutionary effect on the narrative, the role of the Logos in community building, and the responsibilities of the believing community in that role. However, the discussions on the

---

on the topic make brief references to it. Thompson, Watt, and Moloney are among the scholars who have conducted extensive research on the topic. Thompson's interpretation of the Johannine situation and its implications for the disciples is contextualized within Jewish notions of fatherhood and sonship. Moloney utilizes literary analysis as a methodology in his trilogy of works. The author examines the relationship between fathers and sons and its impact on communal relationships, particularly in situations where pertinent narratives are present. On the other hand, Watt's work is notably the most all-encompassing piece of literature regarding the topic. See Thompson, *Gospel of John*; Watt, *Family of the King*; Moloney, *Belief in the Word*.

85. Stovell criticizes his view of the family metaphor as the most prominent for being unhelpful and unnecessary. See Stovel, *Fourth Gospel*, 22.

86. Though John is replete with metaphors, his view of the family metaphor as the most prominent is the substratum for his concentration on the subject. Watt, *Family of the King*, 161–209, 260–377.

87. Watt, *Family of the King*, 161.

88. For instance, Watt, *Family of the King*, 260–377; Ridderbos, *John*, 514–20.

prologue generally focus on its origin, themes, structure, and place in the gospel.[89] Thus, this work seeks to contribute to the debate by analyzing the prologue's development of the theme. Owing to the significant importance of the prologue, its analysis allows the reader to explore the foundation of the community theme.

Furthermore, the account of the miraculous healing of the lame man at the pool of Bethesda is not construed as a narrative that reveals the correlation between communalism and individualism within the Johannine community. The analysis of John 5 and its overall interpretations emphasize the recognition of Jesus' identity as the Lord of the Sabbath and the Sabbath motif.[90] Therefore, an alternative methodology is necessary, one that takes into account the community motif, which has previously been overlooked.

An analysis of John 5 through the lens of community reveals that the healing at Bethesda is a hermeneutical key for an informed understanding of the precarious relationship between individualism and collectivism in Bethesda, a microcosm of the Johannine community. The story makes it imperative to investigate whether some of the cultural values attributed to this community existed in practice or only in theory. For instance, the first-century Mediterranean culture in which John wrote[91] stresses cooperativeness as a cultural value.[92] Cooperativeness, according to Pilch, is best interpreted as "help."[93] It is, consequently, astonishing that the sick man could not get help (John 5:7) at the pool of Bethesda. The attitude of the Bethesda community makes it legitimate to interrogate whether their society was purely communalistic, individualistic, or amphibious. Indeed, Rohrbaugh affirms that two types of seemingly individualistic behavior existed in the Mediterranean culture, even though they were collectivists.[94] Could it be that the "Bethesda community" exhibited traces of individualism? To what degree did it impact the community? Why did the inhabitants exhibit attributes that are antithetical to the tenets of collectivism? In attempting to provide perspicuous answers to this conundrum, the narrative is subjected to a narratological analysis to aid

---

89. See Morris, *John*, 63–100; Köstenberger, *Encountering John*, 44.

90. See Moloney, *Signs and Shadows*, 4–27; Bystrom, *God Among Us*, 98–106; Witherington, *John's Wisdom*, 136–41.

91. Keener, *John*, xxvi.

92. Pilch, "Cooperativeness," 33.

93. Pilch, "Cooperativeness," 33.

94. Rohrbaugh "Ethnocentrism," 35–36.

the reader in appreciating the context of Jesus' message on communality in the farewell discourse of the Book of Glory.

Moreover, since the prologue guides the reader to establish the substratum of the theme and John 5 aids in anticipating and appreciating the discourse on communality in the Book of Glory, the narrative analysis can serve as a lens to ascertain the narrative development of the community theme. It also fills an academic gap that existing studies have not attempted to fill.

Finally, as indicated above, two narratives that address the issue of community in the farewell discourse of the Book of Glory are John 15 and 17. Consequently, the two narratives have been selected for the analysis because of their complementary roles in addressing the community theme. For instance, whereas John 17 is a prayer for unity, John 15 reiterates the source of Christian communalism, reveals how the disciples can replicate the divine community, and establishes the mission of the believing community.[95] Furthermore, both chapters do not present divergent concepts. Rather, they converge at some point; the central theme of love, for instance, is reiterated in both narratives (John 15:9–17; 17:23–26). However, in John 15, love is a commandment (vv. 12–17) that must be demonstrated. Further, the stress on loving one another is more recurrent in John 15 (implicitly in John 15:9–10 and explicitly in John 15:12, 17) than in John 17:26. Indeed, unlike in John 15, where there is a "balanced discussion" on the love between the Father and the Son and between the members of the human community, the theme of love in John 17 focuses more on the love between the Father and the Son (vv. 23–26). Thus, the selected narratives allow the interpreter to prescribe remedies for the societal maladies in the Akan community because of the scope of the issues they examine. Therefore, through narrative analysis of John 15:1—16:3 and John 17, the community theme is analyzed to explore Jesus' paradigm of community and collectivism presented to the disciples for emulation.

---

95. See Köstenberger, *Missions of Jesus*, 15; Ridderbos, *John*, 514–20; Skinner, *John*, 998–1002.

Methodology

Theoretical Framework

The theoretical framework for this research is Ossom-Batsa's communicative approach.[96] The Ghanaian scholar proposes a tripartite level as a frame of interpretation: adherence to the biblical text, attention to the call of action proposed in the text, and the interpreter's context.[97] Adhering to the text, he surmises, is to pay attention to the linguistic and non-linguistic elements to get an informed understanding of the communicative force of the text, which has been deliberately constructed by the author to aid his audience on their journey of reading. The call to action in the text, on the other hand, is the communicative function of the text. Primarily, it is the understanding that emanates from respecting the text and the journey of the implied reader that becomes a call to action for real readers.[98] Furthermore, the interpreter's context is the frame within which the dialogue between God and humanity transpires.[99] The context is pertinent because the realization of the call to action in the text is conditioned by the context of the real readers.[100] It must be noted, however, that the community of readers must guard against "enslaving" the text or rendering it docile to its context. Rather, the text should always have a central position.

The contextual theologian acknowledges that the tripartite levels are not a linear progression but rather a framework for interpretation. Nonetheless, certain procedures are deemed necessary to be carried out prior to others. For example, the identification of the call to action in the text is achieved through analysis. It simply means that before the enculturation of the narrative, the reader should respect the text, discover the call to action, and then enculturate it in his context. Thus, the communicative approach is applied using the tripartite levels as a frame of interpretation.

---

96. Ossom-Batsa, "Biblical Exegesis."
97. Ossom-Batsa, "Biblical Exegesis," 128.
98. Ossom-Batsa, "Biblical Exegesis," 129.
99. Ossom-Batsa, "Biblical Exegesis," 129–30.
100. The real reader is the contemporary reader of the text. See Brown, *Scripture as Communication*, 129–30. Brown further mentions another group of readers: the implied reader. This, she opines, are the textually constructed "reader presupposed by the narrative" or texts. Brown, *Disciples in Narrative Perspective*, 32.

The Application of the Theoretical Framework

In accordance with the communicative approach, the study employed narrative criticism in the *first step* (adherence to the biblical text)—narrative analyses of the prologue, John 5; 15—16:3; and 17—because it analyzes how the author conveys a theological message through narratives.[101] Narrative criticism is a method of reading the text that explores how narrativity is made concrete in a particular text.[102] This is accomplished by studying the narratological components, including but not limited to the settings, plots, characters, narrative time, narrative world, implicit commentaries, the implied narrator, and reader, to discover the journey of the readers or the perlocutionary effect of the text.[103] According to Osborne, there are two aspects that require the reader's attention: poetics, which pertains to the artistic dimension of the text, and meaning, which involves the recreation of the message conveyed by the author.[104] Therefore, the poetics and meaning are studied to ascertain the construction of the narrative and recreate its communicative intentions, allowing us to follow how "the journey" reveals a new image of a community and transforms the "human society" into the image of the divine.

The *second step* is an exegesis of reality. To explicate the community theme in the Akan context, proverbial expressions and cultural values that reflect their presuppositions were selected through purposive sampling and analyzed.[105] The Akan cultural framework is deemed the optimal selection for enculturating the Johannine community concept due to the pivotal role of the community theme in Akan ideology (which is a shared characteristic with the Johannine gospel) and the necessity for a modern sociocultural milieu in the intercultural interpretation of biblical narratives.

Thirdly, the call to action in the text (step one) and the Akan pre-understanding of a community (step two) discovered through both the exegesis of text and reality were engaged, using Loba-Mkole's intercultural

---

101. Marguerat and Bourquin, *How to Read Bible*, 8; cf. Osborne, *Hermeneutical Spiral*, 202; Powell, *Narrative Criticism*, 18.

102. Marguerat and Bourquin, *How to Read Bible*, 3.

103. Osborne, *Hermeneutical Spiral*, 201–12; Powell, *Narrative Criticism*, 18.

104. Osborne, *Hermeneutical Spiral*, 203.

105. According to Dudovskiy, this sampling style allows the researcher to use personal judgement in selecting data that help answer research questions or achieve research objectives. Dudovskiy, "Purposive Sampling."

biblical hermeneutics, to facilitate an engagement between the biblical text and reality (step three).[106] Given the persistent aspiration to enculturate the Bible through intercultural exegesis, many exegetes who study the Bible in the African context employ the term at varying degrees. For instance, Ukpong considers intercultural reading as an "interactive engagement between the biblical text and a particular contemporary sociocultural issue where the gospel message serves as a critique of the culture or the cultural perspective enriches the understanding of the text."[107] The term is utilized by Gatti within the framework of dialogic hermeneutics.[108] This approach views the text and culture as interactive entities engaged in a dialogue that generates a call to action directed towards the believing community. The use of the term in the communicative approach by Ossom-Batsa is comparable to the aforementioned statement.[109] Therefore, in the awareness of the application of intercultural exegesis on different levels, this study follows the definition of Loba-Mkole. He refers to intercultural reading as "the constructive dialogue between an original biblical culture and a receptive audience."[110] Thus, the study employs intercultural reading as a constructive dialogue between the Johannine and Akan community concepts. The purpose is to allow the gospel message to critique the culture or the cultural perspective to enlarge and enrich the understanding of the text.[111]

Chapter Outline

This study consists of six chapters. Chapter 1 provides an overview of introductory matters, including the background of the study, statement of the problem, research questions and objectives, literature review, theoretical framework, research methodology, and organization of chapters. The second chapter of the study focuses on the narrative analyses of specific narratives, which are comprised of the Johannine prologue, John 5; 15:1—16:1–3; and 17. Chapter 3 delineates the development of John's

---

106. Loba-Mkole, "Intercultural Biblical Exegesis," 1347–62. Recounting the historicity of this hermeneutical approach, Loba-Mkole traces it to J. S. Ukpong, from whose work the various strands emanate.

107. Ukpong, "Reading the Bible," 6.

108. Gatti, "Toward a Dialogic Hermeneutics."

109. Ossom-Batsa, "Biblical Exegesis."

110. Loba-Mkole, "Intercultural Biblical Exegesis," 1359.

111. See Ukpong, "Reading the Bible," 6.

community theme. Chapter 4 provides an exegesis of Akan reality. The discourse centers on the Akan notion of communalism. Additionally, the fifth chapter involves an intercultural reading that draws upon the results of the analyses of the narratives (chapters 2–3) and Akan reality (chapter 4). The final chapter of the study encompasses a summary of the findings, conclusions drawn from the research, and recommendations for future research.

2

Analyses of Four Community-Centred Narratives

THIS CHAPTER PRESENTS THE first step of the tripartite levels (frame) of interpretation proposed by Ossom-Batsa—adherence to the biblical text.[1] Ossom-Batsa explicates that adhering to the text means paying attention to the verbal and non-verbal elements to ascertain the communicative force of the text.[2] Narrative analyses of these narratives (the prologue, John 5; 15:1—16:3; 17) through the prism of the community theme demonstrate that it is one of their communicative intentions. Thus, considering the hermeneutical impact of the prologue on any academic autopsy on the themes in John, what follows commences with the narrative analysis of the prologue.[3] The analysis aims to establish the legitimacy of the community theme and its perlocutionary effect on the narrative. It further explores the theme in John 5 to unearth the incarnate Word's expositions of the divine community at Bethesda (a microcosm of the Johannine community) as a remedy for the problem of community: the quality of relationships.[4] Lastly, it analyzes John 15:1–16:3 and John 17 for the participation of the new covenant community in the mission of the divine community.

---

1. Ossom-Batsa, "Biblical Exegesis," 128.

2. Ossom-Batsa, "Biblical Exegesis," 128.

3. See Köstenberger, *Encountering John*, 44; *Missions of Jesus*, 87; Beasley-Murray, *John*, 5; Moloney, *Belief in the Word*, 24; Morris, *John*, 63; Carson, *John*, 111.

4. For the meaning of community, see Gusfield, *Community*, xv–xvi; Cohen, *Symbolic Construction*, 12.

Consequently, narrative criticism by Marguerat and Bourquin is applied because it concentrates on the method employed by the author to express his theological message through narratives.[5] To use this proposed approach, the interpreter must focus on two things: the construction of the text (poetics) and the recreation of the author's message (meaning).[6] However, identifying the structure is key to ascertaining the construction of narratives.[7] Additionally, structuring requires the delimitation of the narrative. Whereas delimitation helps to establish boundaries and context, structuring narratives aims to discern the units and grasp the message being communicated. Consequently, after structuring them, the poetics and meaning are then established through narrative analysis.[8] Thus, the narratives are delimited, structured, and analyzed to explore the community theme.

The Narrative Analysis of the Prologue (John 1:1–18)

The general view among scholars is that the prologue is a repository of the themes in John.[9] Consequently, it is indispensable in any academic exploration of the themes because they are traceable to it. Similarly, to progress with the community discourse in John, the analysis must demonstrate sufficient proof in the prologue to warrant it. Consequently, to ascertain the presence of the community theme in the prologue and establish its legitimacy, the analysis focuses on the narrative function of the prologue in unearthing the substratum and development of John's theology of community.

The Delimitation of the Prologue

In modern Johannine scholarship, it is ubiquitously acknowledged that the prologue refers to John 1:1–18.[10] Conversely, others rely predomi-

---

5. Marguerat and Bourquin, *How to Read Bible*, 3.

6. Osborne, *Hermeneutical Spiral*, 203; cf. Powell, *Narrative Criticism*, 18.

7. See Fuhr and Köstenberger, *Inductive Bible Study*, 158; Marguerat and Bourquin, *How to Read Bible*, 5.

8. See Osborne, *Hermeneutical Spiral*, 203; Powell, *Narrative Criticism*, 18.

9. See Köstenberger, *John*, 44; Moloney, *Belief in the Word*, 24; Robinson, "John," 122; Morris, *John*, 63; Carson, *John*, 111.

10. Moloney, *Belief in the Word*, 23–25; Servotte, *According to John*, 4–8; Morris, *John*, 63; Culpepper, *Gospel and Letters*, 110–11; Voorwinde, "John's Prologue," 28; Anderson, *Riddles of the Fourth Gospel*, 3; Harris, *Prologue and Gospel*, 9–11.

nantly on the literary genre of the prologue and its concomitant features to explain the above position. Moloney, Culpepper, and Ridderbos delimit John 1:1–18 as a literary unit based on its poetic nature while considering John 1:19–51 (or John 1:19–20:31) as a narrative.[11] Additionally, thematically, John 1:1 and John 1:19 start with different themes. While the former deals with meta-reality, the latter, in Dennison's words, "brings us back down to earth after ranging over the prospects of the Logos (Word)."[12] It is also instructive to note that this "movement of the Logos" or "thematic distinction" further strengthens the argument on the delimitation of the pericope: it provides an envelope structure—the use of θεός (*Theos* or God)—and the intimate relationship between the Logos and God expressed at the beginning (John 1:1) forms an *inclusio* (or inclusion)[13] with its repetition in John 1:18.[14]

Despite the existence of divergent positions, scholars generally hold similar views on the delimitation of the prologue, which is not necessarily similar in its structuring. The subsequent session will explore academic perspectives in order to suggest a framework for conducting a narrative analysis of the prologue.

The Structure of the Prologue

Scholars have identified two typical patterns characterized by the structuring of the prologue by modern scholars: synthetic parallelism and concentric chiasm.[15] Scholars who use the literary model of synthetic parallelism see the prologue as a series of parallel themes.[16] The argument is that a theme from a previous part is repeated and developed with others in its following parallel.[17]

---

11. Moloney, *Belief in the Word*, 23; Culpepper, *Gospel and Letters*, 110–11; Ridderbos, *John*, 22.

12. Dennison, "Prologue," 3.

13. Scholars such as Keener and Osborne refer to this literary technique as *inclusio*. Schubert and others, conversely, refer to it as an inclusion. Therefore, they are either used the way the author has expressed it or interchangeably in this work. See Keener, *John*, 276, 302; Osborne, *Hermeneutical Spiral*, 54; Schubert, *Gospel of John*, 51.

14. Dennison, "Prologue," 3; Keener, *John*, 338, 425–26.

15. See Moloney, *Belief in the Word*, 25; Köstenberger, *John*, 20–21; Coloe, "Structure," 41.

16. See Coloe, "Structure," 42.

17. Lacan, "*Prologue*," 97. See Ridderbos, "Structure," 180–200.

In this regard, some scholars understand the prologue as three chains of uninterrupted "waves."[18] Lacan argues that, just like the waves, John makes a point and returns to it in the following passage to elaborate on it.[19] Below is Lacan's structure:

1.	A (1–2)	B (3)	C (4–5)
2.	A^{I} (6–8)	B^{I} (9–11)	C^{I} (12–14)
3.	A^{II} (15)	B^{II} (16–17)	C^{II} (18)

Building on Lacan's argument, La Potterie sees this threefold division (or "waves") in the prologue: 1. the Word in God becomes the Light of the World (John 1:1–5); 2. the incarnation of the Word (1:6–14); and 3. the Revealer: the only Son turned toward the Father (1:15–18).[20]

Finally, though Moloney follows the "three-wave structure," he presents a modified version as follows: 1. the Word is announced and described (John 1:1–2, 6–8, 5); 2. the revelation brought by the incarnate Word (John 1:3–4, 9); 3. the human response to the gift of the Word (John 1:5b, 10–13, 16); and 4. the description of the object of faith as the Father's only Son (John 1:14, 17–18).[21]

However, most scholars advocate for a chiastic structure, the most popular of all proposed structures concerning the prologue.[22] It is traceable to Lund, the person who identified a concentric structure behind the prologue.[23] After Lund, more elaborate structures were proposed, following that trajectory.[24] With each succeeding proposal, nonetheless, the structure became progressively convoluted.[25] And this has generated disagreements on the precise details of the chiasm and its center point.[26]

---

18. Lacan, "*Prologue*," 96–97; La Potterie, "Structure," 357–59; Moloney, *Belief in the Word*, 25–27.

19. Lacan, "*Prologue*," 97.

20. For detailed elucidations on the divisions, see La Potterie, "Structure," 357–67.

21. Moloney, *Belief in the Word*, 27.

22. Voorwinde, "John's Prologue," 23.

23. Lund, "Influence of Chiasmus," 42–46; cf. Culpepper, "Pivot," 2–3.

24. See Boismard, *Prologue*, 76–81; Lamarche, "Prologue," 529–32; Pryor, "Covenant," 47; *John*, 9. Whereas Moloney thinks that most scholars follow an original suggestion from Boismard, Culpepper argues in favour of Lund. See Moloney, *Belief in the Word*, 25; Culpepper, "Pivot," 2–4.

25. Voorwinde, "John's Prologue," 23; Köstenberger, *John*, 20.

26. Pryor, "Covenant," 47; cf. Boismard, *Prologue*, 76–77; Culpepper, "Pivot," 16.

Even though the prologue has stimulated copious creative structures, the various structural proposals, as demonstrated above, do not accommodate the community theme. Therefore, it is expedient to propose one that serves the aim of this research. As Fuhr and Köstenberger succinctly observe, the goal of a literary structure in analyzing biblical texts is to discern the units and grasp the message communicated through the chosen literary form.[27] The explication proffered by these authors posits a correlation between the structure and meaning of the literary form. Therefore, in the absence of structures that reflect the theme, one is proposed as follows: 1. The divine community (John 1:1–2); 2. Creation: The divine community's collaborative work (John 1:3–5); 3. John testifies about the Light in the community (John 1:6–9, 15); 4. The human community's response to the Light (John 1:10–13); and 5. The incarnation and the human community (John 1:14–18).

The Analysis of the Prologue

The narrative analysis of the prologue is the focus of this section. As indicated above, even though the prologue has aroused a gamut of academic interests and discourses, the community theme has not been given the attention it deserves. Since the academic community has not concentrated on the community theme, the various structures employed as the substratum of their analyses do not focus on it. Therefore, the narrative analysis of the prologue follows the researcher's proposed structure because it focuses on the theme of community.

The Divine Community (John 1:1–2)

Beginning the prologue with Ἐν ἀρχῇ (*ēn archē*),[28] John calls the reader's attention to Genesis 1:1.[29] By echoing the first words of the Old Testament,

---

27. Fuhr and Köstenberger, *Inductive Bible Study*, 158.
28. The phrase means "In the beginning."
29. Vincent, *Word Studies*, 24; Moloney, *Belief in the Word*, 27–29; Hamilton, *Book of Genesis*, 144; Morris, *John*, 72; Köstenberger, *John*, 25; Ngewa, *John*, 11; Harris, *John*, 18; McHugh, *Commentary on John*, 6; Keener, *John*, 365; Beutler, *Judaism and the Jews*, 37; Evans, *Word and Glory*, 77–79; Chennattu, "Scripture," 172. Based on the commonalities between both, Borgen takes the argument further to suggest that the prologue is a Targumic exposition of Genesis 1:1–5. Borgen, "Observations," 288–95; "Logos," 115–30.

John's focus is on what precedes time or eternity before creation.[30] So, the purpose is to establish what predates creation, one of which is the Logos (John 1:1).[31] It is evident in the use of the imperfect tense[32] which shows the continuing existence of a state or situation in the past.[33] Thus, it points to the absolute existence of the Logos before creation.[34] Therefore, by attributing to the Logos a state of continuous existence before creation,[35] John is affirming the eternality of the Logos.[36]

Another communicative intent or illocutionary force of *ēn arche* is to demonstrate that the Logos coexisted with God eternally.[37] The argument for the eternal coexistence of the Logos and God can be made when it is established that there are two distinct persons in John 1:1. Without that, we can only speak of the eternal existence of the Logos and not the coexistence of the Logos with a distinct personality.[38] Thus, John establishes this distinction by the preposition *pros*, which denotes that the Logos did not eternally exist alone but with God,[39] the Father.[40] Therefore, the Logos is distinguished from the Father.[41]

---

30. Ngewa, *John*, 11; Tenney, *John*, 64; Moloney, *Belief in the Word*, 28; Harris, *John*, 18; Vincent, *Word Studies*, 24; Barrett, *Gospel According to St. John*, 152; Westcott, *Gospel According to John*, 4–5.

31. Beasley-Murray, *John*, 10; Köstenberger, *John*, 25.

32. The Greek word ἦν (*ēn*) is the imperfect tense of the verb εἰμι (*eimi*).

33. Ngewa, *John*, 11; Vincent, *Word Studies*, 24; Westcott, *Gospel According to John*, 5.

34. Keener, *John*, 267; Borchert, *John 12—21*, 104; McHugh, *Commentary on John*, 6; Moloney, *Belief in the Word*, 31; Skinner, "Characterization," 124.

35. Vincent, *Word Studies*, 24; Beasley-Murray, *John*, 10; Skinner, "Characterization," 124.

36. Vincent, *Word Studies* 24; Morris, *John*, 70; Ngewa, *John*, 12.

37. Barrett, *Gospel According to St. John*, 156; Ngewa, *John*, 12. In other passages in Scripture, the Spirit, the Third Person of the Trinity is part of the community of essence (Gen 1:2; Matt 3:16–17). For an extensive work on the God of the Gospel of John, see Thompson, *Gospel of John*.

38. Ngewa, *John*, 11; Vincent, *Word Studies*, 24; Keener, *John*, 369; Tenney, *John*, 64.

39. Kanagaraj, *John*, 1–2; Tenney, *John*, 64; Moloney, *Belief in the Word*, 28; McHugh, *Commentary on John*, 9.

40. Harris, *John*, 18; Ngewa, *John*, 12; Kanagaraj, *John*, 2; Gharbin and Van Eck, "Johannine Prologue," 2.

41. Harris, *John*, 18–19; Ridderbos, *John*, 24; Vincent, *Word Studies*, 34–35; Mounce, *Biblical Greek Grammar*, 27; Harris, *Jesus as God*, 64; Kanagaraj, *John*, 1–2; Voorwinde, "John's Prologue," 32.

Even though John does not give us details on the character of the relationship,[42] the preposition furnishes the reader with some information on this eternal relationship.[43] In this context, to be "*with* God" does not merely communicate the coexistence of two separate individuals.[44] The term refers to two distinct persons in communion, association, intimacy, fellowship, or union.[45]

Finally, the third statement concerning the Word reveals that the Logos shares the same nature with God.[46] This is evident in the use of the anarthrous (*Theos*) and the emphatic position of θεὸς (*Theos*).[47] The absence of the article in John 1:1c suggests that θεὸς is in a predicative position; therefore, John's focus is on the Word's nature or quality.[48] By this construction, John ascribes to the Logos all the attributes of the divine essence.[49] Furthermore, the emphatic position of θεὸς is John's way of stressing and strengthening the argument that the Logos enjoys unity of essence with God.[50]

For these reasons, we can describe this relationship as a "divine community." Generally, there are two broad categories identified with the idea of community: territorial and relational.[51] By demonstrating that the Logos and the Father are one in essence[52] and have coexisted eternally[53]

42. Ridderbos, *John*, 25.
43. Vincent, *Word Studies*, 33–34; Harris, *John*, 18; Ngewa, *John*, 12.
44. Vincent, *Word Studies*, 34; Westcott, *Gospel According to John*, 6.
45. Vincent, *Word Studies*, 34; Harris, *John*, 18; Kanagaraj, *John*, 1; Keener, *John*, 369; Tenney, *John*, 64; Voorwinde, "John's Prologue," 32; Wuest, *New Testament*, 209; Newman and Nida, *Gospel of John*, 8.
46. Mounce, *Biblical Greek Grammar*, 27; Vincent, *Word Studies*, 34–35; Harris, *John*, 19; Borchert, *John 12—21*, 103–4; Tenney, *John*, 65.
47. See Mounce, *Biblical Greek Grammar*, 27; Vincent, *Word Studies*, 34–35; Harris, *John*, 19; Ngewa, *John*, 12.
48. Mounce, *Biblical Greek Grammar*, 27; Vincent, *Word Studies*, 34–35; Harris, *John*, 19; *Jesus as God*, 68; Ngewa, *John*, 12.
49. Vincent, *Word Studies*, 35; Harris, *John*, 19; Ngewa, *John*, 12; Mounce, *Biblical Greek Grammar*, 27; Kanagaraj, *John*, 2.
50. Vincent, *Word Studies*, 34–35; Harris, *John*, 19; Mounce, *Biblical Greek Grammar*, 27.
51. Whereas the former encompasses the context of location, physical territory, and geographical continuity, the latter points to the quality of relationships. See Gusfield, *Community*, xv–xvi; Cohen, *Symbolic Construction*, 12; Klink, *Sheep of the Fold*, 52.
52. Mounce, *Biblical Greek Grammar*, 27; Vincent, *Word Studies*, 34–35; Harris, *John*, 19; Ngewa, *John*, 12; Borchert, *John 12—21*, 104; Tenney, *John*, 64.
53. Harris, *John*, 18; Kanagaraj, *John*, 1–2; Tenney, *John*, 64–65.

in union and communion,⁵⁴ John is expressing the quality of relationship that exists between God and the Logos (the relational dimension of community). John is, therefore, postulating a divine community.⁵⁵ Borchert perspicaciously and aptly observes that community and unity are two compatible sides of the eternal God.⁵⁶ The reference to this relationship (and creation) indicates that in John, community is always a starting point.⁵⁷

It is pertinent to note that John establishes this foundation (the unity and community of the divine essence) before discussing creation. The idea is that creation is the outflow of the eternal relationship.⁵⁸ Grenz succinctly puts it as follows: "Just as the triune God is the eternal fellowship of the trinitarian members, so also God's purpose for creation is that the world participates in community."⁵⁹ Similarly, Moltmann affirms that the perichoretic unity of the divine trinity is an open, inviting, and integrating unity; thus, the whole world can find room within it.⁶⁰ So, in John, there is a human community because God, the eternal community, has created the world and invites us to participate in the community of God. As a result, having established the concept of the divine community, he discusses the community motif embedded in creation and how it reflects the work of divine collaboration.⁶¹

Creation: The Divine Community's Collaborative Work (John 1:3–5)

The narrative's structure further exemplifies the cooperation the divine community displayed during the world's creation. To emphasize this collaboration, John states it positively and negatively,⁶² the contribution

---

54. Vincent, *Word Studies*, 34; Harris, *John*, 18; Keener, *John*, 369; Morris, *John*, 70; Borchert, *John 12—21*, 103–4; Kanagaraj, *John*, 2; Tenney, *John*, 64–65.
55. See Borchert, *John 12—21*, 106; Harris, *Jesus as God*, 68.
56. Borchert, *John 12—21*, 106.
57. Kunene, *Communal Holiness*, 188.
58. Grenz, *Community of God*, 112.
59. Grenz, *Community of God*, 112; cf. *Created for Community*, 49.
60. Moltmann, "God," 375.
61. Kanagaraj, *John*, 2.
62. There are unresolved arguments whether the word γέγονεν (*gegonen*) should end the sentence (John 1:3) or begin the next sentence. See Metzger, *Textual Commentary*, 195–96; Borchert, *John 12—21*, 107; Keener, *John*, 381–82. Metzger argues that it is more constant with the Johannine repetitive style and doctrine to punctuate with a full stop after ὃ γέγονεν (*ho gegonen*). Metzger, *Textual Commentary*, 195–96.

of the Logos in the work of creation (John 1:3).[63] Recognizing that the Father is the source of all that is,[64] the Logos is identified as God's agent[65] in creation by the expression "through him."[66]

Furthermore, John demonstrates the relationship between the Logos and creation, revealing that the Logos is the life-giver and light-giver of God's creation (John 1:4). The first section (John 1:4a) ascribes life-giving prerogatives to the Logos.[67] Thus, whatever was created exists because of the self-existing life of the Word that was dispensed at creation.[68] The second part shows that this life (the Logos) is also the light that enlightens the world.[69] It is critical to note that the continuance of this role of the Logos is implied in the linear sense of the present tense, which indicates the continuous shining of the Light.[70] And the darkness could not overpower it.[71] The transition from the present tense to the aorist has stunned many.[72] Considering what a punctiliar aorist repre-

---

63. Ngewa, *John*, 13; Carson, *John*, 118; Köstenberger, *John*, 29; Ridderbos, *John*, 36; Borchert, *John 12-21*, 107; Tenney, *John*, 66.

64. Morris, *John*, 71; Harris, *John*, 22; Grenz, *Community of God*, 102.

65. The term "agent" should be interpreted considering what John has already said about the Logos (John 1:1-3). The Logos is God and not a mere ambassador. See Harris, *John*, 113; Köstenberger, *John*, 184; Carson, *John*, 224-25; Barrett, *Gospel According to St. John*, 260.

66. Vincent, *Word Studies*, 37; Ngewa, *John*, 13; Grenz, *Community of God*, 104; Tenney, *John*, 66. This Johannine disclosure about the Logos' involvement in the creation of "all things" unveils the community motif embedded in creation. Kanagaraj, *John*, 2; cf. Kunene, *Communal Holiness*, 188. According to Kanagaraj, the community-oriented nature of creation flows from the fact that God created "all things" as families according to their kinds. Kanagaraj, *John*, 2; cf. Gen 1-2.

67. Harris, *John*, 23; Köstenberger, *John*, 30; Vincent, *Word Studies*, 37-38; Carson, *John*, 119; Morris, *John*, 73; Barrett, *Gospel According to St. John*, 158.

68. Carson, *John*, 119; Harris, *John*, 23; Morris, *John*, 73.

69. Harris, *John*, 23; cf. Brant, *John*, 32.

70. Harris, *John*, 24; Vincent, *Word Studies*, 40; Waetjen, "Logos," 272.

71. Employing double entendres is one of the idiosyncratic features of John. Nasselqvist, "Style," 29. The word κατέλαβεν is one of them. Scholars are divided on how to apply the double meanings of κατέλαβεν (katelaben) in this context. Keener, *John*, 387; cf. Brown, *Gospel According to John*, 8. Some think that applying both meanings (apprehend and comprehend) is legitimate. See Harris, *John*, 23; Barret, *Gospel*, 158; Brant, *John*, 30. Whereas few scholars translate the word as comprehend, the majority choose "apprehend" as the appropriate interpretation. See Köstenberger, *John*, 31; Waetjen, "Logos," 272; Brant, *John*, 30; Ridderbos, *John*, 39-40; Tenney, *John*, 67; Thompson, *Gospel of John*, 134.

72. A transition from φαίνει (phainei) to the aorist κατέλαβεν (katelaben).

sents, some have proposed that John had in mind an event in the past.[73] However, some disagree for two reasons: First, John mentions no event, and second, the conjunction that connects the two statements has a constative sense: it states as a single fact a continuous struggle between the light and darkness and the former's unceasing victory over the latter.[74]

Finally, Barrett takes the argument of the role of the Logos further by arguing that though Jesus (the Logos) was both life and light in himself, he was also the agent by whom God bestowed life and light upon the world.[75] The theological implication is that the Logos exercises these divine prerogatives because the Father bestowed them upon him.[76] Consequently, creation and its continuance are products of divine collaboration between the Father (source) and the Logos, the agent of creation.[77]

John's Testimony in the Community (John 1:6–9, 15)

John introduces the Baptist into the narrative. In contrast to the Logos, whose eternality is established through the use of imperfect tense,[78] John changes the tense to aorist and describes the witness as ἄνθρωπος (*anthrōpos*)—to denote the humanity of John and the historicity of his assignment.[79] Indeed, John (the witness) testifies to the pre-existence and pre-eminence of the Logos.[80]

---

73. Moloney, *Belief in the Word*, 33; Waetjen, "Logos," 272.

74. Waetjen, "Logos," 272.

75. Barrett, *Gospel According to St. John*, 158; cf. Carson, *John*, 118; Kanagaraj, *John*, 2. Even though John uses the term life predominantly in a soteriological sense, what we have in the prologue is the cosmological aspect. See Barrett, *Gospel According to St. John*, 158.

76. See John 5:21; Harris, *John*, 114; Ngewa, *John*, 93; Thompso, *Gospel of John*, 77–78; Morris, *John*, 279; Wuest, *New Testament*, 222.

77. Morris, *John*, 71; Harris, *John*, 22; Vincent, *Word Studies*, 37; Ngewa, *John*, 13. Though John does not include the Spirit, the third eternal distinction, creation is primarily a Trinitarian act. Grenz, *Community of God*, 101. In the Genesis account, the Spirit is part of the divine collaboration that resulted in the creation of the world (Gen 1:1–2). For further studies on the roles of the Father, the Son, and the Spirit in creation, see Grenz, *Community of God*, 101–6.

78. Ngewa, *John*, 11; Vincent, *Word Studies*, 24; Harris, *John*, 18; Keener, *John*, 267; Borchert, *John 12—21*, 104.

79. Köstenberger, *John*, 32; cf. Morris, *John*, 79.

80. John 1:15; Harris, *John*, 36; Tenney, *John*, 74; Köstenberger, *John*, 45; Ngewa, *John*, 15.

Moreover, despite being differentiated from the Light,[81] the importance of the individual in question is revealed by the references to "*witness*" and the sophisticated literary preface that indicates that he is a man *sent from God* and identified by name.[82] Being a witness serves to mark his unique place in salvation history as the one who pointed to the arrival of the Light.[83] Through the privilege of the divine assignment, he participates in God's mission for creation—the social life of the divine community.[84] Therefore, akin to all other Johannine witnesses, he must be someone who has experienced the divine community to be a true witness.[85] "To witness," according to Brant, "preserves the emphasis on one who identifies Jesus for others by virtue of what the witness has seen and heard."[86] Thus, he is introduced as a man sent from God (John 1:6).

Carson and Barrett posit that the fruit of the witness of John, who was sent from God, does not align with the intended purpose of his witness, which was to facilitate belief in all individuals through him.[87] The argument is founded upon the reaction of the community towards John's ministry, as evidenced by sources such as Barrett and Carson.[88] Although the narrative does not provide any evidence to contradict the notion that all believed through John's witness, ascertaining the numerical outcome of his testimony poses a challenge as it may overlook its qualitative significance. Carson acknowledges this fact by briefly mentioning it and providing an example of John 1:35–37, where John's testimony produced positive outcomes.[89] Nevertheless, upon being situated within

---

81. Vincent, *Word Studies*, 41; Barrett, *Gospel According to St. John*, 150.

82. John 1:6–7, 15; Morris, *John*, 79; Vincent, *Word Studies*, 42; Barrett, *Gospel According to St. John*, 150.

83. Ridderbos, *John*, 42; Smith, *World of the New Testament*, 58.

84. Grenz, *Community of God*, 112.

85. Brant, *John*, 31; Keener, *John*, 392; cf. John 1:6; 15:26–27. Morris lists seven who bear witness to Jesus in John: each of the three persons of the Trinity, Scripture, the Baptist, and a variety of human witnesses. See Morris, *John*, 80. Apart from Scripture and Jesus, all these witnesses have experienced the Logos in one way or another. Jesus' statements attest to this (John 15:26–27). He tells his disciples to testify about him because they have been with him and experienced him from the beginning (15:27). He instructed them to testify after telling them that he would send the Holy Spirit (who has coexisted with him eternally) to witness about him (15:26).

86. Brant, *John*, 31; cf. Keener, *John*, 392.

87. Carson, *John*, 121; Barrett, *Gospel According to St. John*, 159.

88. Carson, *John*, 121; Barrett, *Gospel According to St. John*, 256.

89. Carson, *John*, 121.

its appropriate framework, the instance referenced by Carson exposes the qualitative influence of John's ministry and mission.[90] Initially, the text portrays John as the primary individual to provide testimony regarding Jesus (also known as the Light) to the Jewish leaders, as documented in John 1:19–28. Moreover, he holds the distinction of being the initial individual to publicly express support for and present Jesus to the populace, as well as to testify to the community regarding him (John 1:29–34).

Furthermore, the congregation of the believing community commences in response to this testimony. According to the Gospel (John 1:35–39), a pair of individuals who were followers of John's teachings were the initial adherents to the divine community as a result of his witness. Hence, utilizing a negative response as the sole criterion for evaluating the efficacy of his testimony should be avoided.

In light of this context, John's work showcases the manner in which the human community reacted to the Light, which was the focal point of John the Baptist's testimony. The prologue delineates two distinct reactions that typified the community's disposition towards the Light: an affirmative response (John 1:12–13) and a negative response (1:10–11).

The Human Community's Response to the Light (John 1:10–13)

The Light came into the created world inhabited by humankind,[91] but the world alienated from or hostile to God[92] did not recognize the identity of the Light[93] or comprehend the Logos.[94] John's comment also denotes

---

90. See Carson, *John*, 121.

91. Harris, *John*, 30; Beasley-Murray, *John*, 12; Morris, *John*, 85; Köstenberger, *John*, 36; Barrett, *Gospel According to St. John*, 161. Academic discourse has been engaged in discussions regarding John's utilization of the term, as evidenced by the works of some Johannine scholars. See Köstenberger, *John*, 36; Barrett, *Gospel According to St. John*, 62; Morris, *John*, 85; Carson, *John*, 123. According to Morris, the initial two instances of κόσμος (*kosmos*) pertain to a universal audience, whereas the third instance specifically pertains to individuals who encountered Jesus. According to Carson's findings, the term κόσμος is not utilized in a positive manner in the Gospel of John. Barrett proposes a singular interpretation of the term in question (John 1:10). See Morris, *John*, 85; Carson, *John*, 123; Barrett, *Gospel According to St. John*, 162.

92. Ridderbos, *John*, 44; Köstenberger, *John*, 36; Harris, *John*, 30; Carson, *John*, 123–24; Keener, *John*, 395.

93. Harris, *John*, 30; Köstenberger, *John*, 36; Ridderbos, *John*, 44; Barrett, *Gospel According to St. John*, 162.

94. Tenney, *John*, 68.

the rejection of the right relationship with the Logos[95] or response to the Logos.[96]

Similarly, the Logos encounters rejection even within his own people, a *relational* term referring to Israel.[97] John is intimating that some from "his home"—the covenant community,[98] which should have known and accepted him or had a proper relationship with the Logos—rather did not give him the reception he deserves.[99] "God's chosen people who celebrated Torah rejected Torah in the flesh."[100] It suggests that he is unwelcome in his own home,[101] that is, in the covenant community.[102]

The comments about the response of these groups—the world and Israel—indicate the refusal of the human community to align itself to the purpose of the divine community for it, that is, participating "in the life of the social Trinity."[103]

Conversely, despite the general rejection, there were remnants who "went against the current, who broke with the general pattern by which the world thinks, lives, and acts"[104] and gave the Logos the expected reception.[105] These are people who duly and truly recognized the Logos and accepted him for what he was and manifested.[106] Hence, "accepting" or "receiving" the Word is equated with "believing in his name,"[107] given that "the name" is a circumlocution for God.[108]

---

95. Morris, *John*, 85; Ridderbos, *John*, 44.

96. Barrett, *Gospel According to St. John*, 162.

97. Carson, *John*, 122; Vincent, *Word Studies*, 47; Köstenberger, *John*, 37; Tenney, *John*, 69; Keener, *John*, 398.

98. Carson, *John*, 125; Köstenberger, *John*, 402.

99. Carson, *John*, 122; Morris, *John*, 85–86; Köstenberger, *John*, 37; Harris, *John*, 30.

100. Keener, *John*, 399.

101. Vincent, *Word Studies*, 47; Morris, *John*, 85; Harris, *John*, 30; Ridderbos, *John*, 45.

102. Carson, *John*, 125; Köstenberger, *John*, 402.

103. Grenz, *Community of God*, 112.

104. Ridderbos, *John*, 45.

105. Tenney, *John*, 69; cf. Morris, *John*, 85.

106. Ridderbos, *John*, 45; Carson, *John*, 125–26; Köstenberger, *John*, 38; Brant, *John*, 33.

107. Köstenberger, *John*, 38; Harris, *John*, 31; Ridderbos, *John*, 45.

108. Brant, *John*, 33.

Further, whereas rejecting the Logos is tantamount to a rejection of the social life of the divine community,[109] accepting or believing in his name is an acceptance of this life.[110] Therefore, those who receive him are given the privilege[111] or authorization[112] to become τέκνα θεοῦ (*tekna theou*) but not υἱοὶ θεοῦ (*huioi theou*).[113] John makes this distinction when discussing the relationships between the Son and the Father and believers and the Father through the use of the phrase "υἱός" (*huios*) only for the Son.[114] As Harris rightly notes, God has one son by nature and many adopted sons.[115] This authorization ushers them into a new status[116] or identity[117]—a relationship centered on the community of *nature*.[118] This means they participate in the divine nature.[119] The act of participating in it ensures individuals a position as members of the community of God, resulting in a close familial bond with God.[120] However, it should be noted that this phenomenon is not exclusive to the Johannine community but rather encompasses the communities of believers that emerged after the incarnation, as evidenced by Ngewa.[121] According to Ngewa, the term "those who believe" encompasses a broad group of individuals spanning

---

109. Grenz, *Community of God*, 112, Grenz, *Created for Community*, 49.

110. See Harris, *John*, 31; Ridderbos, *John*, 45–46; Morris, *John*, 87; Watt, *Family of the King*, 166.

111. Carson, *John*, 126; Ridderbos, *John*, 45–46; Brant, *John*, 33.

112. Morris, *John*, 87; Harris, *John*, 31; Köstenberger, *John*, 39; Keener, *John*, 403; Barrett, *Gospel According to St. John*, 163; Beasley-Murray, *John*, 13.

113. Harris, *John*, 31; Morris, *John*, 87; Ridderbos, *John*, 45; Köstenberger, *John*, 39; Vincent, *Word Studies*, 49; Beasley-Murray, *John*, 13; McHugh, *Commentary on John*, 45.

114. Harris, *John*, 31; Morris, *John*, 87; Ridderbos, *John*, 45; Köstenberger, *John*, 39; Vincent, *Word Studies*, 49; Brown, *Gospel According to John*, 11.

115. Harris, *John*, 31.

116. Morris, *John*, 87.

117. Watt, *Family of the King*, 182.

118. Vincent, *Word Studies*, 49; Morris, *John*, 87.

119. See Vincent, *Word Studies*, 49; Morris, *John*, 87.

120. Watt, *Family of the King*, 182; Westcott, *Gospel According to John*, 16. According to Watt, "becoming a child of God" is the metaphor with which the family imagery is activated and the awareness of the possibility of a divine family created. Thus, the reader must anticipate and read the various suggestions of a family in John through this lens. Watt, *Family of the King*, 188.

121. Ngewa, *John*, 17.

across different eras, including the past, present, and future.[122] Ngewa further asserts that belief, in this context, is a recurring phenomenon that varies among people across different historical periods.[123]

John further explicates the substratum of this new identity by defining what it is and what it is not. Three different expressions that focus on human procreation (who were born not of blood, nor the will of the flesh, nor the will of man)[124] are used to demonstrate that they did not become God's children through this medium.[125] And they are contrasted with divine procreation to authenticate their new identity as God's children.[126] As Harris affirms, "the four uses of ἐκ may point to the agency (by) or source (from) or cause (a result) or any combination of these."[127] Consequently, the expression (but born of God)[128] points to God as the source or cause of the procreation.[129]

Against this background, John demonstrates in the section that follows that the Word also assumed a "community of nature with humankind" through the incarnation.[130]

The Incarnation and the Human Community (John 1:14-18)

The statement "and the Word became flesh" demonstrates two forms of incarnation in the prologue (John 1:14a). The first is the incarnation of existing concepts in a specific cultural context. The notion that John used oral and written traditions has received scholarly validation.[131] The Logos concept is one of such traditions present in John's religiously pluralistic

---

122. Ngewa, *John*, 17.

123. Ngewa, *John*, 17.

124. The three expressions are human ancestry, human choice, and human initiative. See Harris, *John*, 33; Köstenberger, *John*, 39; cf. Carson, *John*, 126.

125. Watt, *Family of the King*, 183; Ridderbos, *John*, 47; Köstenberger, *John*, 39; Harris, *John*, 32-33; Brant, *John*, 33-34; Vincent, *Word Studies*, 50; Keener, *John*, 404-5; Ngewa, *John*, 16.

126. See Watt, *Family of the King*, 183; Ridderbos, *John*, 47; Köstenberger, *John*, 39; Harris, *John*, 32-33; Bran, *John*, 33-34.

127. Harris, *John*, 32-33.

128. *All' ek Theou egennēthēsan*.

129. Harris, *John*, 32-33; Westcott, *Gospel According to John*, 17.

130. See Vincent, *Word Studies*, 51.

131. Dodd, *Historical Tradition*, 180; Barrett, *Gospel According to St. John*, 45-47; Borgen, *Gospel of John*, 148.

milieu.¹³² Scholars have therefore proposed possible backgrounds for John's Logos, which include Hellenistic philosophy (Stoicism and Philo), Jewish wisdom literature (personification of wisdom), and the word of God in the Old Testament.¹³³ However, scholars argue that traditions are usually applied uniquely by John.¹³⁴ Similarly, scholarly analyses and juxtapositions of John's Logos concept with its parallels indicate its idiosyncratic application.¹³⁵ Indeed, the application of traditions is associated with the establishment of new meanings.¹³⁶ Likewise, John employs it to enculturate or incarnate his Logos Christology within a cultural context.¹³⁷

Moreover, the statement denotes that the Logos entered into a new mode of existence in time without ceasing to be what he was in eternity;¹³⁸ the Logos became genuinely human,¹³⁹ thereby assuming "a community of nature with humankind."¹⁴⁰ However, it is critical to note that as the Word entered a new *mode* of being, all essential properties were retained.¹⁴¹ Consequently, the incarnate Word is fully divine and human—a theanthropic person.¹⁴² After mentioning that the Logos became flesh, John never refers to him as the Word because he has become audible and visible.¹⁴³

Moreover, to explicate the relationship that existed between the incarnate Word and the historical context of the incarnation, John chooses a word that immediately reminds the reader of the Old Testament

---

132. See Keener, *John*, 339–47; Morris, *John*, 102–8; Ridderbos, *John*, 27–36.

133. Köstenberger, *John*, 26–27; Morris, *John*, 102–8. For a comprehensive discussion on the subject, see Keener, *John*, 339–47.

134. Dodd, *Historical Tradition*, 180.

135. Morris, *John*, 108; Keener, *John*, 339; Waetjen, "Logos," 226–71.

136. Labahn, "Living Word(s)," 61.

137. Keener, *John*, 339.

138. Vincent, *Word Studies*, 50–51; Harris, *John*, 35; Brown, *Gospel According to John I-XII*, 32.

139. Harris, *Jesus as God*, 59; Ridderbos, *John*, 49; Vincent, *Word Studies*, 51; Köstenberger, *John*, 40; Carson, *John*, 127; Keener, *John*, 408.

140. Vincent, *Word Studies*, 51.

141. Harris, *John*, 35; Vincent, *Word Studies*, 51; Morris, *John*, 91; Frey, *Glory of the Crucified*, 280.

142. Harris, *John*, 35; Vincent, *Word Studies*, 51; Morris, *John*, 91; Westcott, *Gospel According to John*, 19–20.

143. Bauckham, *Gospel of Glory*, 45.

wilderness wanderings, where God tabernacled among the children of Israel.[144] Thus, Barrett avows that ἐσκήνωσεν (*eskēnōsen*) is chosen because of the word that follows it: δόξα (*doxa*).[145] According to him, it recalls in sound and meaning the Hebrew word used to denote the dwelling of God with Israel.[146] The argument is based on the "divine dwelling" in the Old Testament wilderness wanderings with its concomitant glory and the apparent replication of these motifs by John.[147] As God dwelt within the community of faith in the wilderness, the bright cloud that settled upon the tabernacle was considered the tangible expression of God's abiding presence—his glory.[148] Thus, John evokes both motifs ("dwell" and "glory") to indicate that through the incarnation, God's glory takes up residence among his people once again.[149]

Further, it is pertinent to state that the reference to δόξαν αὐτοῦ (*doxan autou*) is the only moment in which the "we" of the human community enters the narrative, supporting the testimony of John with hers.[150] As the first witness (John) testified about the Son's pre-eminence (John 1:15, 27), the community testifies about his pre-eminence, noting that his glory corresponds in nature to the glory of the uniquely begotten[151] or only begotten of the Father.[152] Nonetheless, what is expressed during the incarnation is glory "revealed under human limitations both in Himself and in those who beheld Him"[153]—the apostles[154] and/or eye-

---

144. The word ἐσκήνωσεν (*eskēnōsen*) means dwelt or "pitched his tent." See Vincent, *Word Studies*, 51–53; Köstenberger, *John*, 41; Carson, *John*, 127; Ridderbos, *John*, 50–51; Moloney, *Belief in the Word*, 42.

145. Barrett, *Gospel According to St. John*, 165.

146. Barrett, *Gospel According to St. John*, 165; cf. Morris, *John*, 91; Ridderbos, *John*, 50–51.

147. Barrett, *Gospel According to St. John*, 165; Morris, *John*, 91; cf. Köstenberger, *John*, 42.

148. Barrett, *Gospel According to St. John*, 165.

149. Köstenberger, *John*, 42; cf. Harris, *John*, 35; Vincent, *Word Studies*, 52–53; Ridderbos, *John*, 51; Keener, *John*, 411; Morris, *John*, 91–92.

150. See Ridderbos, *John*, 51.

151. Keener, *John*, 416; Ridderbos, *John*, 53; Morris, *John*, 93. For an elaborate discussion on the subject, see Harris, *Jesus as God*, 84–88.

152. Harris, *John*, 35; Harris, *Jesus as God*, 85–87; Vincent, *Word Studies*, 53; Morris, *John*, 93; Brant, *John*, 35.

153. Vincent, *Word Studies*, 52; cf. Moloney, *Belief in the Word*, 43.

154. Köstenberger, *John*, 42; Keener, *John*, 411; Tenney, *John*, 71.

witnesses.[155] And it was manifested through his works or sign,[156] death, and resurrection.[157]

Additionally, John declares that the Son is "full of grace and truth" (John 1:14d). The term is a composite expression that indicates an evocation of the Old Testament concept of God.[158] It serves as a designation by which Yahweh reveals himself in his magnificence.[159] It also symbolizes the faithfulness of God to God's people.[160] Consequently, the elementary ramification is that the faithfulness of God finds ultimate expression in the community through the incarnation.[161] The incarnate Word becomes God's revelation to the community.[162] And the believing community receives continuous grace out of his (the incarnate Word) fullness.[163]

John further explicates the significance of the incarnation to the human community (John 1:17).[164] By way of contrast, he reveals that whereas Moses served as an intermediary for the reception of the law, Jesus Christ brought grace and truth—his intrinsic possession.[165]

The Son's significant accomplishment in the human community serves as the prologue's climax. John emphatically states that no man has seen God[166]—not even Moses.[167] Nevertheless, the theanthropic Jesus, though truly man, is exempted.[168] Being God uniquely begotten, or

---

155. Ridderbos, *John*, 52; Carson, *John*, 128; Harris, *John*, 35; Westcott, *Gospel According to John*, 22; Keener, "We Beheld His Glory," 16–17.

156. Carson, *John*, 128; Morris, *John*, 93; Köstenberger, *John*, 42; Beasley-Murray, *John*, 14; Harris, *John*, 35.

157. Morris, *John*, 93; Carson, *John*, 128.

158. Vincent, *Word Studies*, 54; Ridderbos, *John*, 54; Köstenberger, *John*, 44.

159. Ridderbos, *John*, 56.

160. Barrett, *Gospel According to St. John*, 167; Köstenberger, *John*, 44.

161. Köstenberger, *John*, 45.

162. Barrett, *Gospel According to St. John*, 167; Westcott, *Gospel According to John*, 24; Vincent, *Word Studies*, 54.

163. Vincent, *Word Studies*, 57; Ridderbos, *John*, 56; Köstenberger, *John*, 46–47.

164. Ridderbos, *John*, 57; Köstenberger, *John*, 48; Vincent, *Word Studies*, 55; Barrett, *Gospel According to St. John*, 169.

165. Harris, *John*, 37; Ridderbos, *John*, 58.

166. Morris, *John*, 100; Köstenberger, *John*, 48; Harris, *John*, 38; *Jesus as God*, 93–94.

167. Ridderbos, *John*, 58–59; Köstenberger, *John*, 48.

168. Harris, *John*, 35; Vincent, *Word Studies*, 51; Morris, *John*, 91.

μονογενὴς θεός,[169] he enjoys unparalleled and timeless intimacy with the Father.[170]

Most importantly, this eternal relationship makes the Son the only legitimate and authoritative expositor of the Father and the community he represents.[171] Consequently, John presents him as the exegete of the Father and, by implication, the divine community.[172] And the incarnation was the vehicle through which the Son exegeted (revealed or explained) God to the human community.[173] Harris rightly affirms that ἐξηγήσατο (exēgēsato) encompasses in a single glance the whole span of Christ's earthly life, including his death and resurrection.[174] Thus, by concluding the prologue with the summary of Christ's earthly life, John is indicating that what follows (the entire gospel) "should be read as an account of Jesus 'telling the whole story' of God the Father."[175] In other words, the narrative (the rest of the gospel) "*shows*" what the prologue "*tells*."[176]

The Perlocutionary Effect of the Prologue on the Theme

John lays the foundation for the community theme in the prologue. The prologue helps to establish that community is a divine intention and not a human invention. It opens with some interrelated concepts to this

169. Harris lists four variant readings as follows: ὁ μονογενὴς (ho monogenēs), ὁ μονογενὴς υἱός (ho monogenēs huios), ὁ μονογενὴς θεός (ho monogenēs Theos), μονογενὴς θεός (monogenēs Theos). See Harris, *John*, 38; *Jesus as God*, 74–83. However, μονογενὴς θεός has better attestation than the others. Harris, *John*, 38; *Jesus as God*, 74–83; Carson, *John*, 139; Morris, *John*, 100; Vincent, *Word Studies*, 59; Voorwinde, "John's Prologue," 31; Barrett, *Gospel According to St. John*, 169; Metzger, *Textual Commentary*, 198. Some also avow that there are compelling reasons for taking μονογενὴς as equivalent to (ὁ) μονογενὴς υἱός and translating the phrase as "the only Son, who is God." See Carson, *John*, 139; Harris, *John*, 38; *Jesus as God*, 88–92. However, Vincent argues that the sense of the passage is not affected whether we read the only begotten Son or God only begotten. Vincent, *Word Studies*, 59.

170. Köstenberger, *John*, 49; Voorwinde, "John's Prologue," 32; Vincent, *Word Studies*, 60.

171. Voorwinde, "John's Prologue," 32.

172. Vincent, *Word Studies*, 61; Brant, *John*, 37; Harris, *John*, 39; Morris, *John*, 101; Köstenberger, *John*, 50; Beasley-Murray, *John*, 16; Wuest, *New Testament*, 210.

173. Vincent, *Word Studies*, 61; Wuest, *New Testament*, 210; Skinner, "Characterization," 124.

174. Harris, *John*, 39.

175. Köstenberger, *John*, 50.

176. Moloney, *Belief in the Word*, 24.

effect. First, it presents God as a community.[177] Additionally, it considers the concept of community as a starting point.[178] The reason is that John begins with the concept of an eternal community constituted by God and the Logos.

Against this backdrop, John presents creation as the product of collaboration and an extension of the divine relationship. Since creation outflows from this relationship, humanity exists to participate in it: the community of God.[179] However, this divine purpose cannot be fulfilled independent of God; a world that does not know God is not conscious of the will of God (cf. John 1:10). Consequently, a genuine relationship with God is a prerequisite for the revelation and manifestation of the divine intentions for humanity. Therefore, God sends John the Baptist, the witness who has experienced this relationship, to testify about the revelation of God to humanity—the Light (or the Logos).[180]

Through the incarnation, the Logos assumes a community of nature with humankind and exegetes his community to the world,[181] thereby granting the members of the believing community the authorization to become the community of God.[182] The incarnation is also a conduit for the exegesis of God and the eternal community.[183] The entire gospel, which contains what the incarnation entails, provides the framework for the exegesis.[184]

It is important to stress that the idea of telling the whole story encompasses (but is not limited to) ontological equivalence with the Father,[185] the unparalleled and timeless relationship they enjoy, and the functional unity that proceeds from that union,[186] an extension of the community

---

177. See Borchert, *John 12—21*, 106; Harris, *Jesus as God*, 68.

178. Kunene, *Communal Holiness*, 188; Kanagaraj, *John*, 2.

179. Grenz, *Community of God*, 112; cf. Kanagaraj, *John*, 2.

180. Brant, *John*, 31; Keene, *John*, 392.

181. Vincent, *Word Studies*, 61; Brant, *John*, 37; Harris, *John*, 39; Morris, *John*, 101; Köstenberger, *John*, 50.

182. Vincent, *Word Studies*, 49; Morris, *John*, 87; Watt, *Family of the King*, 182; Keener, *John*, 403.

183. Vincent, *Word Studies*, 61; Brant, *John*, 37; Harris, *John*, 39; Morris, *John*, 101; Köstenberger, *John*, 50.

184. Köstenberger, *John*, 50.

185. Ridderbos, *John*, 191; Köstenberger, *John*, 185; Harris, *John*, 110; Brant, *John*, 105.

186. Vincent, *Word Studies*, 135.

theme in the prologue. Thus, we can safely conclude that the exegesis of the Father by the Son includes his revelations concerning the community. Therefore, what follows is a narrative analysis of John 5 as a paradigm of the incarnate Word's exegesis and expression of the community.

Narrative Analysis of John 5

John 5 shares some commonalities with the prologue. Like the prologue, it allows the reader to appreciate the revelation of the community of God in the human community. It also reveals human society's failure to manifest its divine intentions. Beyond these, the disposition exhibited by the characters at Bethesda prompts inquiries into certain principles and practices of collectivism, which is a commonly accepted academic portrayal of Mediterranean society in the first century.[187] The analysis of the narrative is conducted from a community-oriented perspective to reveal the societal maladies present at Bethesda as well as the divine remedy provided by God to address them.

The Delimitation of John 5

The consensus among scholars is that the narrative (John 5) begins with the first verse of the fifth chapter.[188] On the other hand, two scholarly opinions exist concerning the end of the literary unit. Borgen and like-minded scholars avow that John 5:1–18 forms an independent unit.[189] On the contrary, other scholars confirm the literary coherence of John 5:1–47.[190] On the reasons for the divergent positions, Borgen contends that John 5:1–18 is a documented oral unit and not just something extrapolated from oral tradition.[191] His argument emanates from using a diachronic approach—a historical-critical method—to analyze the historical development or utilization of the material. Indeed, John used existing traditions.[192] But has Borgen not stretched the argument beyond

---

187. Malina, *New Testament*, 67; Malina, "Collectivism," 19.

188. Köstenberger, *John*, 174; Moloney, *Signs and Shadows*, 2; Talbert, *Reading John*, 127; Asiedu-Peprah, *Johannine Sabbath*, 52; Kok, *Healing*, 95.

189. Borgen, *Gospel of John*, 138.

190. Köstenberger, *John*, 174; Moloney, *Signs and Shadows*, 2; Talbert, *Reading John*, 127; Schubert, *Gospel*, 51; Asiedu-Peprah, *Johannine Sabbath*, 52; Brant, *John*, 97.

191. Borgen, *Gospel of John*, 138.

192. Dodd, *Historical Tradition*, 180.

its elasticity? For instance, Dodd contends that traditions are employed uniquely by John.[193] Labahn corroborates that using traditions involves forming unfamiliar meanings.[194] Consequently, Borgen's position is incomplete because it ignores the inventive application of the material in John 5. In chapter 5, the healing (John 1:1–18) is not the centre stage but a catalyst for the discussions that follow.[195]

Indeed, the prevailing perspective (literary coherence of John 5:1–47) does not dispute the plausibility of John 5:1–18 constituting a cohesive unit. It studies the text using a synchronic approach and concentrates on the Johannine application of the material in its final form.[196] Further, to advance their position, they focus on the thematic unity of John 5:1–47. Their studies[197] indicate that the Sabbath theme is the unifying element in the chapter. John demonstrates this by stating that the healing occurred on a Sabbath day and making the subsequent events in the narrative traceable to it.[198]

Furthermore, certain academics assert that the narrative in John 5 exhibits similarities with other accounts of miraculous healings.[199] According to Talbert's perspective, the narrative can be interpreted as a manifestation of the conventional tripartite framework, wherein the author presents an issue, its resolution, and the corresponding reaction.[200] Witherington proposes an expanded model that encompasses four key elements: a declaration of the illness, an encounter between Jesus and the afflicted individual, an act of authentication to confirm the healing, and the responses of witnesses to the event.[201] The inference can be drawn that the narrative's conclusion is not limited to John 5:18 due to its failure to encompass all the prescribed characteristics.

Furthermore, academics employ the term "μετὰ ταῦτα" (meta tauta) to demarcate the narrative, as noted by Moloney, Culpepper, Talbert,

---

193. Dodd, *Historical Tradition*, 179.

194. Labahn, "Living Word(s)," 61.

195. Schubert, *Gospel of John*, 51.

196. Köstenberger, *John*, 174; Moloney, *Signs and Shadows*, 27; Witherington, *John's Wisdom*, 134; Schubert, *Gospel of John*, 51.

197. Köstenberger, *John*, 174; Moloney, *Signs and Shadows*, 27; Witherington, *John's Wisdom*, 134; Schubert, *Gospel of John*, 51; Asiedu-Peprah, *Johannine Sabbath*, 52.

198. Köstenberger, *John*, 181–83; Witherington, *John's Wisdom*, 134.

199. Witherington, *John's Wisdom*, 134; Talbert, *Reading John*, 127.

200. Talbert, *Reading John*, 127.

201. Witherington, *John's Wisdom*, 134.

and Schubert.²⁰² The aforementioned scholars assert that the expression "after this" present in John 5:1 and John 6:1 serves as an affirmation of the literary unity of John 5. The orthographical device is regarded as an initial demarcation point, leading to the deduction that the narrative culminates at John 5:47 due to its recurrence in John 6:1, which serves as the commencement of a distinct narrative.

Undoubtedly, there exists ample evidence substantiating the literary coherence of John 5. First, the position of μετὰ ταῦτα (John 5:1; 6:1) creates an *inclusio* (or inclusion).²⁰³ Moloney and Culpepper confirm that the device is employed predominantly to indicate the commencement of new narratives to the reader.²⁰⁴ Thus, because μετὰ ταῦτα is used in John 6:1 to commence another narrative, John 5:1–47 belongs to the previous section. However, there exist certain instances that deviate from the aforementioned pattern, such as those found in John 13:7 and 19:28. In such cases, the phrase "μετὰ ταῦτα" does not connote a distinct section but rather denotes a temporal sequence, signifying "later" (cf. John 13:7; 19:28). Similarly, John 5:14 does not begin a new narrative; rather, it just indicates what transpired "later" or "later the same day."²⁰⁵

On the other hand, more evidence points to the conclusion that in John 6:1, the expression heralds the beginning of a new narrative.²⁰⁶ First, there is a change in geographical location from Jerusalem (John 5:1) to "over the sea of Galilee" (6:1). Additionally, the theme is changed; the Sabbath and its related events and discourse disappear in the fifth chapter, and a new one commences in the next chapter. Thus, we can safely agree with Moloney that the unity of John 5 is certain because of the unity of place, time, characters, and theme.

Finally, seeing the narrative as a thematic unit also influences the structuring of the pericope.

---

202. Moloney, *John*, 165; Culpepper, "John 5:1–18," 196; Talbert, *Reading John*, 127; Schubert, *Gospel of John*, 51.

203. Schubert, *Gospel of John*, 51; Coxon, *Exploring the New Exodus*, 99; Witherington, *John's Wisdom*, 133.

204. Moloney, *John*, 165; Culpepper, "John 5:1–18," 196.

205. Carson, *John*, 245; Ridderbos, *John*, 190; Köstenberger, *John*, 174.

206. See Osborne, *Hermeneutical Spiral*, 217.

The Structure of John 5

Since scholars who accept the literary unity of John 5 predominantly use the Sabbath theme as the premise of their arguments, their proposed structures (though distinct) stress the theme and Jesus' identity as the Son and Lord of the Sabbath.[207] Köstenberger proposes a concise structure as follows: 1. The setting (John 5:1–3); 2. The healing (5:5–9a); 3. The aftermath (5:9b–15); 4. The Sabbath controversy (5:16–47) a. Jesus' response to the charges of Sabbath-breaking and blasphemy (5:16–30); b. Testimony regarding Jesus (5:1–47).[208] Harris also structures the narrative distinctively:1. He heals the man at the pool of Bethesda (5:1–15); 2. Jesus replies to his opponents (5:16–47); a. Jesus and the Sabbath (5:16–18); b. Jesus grants life and exercises judgment (5:19–30); c. Witnesses to Jesus (5:31–47).[209]

Further, because no one has studied the narrative through the lens of community, no structure focuses on that. Thus, this work proposes one that takes into consideration the communicative force of the theme of community: 1. The Bethesda community (John 5:1–3); 2. The divine remedy for Bethesda community (5:5–9a); 3. The religious community concentrates on the Sabbath (5:9b–13); 4. The religious community identifies the "Sabbath breaker" (5:14–16); 5. Jesus exegetes the divine community (5:17–47).

The Analysis of John 5

The Bethesda Community (John 5:1–3a)

The narrator introduces the narrative (John 5:1) using μετὰ ταῦτα (*meta tauta*). By this Johannine phrase, the real reader is signaled to anticipate a new section.[210] Whereas Keener considers the phrase a chronological marker, Schubert opines that John uses these words primarily to indicate

---

207. See Moloney, *Signs and Shadows*, 2–27; Bystrom, *God Among Us*, 98–106; Witherington, *John's Wisdom*, 136–41; Köstenberger, *John*, 175; Harris, *John*, 104–17; cf. Gharbin and Van Eck, "Solitude," 2.

208. Köstenberger, *John*, 175.

209. Harris, *John*, 104–17.

210. Moloney, *Signs and Shadows*, 4; *John*, 165; Talbert, *Reading John*, 127; Schubert, *Gospel of John*, 40–41; Witherington, *John's Wisdom*, 133; Brant, *John*, 100; Kok, *Healing*, 95.

a change of subject or geographical location.²¹¹ In this case, however, the phrase occasioned both topographical and thematic changes.²¹² The narrative indicates that there is a geographical change from Galilee (John 4:54) to Jerusalem (5:1). Additionally, a thematic change is announced through the healing of the paralytic on a Sabbath day, introducing the Sabbath theme (5:9).

John proceeds to explain the reason for the topographical and thematic changes. "A feast of the Jews" is cited as the justification for Jesus' voyage from Galilee to Jerusalem (John 5:1). The narrator's unconventional labeling of the feast has precipitated speculation and a gamut of suggestions from Johannine scholars.²¹³ The reason is that John is known for connecting feasts to his narrative because of their significance in the piety of the believing community.²¹⁴ Consequently, the conjectures aim at uncovering the communicative force of the "feast of the Jews" in this narrative. Nonetheless, it appears that John's silence, in this case, could be attributed to the fact that he mentioned "a feast" just to indicate the purpose of the directional change.²¹⁵ Again, the mention of a Jewish religious feast places the event within a religious context.²¹⁶ It also introduces the theme of feasts and demonstrates how feasts inform John's Christology.²¹⁷

Having established Jesus' mission in Jerusalem, bewilderingly, John describes a location in Jerusalem without demonstrating its connection to the religious feast in question: a place near the "Sheep Gate"²¹⁸ And

211. Keener, *John*, 635; Schubert, *Gospel of John*, 40–41.

212. The same thing is repeated in John 6 and 7 where the phrase occasioned both a change in theme and location. In John 6, Jesus departs from his location in Jerusalem and traverses across the sea of Galilee (6:1). Additionally, the predominant theme in John 5 (Sabbath) is replaced by the feeding of the multitude. Similarly, in John 7, Jesus is seen in Galilee debating with his brothers on the right time to go to Judaea (7:3).

213. Some scholars associate "the feast" with the Passover, Pentecost, and Feast of Tabernacles, e.g., Morris, *John*, 265; Barnes, "John 5"; Boismard, "Bethzatha," 208–18. For a comprehensive discussion on the subject, see Kok, *Healing*, 99–101.

214. Yee, *Jewish Feasts*, 27, 30; cf. Carson, *John*, 240; Keener, *John*, 634. John attaches John 2:13; 6:4; 11:35 to the Passover; John 7:2 to the Feast of Tabernacles; and John 10:22 to the Feast of Dedications.

215. Moloney, *Signs and Shadows*, 2–3; Carson, *John*, 241.

216. Yee, *Jewish Feasts*, 16.

217. Moloney, *Signs and Shadows*, 2; Daise, *Feasts in John*, 68.

218. Köstenberger, *John*, 179; Carson, *John*, 241; Bruce, *Gospel of John*, 122; Estes, *Questions of Jesus*, 116; Keener, *John*, 636. These scholars agree that instead of sheep market, it should read "Sheep Gate." What they have in mind is the Sheep Gate Nehemiah mentions (Neh 3:1, 32).

unlike the feast that occasioned the visit, the location is named. Scholars are, however, divided on the right reading of the name of the pool. Thus, some suggested names are Bethesda, Bethzatha, or Bethsaida.[219] Based on the corresponding Hebrew name in the Qumran Copper Scroll, "Bethesda" is widely accepted among them.[220] Additionally, the meaning of the name—House of (Divine) mercy—could be one of the reasons for its wide acceptance.[221] It derives its significance from the deliverances at the pool, which are considered products of God's mercy.[222]

Again, since the setting of a narrative has a figurative tenor,[223] the idea of situating the event in a religious context is reiterated and further heightened by this labeling and representation.[224] Thus, to legitimize its name as a place where God shows mercy, a community constituted by the sick (invalids, blind, lame, and paralyzed) and searching for divine mercy or healing is indicated as occupants of the colonnades at Bethesda.[225]

The Divine Remedy for Bethesda Community (John 5:5–9a)

Having established the different groups that constitute the community and the purpose of congregating there, the attention of the reader

---

219. Metzger, *Textual Commentary*, 208; Moloney, *John*, 171; Siebald, "Bethesda," 84. Bethzatha is accepted by some scholars because the name resembles a northern suburb of Jerusalem. Siebald, "Bethesda," 84. Conversely, others accept Bethsaida because it is confused with a town in John 1:44. See Bruce, *Gospel of John*, 122; Metzger, *Textual Commentary*, 208.

220. Bruce, *Gospel of John*, 122; Moloney, *John*, 171; Carson, *John*, 241; Metzger, *Textual Commentary*, 208; Keener, *John*, 636; Talbert, *Reading John*, 127.

221. Metzger, *Textual Commentary*, 208.

222. Köstenberger, *John*, 178.

223. Marguerat and Bourquin, *How to Read Bible*, 79.

224. See John 5:1; Yee, *Jewish Feasts*, 16; Asiedu-Peprah, *Johannine Sabbath*, 52.

225. John 5:3b–4 attempts to demonstrate the mode of healing. Textual critics agree that the poor external attestations and the presence of non-Johannine words in the verse render it inauthentic. See Metzger, *Textual Commentary*, 209; Harris, *John*, 105; Köstenberger, *John*, 195. Thus, they are considered scribal insertions, serving as marginal glosses to capture the popular belief of the people about the reason behind the stirring of the water and its consequence. Carson, *John*, 242; Bruce, *Gospel of John*, 122; Moloney, *John*, 171; Bultmann, *Gospel of John*, 240–41; Barrett, *Gospel According to St. John*, 251. Therefore, most scholars suggest that it must be omitted due to its absence in the best and earliest manuscripts, such as P66, P75, Vaticanus, Sinaiticus, and others. Metzger, *Textual Commentary*, 209; Harris, *John*, 105; Talbert, *Reading John*, 128; Jones, *Symbol of Water*, 124.

is drawn to a particular case after a general, pictorial, and panoramic presentation of the conditions at Bethesda. This character, who is a member of the Bethesda community, is merely identified as τις ἄνθρωπος (*tis anthrōpos*, a certain man). In a status-conscious social system such as the first-century world,[226] introducing a character with such a description must be regarded with suspicion. Also, it is noteworthy that this identification marker is characteristic of John (John 1:6; 3:1; 5:5; 9:1; 11:1). Out of the five instances, the narrative describes three of them by their names and "social standing."[227] Nicodemus was a Pharisee, a teacher of Israel (John 3:1–10). That denotes a man of high social standing.[228] Further, Lazarus was Jesus' friend, an anticipation of the later elevation of the status of the disciples.[229] John the Baptist was also God's authorized personal representative,[230] a man with high social standing.[231] On the other hand, the name and status of this man (and the congenitally blind man in John 9) are unknown. The absence of such identification reflects his social condition: an impoverished man[232] who had no status in his society.[233]

Apart from the social malady, his condition is known. He is suffering from long-term lameness, a disvalued state.[234] Many people in antiquity did not even live for thirty-eight years.[235] Thus, the "thirty-eight years" is purposefully stated to highlight both the severity and hopelessness of his condition.[236]

Against this background, John introduces Jesus' response to the problem through various actions. Consequently, the verbs ὁράω (*horáō*, to see), γινώσκω (*ginōskō*, to know), and λέγω (*légō*, to say) are worth mentioning because of how John employs them interconnectedly to unveil the actions of Jesus targeted at alleviating the problem (John 5:6). The

226. Malina, *New Testament*, 107.
227. They are John the Baptist (John 1:6), Nicodemus (3:1), and Lazarus (11:1).
228. Skinner, *John*, 128.
229. Esler and Piper, *Lazarus, Mary, and Martha*, 91.
230. Harris, *John*, 26.
231. Webb has done an extensive sociohistorical study on John the Baptist, considering his significance in the narrative. Webb, *John the Baptizer*, 349–77.
232. According to some scholars, the man's mat reveals his economic status: poor. Köstenberger, *John*, 180; Keener, *John*, 640; Harris, *John*, 106.
233. Porter, *John*, 54; Keener, *John*, 640.
234. John 5:5, 8–9; Pilch, *Healing*, 13.
235. Köstenberger, *John*, 179.
236. Ridderbos, *John*, 185; Tenney, *John*, 104; Köstenberger, *John*, 179.

process of healing commences with Jesus seeing the man (5:6). However, the expression does not merely indicate that Jesus caught a glimpse of him.[237] In some instances, John (and the gospel traditions) indicate Jesus seeing a sick person before the healing as an introduction to action.[238] This approach poses no problems for his audience because it is grounded in a thorough knowledge of their background. The Mediterranean culture establishes a link between what one sees and the positive actions it triggers when one observes through the eyes of pity.[239] The quality of pity is said to inhere in a person's eyes or heart and is revealed by what a person does on behalf of others in need.[240] It indicates that positive actions are provoked when people in need are viewed through the lens of pity.[241]

The significance of this concept lies in its inextricable connection to honor, a pivotal value in Mediterranean society.[242] According to Malina,[243] pity is a means of achieving honor; it provokes honorable acts towards those in need. The individual who acts out of pity is also said to be compassionate.[244] Finally, pity is also a theological value—a quality of God.[245] Thus, we can safely conclude that John is evoking one of their culturally held values to explain Jesus' response. Therefore, the relationship established between "seeing" and "acting" suggests that Jesus personifies the various representations of the quality of pity in that community. Through the eyes of compassion, he becomes the merciful one who demonstrates pity in a house of mercy devoid of mercy, "seeing" the man in the depths of his misery.[246]

Further, the import of John's christological perspective on lameness becomes more conspicuous when juxtaposed with the first-century

237. See Brown, *Gospel According to John*, 207; Ridderbos, *John*, 185.

238. Brown, *Gospel According to John*, 207; Ridderbos, *John*, 185; cf. John 9:1. Luke 7:13 records a similar case where Jesus was moved with compassion to raise the son of the widow of Nain after seeing her. Thus, the idea of tracing Jesus' compassionate actions to "seeing" the individual first is characteristic of the gospel traditions and not just a Johannine style.

239. Malina, "Pity," 139.

240. Malina, "Pity," 139.

241. See Malina, "Pity," 139.

242. See Malina, *New Testament*, 28; Van Eck, "When Neighbours," 4; Malina and Rohrbaugh, *Social Science Commentary*, 369.

243. Malina, "Pity," 139.

244. Malina, "Pity," 139.

245. Malina, "Pity," 139.

246. Ridderbos, *John*, 185; cf. Malina, "Pity," 139.

Mediterranean view on lameness. Despite the significant place of pity in their cultural ethos, people who needed it most (such as the lame) did not always receive it. On the contrary, some viewed them with contempt[247] because being lame was considered a disvalued state.[248] And in a society where a person's honor is his publicly acknowledged worth, this is tantamount to shame.[249] Thus, Jesus' response to the situation challenges the culture to reevaluate its views on this marginalized group.

Moreover, even though John invokes a theological and cultural value, he builds upon that knowledge. The verbs ὁράω (horáō) and γινώσκω (ginōskō) are connected to demonstrate that, though "seeing" is an introduction to action in John,[250] in this case, the awareness of the problem prompted his actions.[251] The knowledge of the condition influenced Jesus' view of the man's reality.[252]

Having established these premises, John proceeds to detail additional actions carried out by Jesus. First, Jesus initiates a conversation with the man to elicit his response.[253] It is noteworthy that, characteristic of the gospel traditions, the sick usually come to Jesus to ask for healing.[254] In this narrative, the converse is true.[255] Jesus seeks the man's attention by asking him a polar question.[256] In his examination of the interrogative force of Jesus' questions in John, Estes establishes that though polar questions require either a positive or negative response (yes or no), the use of ὑγιὴς (hugiēs) coupled with the compassion that occasioned

---

247. Keener, *John*, 640.
248. Pilch, *Healing*, 13.
249. Plevnik, "Honour," 96; Rohrbaugh, "Honor," 109; cf. Lev 21:18.
250. Brown, *Gospel According to John*, 207; Ridderbos, *John*, 185.
251. Morris, *John*, 268; Ridderbos, *John*, 185. Since John does not indicate how Jesus received information about the man's predicament, scholars have sought to explain the source of his information by showing that it was through supernatural knowledge. Moloney, *Signs and Shadows*, 5; Brown, *Gospel According to John*, 207; Morris, *John*, 268; Witherington, *John's Wisdom*, 137. Köstenberger and Carson, on the other hand, assert that Jesus asked for the information, even though they admit that the word is used for both supernatural knowledge and knowledge gained through inquiry. Köstenberger, *John*, 180; Carson, *John*, 243.
252. Ridderbos, *John*, 185.
253. Estes, *Questions of Jesus*, 117; Köstenberger, *John*, 180.
254. Witherington, *John's Wisdom*, 134; Keener, *John*, 640.
255. Carson, *John*, 243; Witherington, *John's Wisdom*, 134; Keener, *John*, 640.
256. Estes, *Questions of Jesus*, 117.

the question makes a positive response the only expected answer.[257] The man answers differently; he explains the futility of his attempts at procuring his healing and the cause of the long-term debilitation instead (John 5:7).[258] Indeed, his persistent presence at the pool and the several unproductive attempts to step into it demonstrate his willingness for healing.[259] It also makes conspicuous the absence of human help as the cause of his failed expectations.[260]

His answer is astounding. It establishes the cause of his exacerbated condition and the "colossal cultural failure" that helped to perpetuate it.[261] By that statement, John is indicating that the impoverished[262] and hopeless lame man[263] who has no social position[264] is unable to receive assistance even in the house of mercy.[265]

There are valid reasons why his answer is astonishing. First, John develops the narrative within a religious-cultural context.[266] Jesus comes to Jerusalem to celebrate a religious feast. Asiedu-Peprah argues that "the mention of a feast is intended to place the whole of chapter 5 within a specific religious-cultural setting."[267] In Jerusalem, Jesus enters a society with a religious identity (Bethesda), a place where members live in expectation of God's omnibenevolence.[268] So, it is reasonable to expect that people who live in anticipation of days of personal experiences of the mercies of God will incarnate this attribute or one worthy of their identity. Indeed, in the ancient Mediterranean world, religion meant "the attitude one must have and the behavior one is expected to follow

---

257. Estes, *Questions of Jesus*, 117.

258. The notion that miraculous healings transpired after the angelic stirring of the pool (a follow-up of John 5:3b–4) is considered inauthentic due to the absence of sufficient external evidence. Metzger, *Textual Commentary*, 209; Köstenberger, *John*, 195. Since they are considered scribal insertions, the explanation in John 5:7 forms part of the marginal glosses. Carson, *John*, 242; Bruce, *Gospel of John*, 122; Moloney, *John*, 171; Brown, *Gospel According to John*, 207.

259. Bruce, *Gospel of John*, 124; Carson, *John*, 243; Tenney, *John*, 105.

260. Moloney, *Signs and Shadows*, 5; Tenney, *John*, 105.

261. Pilch, *Healing*, 13. See also Pilch, "Cooperativeness," 33.

262. Köstenberger, *John*, 180; Keener, *John*, 640.

263. Ridderbos, *John*, 185; Tenney, *John*, 104; Brown, *Gospel According to John*, 207.

264. Porter, *John*, 54; Köstenberger, *John*, 180; Keener, *John*, 640.

265. Moloney, *Signs and Shadows*, 5; Tenney, *John*, 105.

266. Asiedu-Peprah, *Johannine Sabbath*, 52; Yee, *Jewish Feasts*, 16.

267. Asiedu-Peprah, *Johannine Sabbath*, 52.

268. See Köstenberger, *John*, 178.

relative to those who control one's existence."²⁶⁹ It implies that God, the controller of life, expects humans to demonstrate an expected attitude. Malina argues that Bible translations sometimes refer to this behavior as justice.²⁷⁰ As a virtue, justice refers to how community members relate to one another and reminds members to treat each other as they wish that God might treat them.²⁷¹ Again, it manifests special care for the poor and marginalized in society.²⁷²

Regrettably, there was no justice at Bethesda. Instead, what was present were acts of injustice perpetrated against the disenfranchised and most vulnerable members of that community.²⁷³ The word βάλῃ (bale; John 5:7) indicates that a certain degree of agility is a prerequisite for healing in the water before the cessation of its agitations.²⁷⁴ And since the lame man and other weak members of that community were incapacitated and immobilized by their sicknesses, those who needed healing most were hindered by those whose sicknesses did not immobilize them.²⁷⁵ Thus, healings obtained at Bethesda are not products of communal or collective efforts but are contingent on the individual's competitive spirit, level of fitness, swiftness, and probably connections (John 5:7).²⁷⁶

The strong presence of individualism at Bethesda is antithetical to the first-century Mediterranean culture. Scholars agree that the Mediterranean selves were communalistic.²⁷⁷ The practice of collectivism in their cultural context is rooted in their appreciation of group orientation as a primary value.²⁷⁸ It indicates that individuals should always "seek the good of the neighbour" and not pursue individualistic goals.²⁷⁹ Therefore, unless for the benefit of the group, competition is considered disruptive to social harmony.²⁸⁰ Individualistic goals coupled with competition do

269. Malina, *New Testament*, 31.

270. Malina, *New Testament*, 31; cf. Downs, "Economics," 163. Jesus refers to justice and mercy as the weightier matters of the law (Matt 23:23).

271. Keenan, "Justice," 121.

272. Keenan, "Justice," 121–22, 126; Harrington, "*Biblical Perspectives*," 126.

273. Witherington, *John's Wisdom*, 137.

274. Vincent, *Word Studies*, 132.

275. Witherington, *John's Wisdom*, 137.

276. See Witherington, *John's Wisdom*, 137.

277. Malina, *New Testament*, 67; Malina, "Who Are We?," 106; "Collectivism," 19.

278. Neyrey, "Group Orientation," 91.

279. Neyrey, "Group Orientation," 89.

280. Malina, "Collectivism," 22.

not encourage cooperativeness—the urge to help one another, especially those in need.[281] Further, since cooperativeness is governed by family-centeredness,[282] expressing this cultural value, in turn, breeds family-centeredness, making it possible for the community to enjoy "justice."[283] Thus, the privation of help to those who needed it most betrays the tenets of collectivism and makes individualism the root of the enormous religious-cultural disappointment displayed at Bethesda.[284]

Moreover, there are sufficient proofs of their cultural values to warrant the needed support. For instance, justice—loyalty—was also appreciated in the family institution, the dominant institution in the first-century Mediterranean world.[285] Within a kinship group, justice also means enduring loyalty to one's kin.[286] Malina argues that this enduring loyalty is demonstrated to the individual regardless of their conduct.[287] Thus, family members were to support each other.[288] In this narrative, John is silent about the family of the man. Consequently, he leaves a gap for other "family members" to occupy—friends.[289]

In the absence of kinsmen, friends could have helped him.[290] In the first-century Mediterranean world, one's survival depended on making friends.[291] An important reason was that friends were "persons who treated each other as if they were family."[292] Implicit in this definition is the idea that friendship requires commitment, which makes it a moral obligation to help a friend in need.[293] Therefore, being friendless means the deprivation of friendship and "family," with all its associated

---

281. Pilch, "Cooperativeness," 33.
282. Pilch, "Cooperativeness," 33.
283. See Malina, "Patronage," 136.
284. See Pilch, "Cooperativeness," 33.
285. Malina, "Patronage," 136; Van Eck, "Inclusivity," 61.
286. Malina, "Patronage," 136.
287. Malina, "Patronage," 136.
288. Malina, "Patronage," 136.
289. See Pilch, *Healing*, 13.
290. See Pilch, *Healing*, 13. The Synoptic Gospels record a case where the narrative changed because a group of people carried a sick friend to Jesus (Matt 9:1; Mark 2:1–12; Luke 5:17–26).
291. Pilch, *Healing*, 13.
292. Van Eck, "When Neighbours," 5.
293. Van Eck, "When Neighbours," 5; Moxnes, *Economy of the Kingdom*, 62.

benefits—accessing help from deeply committed members in times of need.[294]

The above reasons show that viewing the man's answer (I have no one) through the lens of first-century Mediterranean cultural values leads to an agreement with Pilch that the narrative points to the restoration of the paralytic's disvalued states and the "colossal cultural failure" that helped to perpetuate it.[295] First, the healing, confirmed by lifting the mat,[296] shows the restoration of his disvalued state.[297] The actions of Jesus also remind the community to demonstrate its religious and cultural values to the marginalized among them.

The Religious Community Concentrate on the Sabbath (John 5:9b–13)

John introduces two new themes in the narrative: the Sabbath[298] and "the Jews." The Sabbath is crucial because it gives the new scene a religious-cultural context.[299] The religious dimension of the Sabbath is that it must be observed and sanctified to the Lord (cf. Deut 5:12). The cultural significance is the provision of liberation from work and any form of servitude within one's society, irrespective of one's social classification.[300] Thus, one of the divine intentions for observing the Sabbath is to break down the wall of discrimination in a stratified society that grouped individuals into classes by one's gender or achievements and re-enact in the community humankind's original status.[301]

Moreover, the community's responsibility towards the marginalized is attached to the observance of the Sabbath (cf. Deut 5:12–15). The Old

---

294. See Pilch, *Healing*, 13; Moxnes, *Economy of the Kingdom*, 62.

295. Pilch admits that the man's response is tantamount to a colossal cultural failure. However, he argues that in this healing story, Jesus improves the man's disvalued state by restoring him to wholeness and becoming his first friend. Pilch, *Healing*, 13. This seems to narrow the "colossal cultural failure" to friendship. Friendship is not the only Mediterranean value that is not evident at Bethesda. Therefore, I argue that the encounter between Jesus and the paralytic exposes the missing link between the theory and practise of collectivism and its interrelated Mediterranean values.

296. Köstenberger, *John*, 180; Beutler, *Commentary*, 148; Beasley-Murray, *John*, 74.

297. Pilch, *Healing*, 13; cf. Keener, *John*, 640; Lev 21:18.

298. In this narrative, John deviates from the Synoptics, which usually place the Sabbath theme before the healing. O'Day and Hylen, *John*, 64.

299. Asiedu-Peprah, *Johannine Sabbath*, 52; cf. Keener, *John*, 641–42.

300. Nelson, *Deuteronomy*, 83; Hasel, "Sabbath," 32.

301. Nelson, *Deuteronomy*, 83; Hasel, "Sabbath," 32.

Testament gives two motivations for the command to observe the Sabbath: creation and the liberation from slavery in Egypt (cf. Deut 5:12–15; Exod 20:8–11; 23:12). The freedom from Egypt serves as the basis for a social motivation: to prompt the people to allow those in bondage to participate in the communal rest provided by the Sabbath (Deut 5:14–15). So, indicating that the healing occurred on a Sabbath day, considering the abovementioned cultural import, the man's liberation from sickness is a way of reminding the community of its emancipatory role (cf. Deut 5:14–15).

Further, since the narrative has progressed from one "religious-cultural scene" (Bethesda) to another, where Jewish religious authorities have been introduced,[302] the Sabbath establishes the religious context of the narrative and sets the stage for the drama that follows.[303]

Therefore, the reader is prepared to anticipate a corresponding response. However, the attitude of the authorities shows the intensity of the societal maladies. The leaders demonstrate through their responses that they are interested in the violation of the religious law and not the liberation of the man.[304] John's words indicate that they acted purposely because of what had transpired on a Sabbath day. Unlike the introduction of Jesus that occasioned compassion and culminated in healing, the religious leaders, from whom much is expected, paid no attention to the cure of an impoverished man[305] who had endured 38 years of living in a disvalued state.[306] Their behavior has been described as extraordinary,[307] unimaginable, and shortsighted for forgetting the true intent of the law.[308] They had jettisoned the weightier matters of the law (one of which is mercy) but promoted strict adherence to the law.[309] The narrative flow

---

302. Harris, *John*, 106; Köstenberger, *Encountering John*, 79; Stibbe, *John's Gospel*, 78; Morris, *John*, 357; Moloney, *John*, 97.

303. Martyn, *History and Theology*, 74; Carson, *John*, 244.

304. Harris, *John*, 106; Moloney, *John*, 168–69; Köstenberger, *Encountering John*, 79; Witherington, *John's Wisdom*, 138. Since the Sabbath was included in the three religious rituals that characterized the life of first-century Judaism, issues concerning it were of great interest. Breaking it was practically the same as touching their communal identity. O'Day and Hylen, *John*, 64.

305. Köstenberger, *John*, 180; Keener, *John*, 640; Harris, *John*, 106.

306. Pilch, *Healing*, 13; cf. Köstenberger, *Encountering John*, 79.

307. Beasley-Murray, *John*, 74.

308. Köstenberger, *Encountering John*, 79.

309. See Matt 23:23; Köstenberger, *Encountering John*, 96.

brings the reader to another discovery: the absence of mercy from the religious community. And this helps to appreciate the problems of the Bethesda community.

The man's response to the leaders for the violation of the law was that he was acting at the command of an authoritative[310] but unfamiliar man.[311] John's comment that the cured man was oblivious to Jesus' identity could be his way of further stressing that the healing was purely an act of mercy (what is lacking in the community) and not based on any prior relationship (cf. John 5:13).

The Religious Community Identifies the "Sabbath Breaker" (John 5:14–16)

A new scene (not a new section) is introduced in John 5:14 using μετὰ ταῦτα (*meta tauta*).[312] The aforementioned expression denotes temporal posteriority,[313] conveys the idea of a subsequent occurrence on the same day,[314] or implies temporal ambiguity.[315] Thus, the event—the encounter between Jesus and the healed man—is separated from the surrounding narrative.[316] John creates a critical narrative event—a space in the plot—to see how the man responds to his new life. And the first place he enters is the temple (John 5:14). Interestingly, Jesus finds him in the temple and cautions him not to continue sinning.[317] The nature of Jesus' instruction stems from the repercussions of living in sin: something more terrible would happen to him.[318] This possibly refers to either another physical illness[319] or eternal damnation.[320]

Nevertheless, unlike the man healed from congenital blindness who defends Jesus in the presence of the Jewish leaders (John 9:15–17, 24–34),

310. Harris, *John*, 106.
311. Bultmann, *Gospel of John*, 243; Brant, *John*, 104.
312. Moloney, *Signs and Shadows*, 6; cf. Ridderbos, *John*, 181.
313. Carson, *John*, 245; Ridderbos, *John*, 190.
314. Köstenberger, *John*, 174.
315. Morris, *John*, 272.
316. Moloney, *Signs and Shadows*, 6.
317. Beasley-Murray, *John*, 74; Morris, *John*, 272.
318. Köstenberger, *John*, 181; Harris, *John*, 107.
319. Moloney, *John*, 169; Morris, *John*, 272.
320. Morris, *John*, 272; Ridderbos, *John*, 189.

he decides to go and report (*anaggéllō*) Jesus to the authorities.[321] And on account of this report[322] or healing on the Sabbath day, a perceived contravention of the Sabbatical laws,[323] the religious leaders persecuted and sought to kill Jesus.[324]

Jesus Exegetes the Divine Community (John 5:17–47)

Since the leaders could not discern Jesus' authority and the social maladies that the healing exposes and remedies, he "exegetes" the divine community as the ideal response to this colossal cultural failure. He makes statements with illocutionary force to achieve a perlocutionary effect on the authorities.

The verb ἀπεκρίνατο (*apekrinato*) has a legal undertone and indicates that what follows (John 5:17) is Jesus' reply to the leaders.[325] For this reason, it indicates Jesus' response to the charges leveled against him (5:17). Using the family metaphor ὁ πατήρ μου (*ho Patēr mou*), Jesus appeals to his unique relationship with God as the substratum of his work.[326] The expression ὁ πατήρ μου aims to assert that he enjoys ontological equality with the father.[327] Again, the conjunction καὶ (*kai*, which in this context means "and so") and the emphatic ἐγὼ (*egō*)[328] suggest that by working on the Sabbath, Jesus is only replicating his father.[329] It is an adoption of a Jewish rabbinic opinion that some divine activities continue even on

---

321. Harris, *John*, 107; Ridderbos, *John*, 189.

322. Brant, *John*, 104–5; Ridderbos, *John*, 189.

323. See Talbert, *Reading John*, 129; Harris, *John*, 109; Moloney, *Signs and Shadows*, 8; Brant, *John*, 105.

324. Though the imperfect tense indicates a repeated action, scholars disagree on the nature of the persecution. Cf. Mounce, *Biblical Greek Grammar*, 181; Köstenberger, *John*, 115. For instance, whereas Moloney and Carson agree that the imperfect tense suggests that the persecution was a repeated action, Harris thinks that the imperfect tense here is less likely to be customary. See Moloney, *Signs and Shadows*, 8; Carson, *John*, 247; Harris, *John*, 109.

325. Abbott, *Johannine Vocabulary*, 186; Bruner, *Gospel of John*, 321; Carson, *John*, 247. The word appears only in John 5:19 apart from John 5:17.

326. Harris, *John*, 110; Köstenberger, *Encountering John*, 97; Keener, *John*, 646.

327. Ridderbos, *John*, 191; Köstenberger, *John*, 185; Moloney, *John*, 174; Harris, *John*, 110; Beasley-Murray, *John*, 74–75; Brant, *John*, 105; Dalcour, *Oneness Theology*, 2.

328. Both from the crasis κἀγὼ (*kagō*).

329. Harris, *John*, 109; Bruce, *Gospel of John*, 127.

the Sabbath.³³⁰ Therefore, his participation in the self-evident axiom of the constancy of divine activity is employed as an oblique claim to deity: doing what his Father does makes the Son as divine as the Father.³³¹ The interlocutors perfectly understood the perlocutionary effect of his illocutionary act and hence charged him with blasphemy.³³²

Consequently, prefixing his argument with ἀμὴν ἀμὴν (*amen amen*) to establish the emphatic and supremely authoritative nature of his answer,³³³ Jesus begins to correct these misconceptions (from John 5:19) by exegeting the divine community, focusing on collectivism, love, partnership, equality, and functional unity.³³⁴

"The Jews" understood equality with God as independence from God,³³⁵ whereas Jesus viewed it as the very opposite.³³⁶ Though they are one in being, the Son submits to the Father functionally.³³⁷ And accordingly, his works (both present and future works)³³⁸ proceed from what

330. Carson, *John*, 247; Keener, *John*, 646; Harris, *John*, 110; Talbert, *Reading John*, 129.

331. Carson, *John*, 251; Barret, *Gospel*, 256. The word κἀγώ (*kagō*) places Jesus on the same level as God. See John 5:17.

332. Ridderbos, *John*, 191; Köstenberger, *John*, 185; Moloney, *John*, 174; Brant, *John*, 105. Bultmann argues that even though "the Jews" understood what Jesus meant, their understanding of equality with God was different; whereas they saw equality with God as independence from God, Jesus meant the very opposite. Bultmann, *Gospel of John*, 245; cf. Moloney, *John*, 174; Morris, *John*, 274–75.

333. Ridderbos, *John*, 192; Brodie, *Gospel According to John*, 280. In the New Testament, the double amen appears exclusively in John and from the mouth of Jesus. Ridderbos, *John*, 92; Kysar, *John*, 3; Brodie, *Gospel According to John*, 280.

334. Thompson, *Gospel of John*, 77–78; Ngewa, *John*, 88–89. In describing the father-son relationship, Ngewa lists partnership, love, transparency, equality of power and honour, and delegated authority as parts of the attributes evident in Jesus' response.

335. To be "equal to God" is a close equivalent of a later rabbinic phrase meaning to make oneself independent from God. Odeberg, *Fourth Gospel*, 203; cf. Keener, *John*, 647.

336. Bultmann, *Gospel of John*, 245. See Moloney, *Signs and Shadows*, 9; Morris, *John*, 274–75; Harris, *John*, 112.

337. Morris, *John*, 277; Carson, *John*, 250; Ridderbos, *John*, 192; Talbert, *Reading John*, 131. Jesus is using his experiences with his adoptive father to argue that functional subordination is not at variance with ontological equality in a father-son relationship. Harris, *John*, 112; Carson, *John*, 251; Köstenberger, *John*, 182.

338. Given the fact that he used both a present tense verb and its future tense, the change of tense logically implies the continuance of the divine works. First and foremost, the Son submits to his Father and does what he sees. Therefore, future "showing" warrants future actions. Morris, *John*, 277; Carson, *John*, 250; cf. Köstenberger, *John*, 182.

the Father does and continuously show him out of a perfect, continuing, and habitual love.[339] And whatever the Son sees the Father doing, he does likewise (John 5:19). The adverb ὁμοίως (likewise) indicates the "identity of *action* (functional unity) based upon the identity of nature (ontological equality)."[340] The ontological equality that exists between the two precipitates functional unity, thereby producing exact or perfect parallelism between the Father and the Son.[341] Therefore, the functions of the Son are the functions of the Father; their works are one.[342] As a result, the Son's replication of the Father is a conduit for explicating the communal attributes that exist within the community of divine essence[343] and for "exegeting" the father's will and works to the religious community.[344]

When talking about works, John makes it conspicuous that Jesus is referring to judgment and life-giving prerogatives.[345] Jewish theology ascribes these rights exclusively to God.[346] But Jesus reveals something new, namely, that the Son also has the divine prerogative of giving life,[347] presently and eschatologically.[348] Nonetheless, the Son's exercise of exclusively divine functions is grounded in the Father's eternal investiture of life in him.[349] And the eternal investiture gives the Son the complete

---

339. Bruce, *Gospel of John*, 128; Morris, *John*, 278; Talbert, *Reading John*, 131; Wuest, *New Testament*, 221. Even though this is the only time the word φιλέω (*phileō*) is used to describe the love of the Father for the Son, Bruce and Carson argue that it is immaterial because the Father's love is affirmed already in this gospel (John 3:35) and expressed as ἀγαπαω (*agapaō*). Morris, *John*, 278; Bruce, *Gospel of John*, 128; Carson, *John*, 251. See also Westcott, *Gospel According to John*, 190.

340. Vincent, *Word Studies*, 135.

341. Carson, *John*, 252; Vincent, *Word Studies*, 135.

342. Kysar, *John*, 43; Thompson, *Gospel of John*, 77–78; Ngewa, *John*, 88.

343. Thompson, *Gospel of John*, 77–78.

344. Carson, *John*, 251–52; Ridderbos, *John*, 193. Jesus was "exegeting" the Father to the religious community, which claimed to know and represent God (John 9:28–34), and yet could neither discern his voice (5:37) nor his deeds (5:16; 9:16–28).

345. John 5:20–30; Morris, *John*, 278; Moloney, *John*, 178, 182; Köstenberger, *John*, 183; Harris, *John*, 113; Beutler, *Commentary*, 154. Carson argues that "raises the dead" and "gives life" are the same. Carson, *John*, 253.

346. Barrett, *Gospel According to St. John*, 260; Morris, *John*, 279; Thompson, *Gospel of John*, 77; Ngewa, *John*, 93.

347. John 5:21, 26; Harris, *John*, 114; Thompson, *Gospel of John*, 77; Morris, *John*, 279.

348. Beasley-Murray, *John*, 77; Barrett, *Gospel According to St. John*, 260; Brant, *John*, 104.

349. Harris, *John*, 114; Ngewa, *John*, 93.

freedom to dispense life to whomever he pleases.³⁵⁰ Thus, the healing of the paralytic at Bethesda is not a violation of law but an exercise of the life-giving prerogative vested in the Son.³⁵¹ Furthermore, since the Son establishes that the ontological equality which he enjoys with the Father is the substratum of their functional unity, he works in partnership with the Father.³⁵² So, to question his authority and right to give life is to be guilty of questioning the authority of God. Therefore, having established this, he discusses judgment—another divine prerogative—with these "judges" (John 5:22, 27).³⁵³ According to the Son, this has also been conferred on him.³⁵⁴ Just like the life-giving prerogative, the judgment (5:22, 27–30) belongs to both the present and the future, making him the "present" and eschatological judge.³⁵⁵

John indicates that the Father vested these in him for two reasons (John 5:23, 27). One of them is that Jesus is the Son of Man (5:27). However, primarily, the Father bestowed these divine privileges on him because he wants the Son to be one in honour with him (5:23): honoring the Father (who sent the Son) and honoring the Son stand or fall together.³⁵⁶ His response again returns the charge against the leaders, who are rather dishonoring God by dishonoring him and judging the one appointed by

350. Morris, *John*, 279; Barret, *Gospel According to St. John*, 260; Westcott, *Gospel According to John*, 191.

351. Barrett, *Gospel According to St. John*, 260; Westcott, *Gospel According to John*, 191; Brant, *John*, 104, 106. The healing is considered by many as a resurrection or the exercise of the life-giving prerogative. Barrett, *Gospel According to St. John*, 260; Westcott, *Gospel According to John*, 191; Brant, *John*, 104, 106. Brant, for instance, argues that the verb ἔγείρω and the language of healing used in John only in this case (John 5:6, 9, 11, 14, 15; 7:23), may render this healing a sort of resurrection. In ancient conception, a limb that was not usable was dead, and so its restoration would be a restoration of life itself. According to him, this position is supported by the reference to resurrection. Brant, *John*, 104–6.

352. Kysar, *John*, 43; Thompson, *Gospel of John*, 77–78; Ngewa, *John*, 88.

353. See Barrett, *Gospel According to St. John*, 260; Morris, *John*, 279; Thompson, *Gospel of John*, 77.

354. Vincent, *Word Studies*, 137; Barrett, *Gospel According to St. John*, 260; Köstenberger, *John*, 184; Carson, *John*, 254.

355. Barrett, *Gospel According to St. John*, 260.

356. Harris, *John*, 113; Keener, *John*, 652; Ngewa, *John*, 90; Carson, *John*, 254; Barrett, *Gospel According to St. John*, 260. But this is not to be understood as the universally recognised principle that "a person's agent is as the person himself," or the Jewish concept of the sender and the sent; he is God and not a mere ambassador. Harris, *John*, 113; Beasley-Murray, *John*, 76; Köstenberger, *John*, 184; Carson, *John*, 224–25; Barrett, *Gospel According to St. John*, 260.

God as their judge.[357] Men are bound to respect their judge.[358] But these leaders were judging their judge.[359]

Thus, Jesus mentions his witnesses to cement and conclude his argument.[360] In biblical Jewish judicial proceedings, witnesses are crucial because a solo witness is untrue.[361] Jesus' statement (John 5:31) is therefore not suggesting that his claims thus far are false; the emphasis is (in line with Jewish judicial proceedings) on the veracity of uncorroborated claims by a solo witness.[362] The requirement is to provide two or three witnesses.[363] As a result, Jesus presents "another" whose testimony is true (5:32) and greater (5:36–37): the Father.[364]

How did the Father bear witness to the Son? The predominant view is that he received authorization from the Father to perform these tasks.[365] However, while some scholars opine that the statement refers to the Old Testament Scriptures,[366] others mention the voice at Jesus' baptism (an unstated event in John) as the testimony in view.[367]

Moreover, the perfect tense used to explicate the father's testimony stresses its perpetual significance.[368] Therefore, his testimony is conclusive for the son.[369] Nonetheless, for the sake and salvation of his interlocutors, he presents a human witness (John the Baptist) who had a unique place in the community because of his mission.[370]

The purpose of John the Baptist is to bear witness concerning the Light so that all might believe through his intermediate agency (John

---

357. Keener, *John*, 652; Ngewa, *John*, 90; Köstenberger, *John*, 184.

358. Barrett, *Gospel According to St. John*, 260.

359. Ngewa, *John*, 90.

360. Ridderbos, *John*, 202.

361. Bruner, *Gospel of John*, 336; Ridderbos, *John*, 202; Carson, *John*, 259; Morris, *John*, 287; Ngewa, *John*, 94.

362. Vincent, *Word Studies*, 138; Brunner, *Gospel*, 336; Harris, *John*, 117; Morris, *John*, 287; Carson, *John*, 259; Ngewa, *John*, 94.

363. Ngewa, *John*, 94; Morris, *John*, 287.

364. Carson, *John*, 260; Moloney, *Signs and Shadows*, 20; Ngewa, *John*, 95.

365. Ridderbos, *John*, 203; Bruce, *Gospel of John*, 135–36; Carson, *John*, 261.

366. Bultmann, *Gospel of John*, 266; Vincent, *Word Studies*, 139–40; Beasley-Murray, *John*, 78; Köstenberger, *John*, 192.

367. Beasley-Murray, *John*, 79; Harris, *John*, 118.

368. Bruner, *Gospel of John*, 340; Köstenberger, *John*, 192.

369. Ridderbos, *John*, 202; Beasley-Murray, *John*, 78.

370. Ridderbos, *John*, 42; Bruce, *Gospel of John*, 135; Ngewa, *John*, 95.

ANALYSES OF FOUR COMMUNITY-CENTRED NARRATIVES   63

1:7).[371] Indeed, it was on record that he had borne witness of the Son to the delegation sent by the leaders (1:19–28). So, his testimony is "presented as an established datum," taking into consideration the effect of the perfect tense.[372] Yet, it does not achieve its intended aim of leading to faith in the Son (1:7) because "the Jews" preferred "the brief religious excitement of John's ministry to faith in whom God sent and to whom John bore witness, and the eternal life which he offered."[373] Therefore, Jesus brings it up and appeals to more witnesses.

The idea that the works of the Son validate his claims is evident in the narrative. The term (works) refers to all that the Father has given to him or assigned him to accomplish.[374] The Son stresses that even though the Father has entrusted these to him, he relies on him continuously to see what the Father does and replicate it.[375] As a result, their works are the same.[376] And since the Father who assigned him to work is working with him as his partner and testifying about him, the works testify of him as one sent by the Father (John 5:36).

Finally, Jesus presents the Scriptures as his witness (John 5:39–40). Most scholars affirm that "the Jews" were people who studied the Scriptures diligently.[377] The problem is that their exploration of the Scriptures was misguided because they judged it to be inherently life-sustaining.[378] Additionally, most people in the rabbinic schools studied merely for self-advancement.[379] So, the possibility of examining and expounding the Scriptures for public admiration is inevitable.[380] Hence, they failed to see the testimony it bears about the one in whom eternal life is vested.[381]

371. Wuest, *New Testament*, 209.
372. Barrett, *Gospel According to St. John*, 264.
373. Barrett, *Gospel According to St. John*, 265.
374. Ridderbos, *John*, 203; Ngewa, *John*, 95; Bruce, *Gospel of John*, 135; Beutler, *Judaism and the Jews*, 160; Barrett, *Gospel According to St. John*, 266.
375. Bruce, *Gospel of John*, 128; Morris, *John*, 278; Talbert, *Reading John*, 131; Wuest, *New Testament*, 221; Westcott, *Gospel According to John*, 190.
376. Kysar, *John*, 43; Thompson, *Gospel of John*, 77–78; Barrett, *Gospel According to St. John*, 260; Ngewa, *John*, 88; Vincent, *Word Studies*, 135.
377. Carson, *John*, 263; Köstenberger, *John*, 192; Morris, *John*, 292; Bruce, *Gospel of John*, 136; Ridderbos, *John*, 204; Ngewa, *John*, 96.
378. Köstenberger, *John*, 193; Carson, *John*, 263; Barrett, *Gospel According to St. John*, 267; Ridderbos, *John*, 204; Bruce, *Gospel of John*, 136.
379. Köstenberger, *John*, 194.
380. Köstenberger, *John*, 194; cf. Ngewa, *John*, 97.
381. Bruce, *Gospel of John*, 136; Moloney, *Signs and Shadows*, 23–24; Ngewa, *John*, 96.

For that reason, Moses will be their accuser[382] since their study could not guide them to ascertain the import of his message[383] despite the inextricable bond that exists between Moses' writings and Jesus' words.[384] Thus, they cannot believe the words of Jesus since they have neglected Moses' testimony (John 5:47).[385]

The Perlocutionary Effect on the Community Theme

Studying the narrative through the eyes of the community theme, the reader discovers that John set out to illustrate the exegesis of the community of God as a paradigm for emulation. Therefore, he selects the marginalized (the paralytic) and the magnified (religious authorities) to demonstrate how the community fails to fulfill the divine intentions for establishing it. These groups have some commonalities worth noting. To begin with, they place the narrative in a religious-cultural context. The lame is at Bethesda (the house of mercy). "The Jews" are also custodians of the Law. In addition, despite the above, the two communities fail to fulfill the divine intention for establishing them.

The exegesis of the eternal community exposes the problems in the community. It brings to light the enormous religious-cultural failure at Bethesda.[386] Additionally, it discloses the exacerbated nature of the problem: the custodians of the Law are neither willing to accept the incarnate Logos nor have the word of God abiding in them (John 4:38–40). Thus, a suitable replacement is necessary—a new community that endeavors to imitate the eternal community.[387] To investigate how the narrative fills the lacuna created by the failure, John 15:1—16:3 is analyzed to ascertain how Jesus demonstrates to his friends (the disciples) and "family members" (John 1:12–13) how to imitate the community. It also allows us to see the elaboration of the theme in the prologue: the community of God. Finally, it reveals how the new community fills the gap.

---

382. It is contrary to their belief that Moses is their intercessor or defender. Beasley-Murray, *John*, 79.

383. Köstenberger, *John*, 195; Ridderbos, *John*, 207; Harris, *John*, 120; Vincent, *Word Studies*, 141–43.

384. Carson, *John*, 266; Smith, *Theology*, 76.

385. Morris, *John*, 295.

386. Pilch, *Healing*, 13.

387. Grenz, *Community of God*, 112; Kunene, *Communal Holiness*, 103.

Narrative Analysis of John 15—16:3

The narrative within the farewell discourse provides guidance on how the newly formed community should incarnate God's intended purpose for communal living, thereby reflecting their new identity. Thus, the objective is to explore how the novel community perpetuated the divine mission and embodied the divine notion of community.

The Delimitation of John 15—16:3

The commencement of the narrative is indicated by John 15:1, as noted by various scholars.[388] However, there are various positions concerning where it ends. Whereas some scholars propose succinct narratives, others promulgate lengthy narratives as the delimitation, depending on their emphases.

Scholars who focus only on the "vine metaphor"[389] provide the shortest demarcations.[390] Watt's concentration on the vine metaphor, for instance, allows him to delimit John 15:1–8 as a narrative.[391] The basis of his argument is that the use of semantically related words within this textual locality makes it an independent unit.[392]

However, those who think of this as an extended metaphor agree on the delimitation but present divergent arguments that concentrate on the metaphor and its application.[393] Consequently, in their opinion, the vine metaphor (John 15:1–8) and its application (15:9–17) are one inextricable narrative.[394] It is pertinent to note that Segovia also affirms the literary unity of the narrative; nonetheless, he argues that John 15:1–17 is

---

388. Keener, *John*, 988; Köstenberger, *John*, 448; Harris, *John*, 266; Carson, *John*, 510; Ridderbos, *John*, 514.

389. Even though Watt accepts John 15:1–8 as a metaphor, others have challenged its metaphorical nature and defined it differently. See Watt, *Family of the King*, 27–29.

390. See Watt, *Family of the King*, 30–48; Segovia, "Theology and Provenance," 118; Carson, *John*, 510–24.

391. Watt, *Family of the King*, 30–48.

392. Watt, *Family of the King*, 31; cf. Watt, *Introduction*, 12.

393. Carson, *John*, 510–24; Whitacre, *John*, 371–80. Though Carson opines that the extended metaphor occurs in John 15:1–8, he considers John 15:9–16 (unlike the rest who extend it to John 15:17) as the "unpacking" of the metaphor.

394. Carson, *John*, 510–24; Whitacre, *John*, 371–80; Kunene, *Communal Holiness*, 75; cf. Smith, *John*, 279.

an originally dependent discourse.[395] He discusses further that from John 15:18, an entirely new focus predominates the narrative: the world and its attitude towards Jesus and his disciples.[396] For that reason, he claims that the argument from content supports his position that John 15:1–17 forms a unit on its own.[397]

Nonetheless, most scholars support the delimitation of the narrative: John 15:1—16:4a.[398] For these scholars, John 15:18—6:4a puts John 15:1–17 in a proper context by establishing that the significance of the teachings (on "abiding" and "mutual love") in the vine imagery (15:1–17) is meaningful in their connection to the world's hatred towards Jesus and his disciples.[399] Additionally, Schnackenburg sees the frequently-repeated phrase, "these things have I spoken to you,"[400] as a demarcation marker that points to John 16:4a as the conclusion of the narrative.[401] He contends that the repetition of the phrase in John 16:4a terminates the section.[402]

Others, such as Moloney and Brown, opine that the narrative ends at John 16:3.[403] Moloney, for instance, gives various arguments to substantiate this position. First, he asserts that John 15:21 and 16:3 form an inclusion.[404] Further, Moloney suggests a link between the identical expressions used towards the end of the allegory on the vine and at the

395. Segovia, "Theology and Provenance," 118.

396. Segovia, "John 15:18—16:4a," 217.

397. Segovia, "John 15:18—16:4a," 217.

398. Brodie, *Gospel According to John*, 475; Lindars, "John 15:18—16:4a," 54-55; Harris, *John*, 27. Even though Moloney argues that the narrative ends at John 16:3, he admits that most scholars support the literary coherence of John 15:1—16:4a. See Moloney, "Structure and Message," 36; *Glory Not Dishonor*, 55.

399. Schnackenburg, *Gospel*, 91; Lindars, "John 15:18—16:4a," 54-55; cf. Brant, *John*, 211–19. Brant focuses on the entire farewell discourse as a unit and yet sees the message of consolation (John 14:27–28; 16:4b) as a linguistic feature that makes John 15:1—16:4a a sub-unit. See Brant, *John*, 211.

400. The phrase occurs in various places in the narrative (John 15:11; 16:1, 4, 6, 25, 33).

401. Schnackenburg, *Gospel*, 92.

402. Schnackenburg, *Gospel*, 92.

403. Moloney, "Structure and Message," 36; *Glory Not Dishonor*, 55; Brown, *Gospel and Epistles*, 78–79.

404. Moloney, "Structure and Message," 35. The verses that form the inclusion read as follows: But all this they will do to you on my account because they do not know him who sent me (John 15:21), and they will do this because they have not known the Father nor me (16:3).

end of the section on hatred (John 15:11; 16:1).⁴⁰⁵ He clarifies that even though the same expression appears in John 16:4a, the strong adversative ἀλλά (*alla*) distinguishes John 16:4a from 16:3 and enables us to look towards the conclusion of John 16 (v. 33) for the link with John 16:4a. Finally, there is a shift in content between John 16:3 and 16:4; whereas John 15:1—16:3 develops themes of abiding, love, and hatred, the rest of the narrative focuses on different themes. Against this background, he advocates for the unity of John 15—16:3.⁴⁰⁶

Finally, others consider John 15:1—16:33 as a unit.⁴⁰⁷ This demarcation stems from the view that the entire narrative, constituted by a monologue, forms the second part of the farewell discourse in John.⁴⁰⁸ Consequently, John 16:4b–33 is considered an extension of the narrative from John 15—16:4a.⁴⁰⁹

Given the elucidations by Moloney, the delimitation of the narrative follows his position; it finds his argument more convincing, cogent, and pellucid.⁴¹⁰ It is nevertheless noteworthy that the two views converge and diverge at the same time. For instance, both agree that the last section contains a new discourse.⁴¹¹ However, the disagreement is a conclusion drawn from the implication of the phrase on the demarcation of the narrative.⁴¹² The argument for the repetitive phrase as a clue for the demarcation of the narrative seems to favor Moloney for various reasons.⁴¹³ For instance, though Segovia proposes that John 15:1-17 and 15:18—16:4a are originally dependent discourses and units, he affirms that the phrase that appears in John 16:4a is a concluding formula that points to John 16:33 as the end of the narrative.⁴¹⁴ Thus, one will be required to consider the repetitious phrase in John 16:33 as the conclusion of the section

---

405. The identical phrase is "These things I have spoken to you." See Moloney, "Structure and Message," 35.

406. Moloney, "Structure and Message," 36; *Glory Not Dishonor*, 55.

407. Carson, *John*, 510; Talbert, *Reading John*, 219; Beasley-Murray, *John*, 269.

408. Carson, *John*, 510; Talbert, *Reading John*, 219; Beasley-Murray, *John*, 269.

409. Carson, *John*, 510; Talbert, *Reading John*, 219.

410. Moloney, "Structure and Message," 36; *Glory Not Dishonor*, 55–56.

411. Whereas Moloney refers to John 16:4-33, Schnackenburg refers to John 16:5-33 as the last section. See Moloney, "Structure and Message," 35–36; Schnackenburg, *Gospel*, 92.

412. See Moloney, "Structure and Message," 35–36; Schnackenburg, *Gospel*, 92.

413. Moloney, "Structure and Message," 36.

414. Segovia, "John 15:18—16:4a," 217; cf. Moloney, "Structure and Message," 36.

that begins with John 16:4a if one does not conclude with John 16:3.[415] It explains why even scholars who view the second farewell discourse as a unit (John 15–16) still see John 16:4b–33 as the concluding part of the narrative, even though they consider John 16:4a as the end of the subdivision.[416] Thus, as stated above, the work follows Moloney's delineation of the narrative because it is more cogent, clear, and convincing.

The Structure of John 15—16:3

The proposed structures follow different concepts about the delimitation of the narrative. However, in the following examples, attention is given to the structures that extend beyond the metaphor.[417]

Among them, scholars who see John 15:1–17 as an "extended metaphor" present different structures centered on the metaphor and how John unpacks it in the narrative. For instance, Segovia divides the narrative into two main sections (John 15:1–8 and 15:9–17)[418] and proposes a structure constituted by the following subunits: 1. the introduction of the figure of the vine and branches (15:1–2); 2. a statement concerning the basic origins of all the branches (15:3); 3. an exhortation to the branches to abide in the vine (15:4–7); 4. the results of such an abiding (15:8); 5. the introduction of the different relationships of love and their hierarchy (15:9–10); 6. a statement concerning the joy of the believers (15:11); vii. the exposition of the love command (15:12–17).

Nonetheless, the majority who affirm the coherence of John 15:1—16:4a also propose idiosyncratic structures.[419] Brodie, for instance, divides the narrative into two distinct units: positive (God's purifying of Jesus, the true vine, John 15:1–17) and negative (the world's hatred, John 15:18—16:4a).[420] Keener gives three divisions as follows: the vine and its fruitful branches (15:1–7), the love commandment (15:8–17), and the world's hatred (15:18—16:4).[421] Schnackenburg provides a detailed struc-

---

415. Moloney, "Structure and Message," 36; cf. Segovia, "John 15:18—16:4a," 217.

416. See Carson, *John*, 510; Talbert, *Reading John*, 219; Beasley-Murray, *John*, 269.

417. Segovia, "Theology and Provenance," 119–20; Brodie, *Gospel According to John*, 475; Keener, *John*, 988–1016; Brown, *Gospel and Epistles*, 78–79; Moloney, *Glory Not Dishonor*, 59–70.

418. Segovia, "Theology and Provenance," 119–20.

419. For example, Brodie, *Gospel According to John*, 475; Keener, *John*, 988–1016.

420. Brodie, *Gospel According to John*, 475.

421. Keener, *John*, 988–1016.

ture constituted by these five divisions: a. the figurative discourse of the vine and the branches and the closing words (15:1–11); b. the commandment to love one another (15:12–17); c. the hatred and hostility of the world (15:18–25); d. the witness borne by the Paraclete and the disciples to Jesus (15:26–27); and e. Jewish hostilities (16:1–4a).[422]

Brown and Moloney agree on the unity of John 15:1–16:3. However, the latter presents a more detailed structure than the former. Brown proposes a structure with two divisions: (a) the vine and the branches (15:1–17); and (b) the world's hatred (15:18–16:3).[423] Conversely, Moloney shapes the narrative as follows: 1. To abide in Jesus (15:1–11); 2. The commandment to love (15:12–17); 3. To be hated by the world (15:18–16:3).[424]

From these proposed structures, it has become increasingly clear that, though a group of scholars may agree on the boundary of the narrative, almost everyone presents something idiosyncratic.[425] Because the units discerned from a text have ramifications for the message deduced as its communicative purpose, divergent structuring produces different messages.[426] Therefore, most of the proposed structures do not purely concentrate on the exegesis of the community theme. Consequently, a new one—an adapted form of Moloney's structure—is proposed for the narrative analysis as follows: 1. The vine as a symbol for the believing community (John 15:1–11): a. Abiding in Jesus (15:1–5), b. the effects of abiding and not abiding in Jesus (15:6–8), c. abiding in the love of Jesus (15:9–11); 2. The commandment for the believing community (15:12–17): a. the commandment to love as Jesus loved (15:12–14), b. Jesus' love has established a new relationship (15:15–16), c. the commandment to love (15:17); 3. The world's hatred for the believing community (15:18–16:3): a. an explanation for the hatred of the world (15:18–21), b. the results of the world's hatred (15:22–25), c. witnessing in times of hatred (15:26–27), d. further explanation for the hatred of the world (16:1–3).[427]

---

422. Schnackenburg, *Gospel*, 94–122.
423. Brown, *Gospel and Epistles*, 78–79.
424. Moloney, *Glory Not Dishonor*, 59–70.
425. See Brodie, *Gospel According to John*, 475.
426. See Fuhr and Köstenberger, *Inductive Bible Study*, 158.
427. See Moloney, *Glory Not Dishonor*, 59–70.

The Analysis of John 15—16:3

This section follows the above modified version of Moloney's proposed structure.

The Vine as a Symbol for the Believing Community (John 15:1–11)

Abiding in Jesus (John 15:1–5)

Jesus makes the last of his "I am" statements in John unconventionally: "it is the only one to which an additional predicate is conjoined ('and my Father is the Vinedresser')."[428] Despite the idiosyncratic nature of this statement, the vine imagery connected to it—the symbol of the community—is not peculiar to this narrative.[429] The difference is, nonetheless, that he refers to himself as the true vine. What Jesus evokes with this affirmation is the Old Testament vine imagery.[430] The Old Testament is replete with narratives that depict the believing community—Israel—like a vine or vineyard.[431]

So, why does Jesus evoke the imagery in this narrative? One of the goals of this metaphorical representation in John 15 is that it serves as a reminder of Israel's failure to produce good fruits, a reflection of the religious-cultural context of the time as well, as demonstrated in the prologue and John 5.[432] The prologue from which Israel's failure developed presents the Son as one rejected by many in Israel—the only nation distinguished from the world and identified as his own (John 1:10–11). John 5 also reveals a community where even the marginalized groups are unfruitful in incarnating their religious and cultural values in such a religious-cultural context, where the testimony of John, the Scriptures,

---

428. Beasley-Murray, *John*, 271; cf. Carson, *John*, 513.

429. We see examples in the Gospels (Matt 21:23–41; Mark 12:1–9; Luke 20:9–16), the Old Testament (Ps 80:8–19; Isa 5:1–7), as well as in the ancient world where a vineyard is employed to symbolize Israel. See also Köstenberger, *John*, 448–50; Carson, *John*, 513; Watt, *Family of the King*, 26–29; Whitacre, *John*, 371; Brown, *Gospel According to John*, 669–72.

430. Harris, *John*, 266; Köstenberger, *John*, 449–50; Ridderbos, *John*, 515; Keener, *John*, 988; Talbert, *Reading John*, 220; Carson, *John*, 513.

431. Mooney, *Glory Not Dishonor*, 59; Köstenberger, *John*, 449–50; Keener, *John*, 988; Talbert, *Reading John*, 220.

432. See Köstenberger, *John*, 449–50; Harris, *John*, 266; Carson, *John*, 513; Morris, *John*, 593.

and the works of Jesus do not produce the intended fruits in many religious leaders because of their attitude (John 5:33–39). Consequently, a reminder of the failures of the Old Testament believing community and that of John makes possible the anticipation of something that reflects God's intentions for choosing Israel as God's vineyard.[433]

Against this background, John presents Jesus, the true Vine, as the one to whom Israel pointed.[434] As the true Vine, Jesus "replaces" Israel as the one through whom the blessings of God flow,[435] thereby demystifying the idea of tying the community of faith to a territory.[436] He becomes the perfect representation of the definition of community by epitomizing the territorial dimension through the demystification of the idea of the "holy land" and the relational dimension through the character of relationships expressed using the vine metaphor.[437] Thus, the vine image denotes the new community of God constituted by both gentiles and believing Jews.[438]

Jesus introduces the Father into the discourse as the vinedresser (of the community) and describes his role in two ways: negatively and positively.[439] The Father removes unproductive branches[440] but prunes the ones that bear fruits[441] to fulfill the purpose of the vineyard—fruit-

433. See Isa 5:1–4; Beasley-Murray, *John*, 272; Schnackenburg, *Gospel*, 106.

434. Carson, *John*, 513; Köstenberger, *John*, 15, 448; Burge, *Jesus and the Land*, 54.

435. Köstenberger, *John*, 15; Carson, *John*, 514; Burge, *Jesus and the Land*, 54; Watt, *Family of the King*, 52.

436. Whitacre, *John*, 372; Burge, *Jesus and the Land*, 54; cf. Painter, *Gospel of John*, 5.

437. Whitacre, *John*, 372; Burge, *Jesus and the Land*, 54; Köstenberger, *John*, 449; Brant, *John*, 217.

438. Köstenberger, *John*, 449; Ridderbos, *John*, 516; Keener, *John*, 993.

439. See Harris, *John*, 266–67; Köstenberger, *John*, 448–49; Carson, *John*, 514.

440. Because Jesus indicates that the unproductive branches were in him before their removal, there have been many speculations about the identity of this group. Cf. Carson, *John*, 514; Barrett, *Gospel According to St. John*, 473. Though John does not mention Judas, Carson opines that we need to go no further than Judas Iscariot. See Carson, *John*, 515; cf. Köstenberger, *John*, 452. Many others, however, contend that John is referring to apostate Christians. For instance, Keener, *John*, 1001; Brodie, *Gospel According to John*, 481; Barret, *Gospel According to St. John*, 473.

441. Scholars adduce several factors to explain the meaning of fruitfulness in this context. Some approach it from John's primary usage: the missional activity of leading others to Christ. See Köstenberger, *John*, 453; Schnackenburg, *Gospel*, 100; cf. Keener, *John*, 997. Others opine that it means expressing the life of a Christian disciple. For instance, Barrett, *Gospel According to St. John*, 474; Brodie, *Gospel According to John*, 480. However, it would seem to include love and Christian character. Moloney, *John*, 420–21; Morris, *John*, 595.

bearing.[442] The fruit-bearing branches produce fruits because the message of Jesus prunes them.[443]

In John 15:4, the idea of being in union (or being in the Vine) with the Vine, with its accompanying results, is elaborated further.[444] The fruitfulness of the disciples depends on remaining in the relationship of mutual indwelling, where they abide in the Vine and vice versa.[445] Abiding in the Vine includes but is not limited to "continuing to believe."[446] It connotes a vibrant and intimate spiritual fellowship, continuing to live in union with Jesus.[447] Köstenberger adds that primarily, it is to remain in the love of Jesus by obeying his commandments.[448] However, this should not be considered a moralistic command.[449] The focus is on nurturing one's spiritual communion with Christ, which is the ground for fruitfulness.[450] The application of the metaphor is a reverberation of Jesus' relationship with his Father, intended to produce a perlocutionary effect: fruitfulness flows naturally from "mutual abiding" just as Jesus' works outflow from his union and communion with the Father.[451]

The Effects of Abiding and not Abiding in Jesus (John 15:6–8)

Jesus contrasts the effects of abiding and not abiding in him. The people who do not dwell in him are like unproductive branches: they are thrown away, dried up, gathered, and burned.[452] Though not explicitly mentioned,

---

442. Harris, *John*, 266; Talbert, *Reading John*, 220.

443. Moloney, *Glory Not Dishonor*, 60; Harris, *John*, 267; Keener, *John*, 997.

444. The first sentence of John 15:4 may be interpreted in one of three ways: conditional, comparison, or mutual imperative. See Barrett, *Gospel According to St. John*, 474; Carson, *John*, 516. Barrett contends that the next verse (John 15:5) warrants mutual indwelling as the interpretation.

445. Köstenberger, *John*, 451–53; Brodie, *Gospel According to John*, 480; Harris, *John*, 267.

446. Harris, *John*, 267; Beasley-Murray, *John*, 272.

447. Harris, *John*, 267; Beasley-Murray, *John*, 272.

448. Köstenberger, *John*, 453.

449. Schnackenburg, *Gospel*, 99.

450. Köstenberger, *John*, 454; cf. Carson, *John*, 516–17.

451. Beasley-Murray, *John*, 273; Keener, *John*, 998; cf. Moloney, *Glory Not Dishonor*, 61.

452. Most scholars understand this as judgment. See Carson, *John*, 517; Ridderbos, *John*, 518; Köstenberger, *John*, 455; Brant, *John*, 218; Brodie, *Gospel According to John*, 481; Keener, *John*, 1002; Watt, *Family of the King*, 41. However, Beasley-Murray and

the passive voice employed in describing the condition of the unfruitful branches (John 15:6b) points to the Father as the one who destroys.[453] Conversely, those who abide in Jesus by allowing his teachings to govern their lives and practices receive the assurance of answered prayers.[454] Since God's word governs their lives, the assurance of answered prayers stems from the understanding that they pray according to God's will.[455]

Furthermore, by living and praying within the parameters of the will of God, they bring glory to God (the Vinedresser) for fulfilling God's purpose for the vine,[456] that is, being fruitful.[457] And by this, they show that they are genuine disciples of Jesus,[458] because their mission culminates in bringing glory to the Father just as Jesus did.[459]

Abiding in the Love of Jesus (John 15:9–11)

John establishes a connection between the eternal relationship and the implications for its appropriation by the community of God. The word καθώς (kathōs) implies that the disciples enjoy the same manner of love that the Father lavishes on the Son.[460] The Son patterns his love for them after what he sees the Father display towards him.[461] It is naturally incessant.[462] And in response, the Son keeps the commands of the Father out of love.[463] Similarly, they are required to remain in Jesus' love by obey-

---

Ridderbos find the expression to depict the uselessness of the branches rather than judgment. Beasley-Murray, *John*, 273; Ridderbos, *John*, 517–18.

453. Moloney, *Glory Not Dishonor*, 62; Watt, *Family of the King*, 46.

454. Harris, *John*, 268; Köstenberger, *John*, 455; Carson, *John*, 518.

455. Carson, *John*, 518; Barrett, *Gospel According to St. John*, 475; Beasley-Murray, *John*, 273.

456. Harris, *John*, 266; Talbert, *Reading John*, 220; Watt, *Family of the King*, 44.

457. Harris, *John*, 268; Köstenberger, *John*, 45; Ridderbos, *John*, 518; Keener, *John*, 1003.

458. Köstenberger, *John*, 455; Harris, *John*, 268; Ridderbos, *John*, 518; Beasley-Murray, *John*, 273. The new community demonstrates what the religious authorities lack—bringing honor to God (cf. John 5:44–47).

459. See Moloney, *Glory Not Dishonor*, 62.

460. Harris, *John*, 269.

461. Carson, *John*, 520; Köstenberger, *John*, 456; Barrett, *Gospel According to St. John*, 475.

462. See Barrett, *Gospel According to St. John*, 475; Moloney, *Glory Not Dishonor*, 64.

463. Köstenberger, *John*, 456; cf. Harris, *John*, 269; Keener, *John*, 1003.

ing his commands, not by compulsion but as an expression of love.[464] As Barrett appositely and succinctly notes, "the parallel shows that love and obedience are mutually dependent. Love arises out of obedience, obedience out of love."[465] Further, the obedience is, as Jesus reveals, something that inures to their benefits; just as Jesus' obedience to the Father is the ground of his joy, those who obey him also partake of this joy.[466]

The Commandment for the Believing Community (John 15:12–17)

The Commandment to Love as Jesus Loved (John 15:12–14)

The command to abide in his love is clarified as mutual love.[467] Therefore, a chain of love is created where the divine and community of faith are united.[468] Flowing from and patterned after the divine community, they must imitate it by demonstrating what Jesus exemplified: sacrificial love.[469] Just as he sacrificed his life for his "friends" (in anticipation of the relationship expressed in the following verse), they are to obey this command and express reciprocal sacrificial love.[470] Their obedience to the command identifies them as his friends.[471]

Jesus' Love Establishes New Relationships (John 15:15–16)

The introduction of the theme of friendship establishes a new relationship.[472] Throughout the gospel, the followers of Jesus are considered his disciples. The change of identity to friends thus reflects a more elevated

---

464. Ridderbos, *John*, 519; Carson, *John*, 520; cf. Moloney, *Glory Not Dishonor*, 64.

465. Barrett, *Gospel According to St. John*, 476.

466. Carson, *John*, 506; Ridderbos, *John*, 519.

467. Köstenberger, *John*, 457; Carson, *John*, 521; Ridderbos, *John*, 520; Beasley-Murray, *John*, 274; Barrett, *Gospel According to St. John*, 476.

468. Carson, *John*, 521–22; Moloney, *John*, 424; Barrett, *Gospel According to St. John*, 476.

469. See Schnackenburg, *Gospel*, 103; Brodie, *Gospel According to John*, 483; Keener, *John*, 1004; Moloney, *Glory Not Dishonor*, 64.

470. Barrett, *Gospel According to St. John*, 476; Carson, *John*, 521–22; cf. Beasley-Murray, *John*, 274.

471. Harris, *John*, 269; Carson, *John*, 522.

472. Beasley-Murray, *John*, 274; cf. Moloney, *Glory Not Dishonor*, 65.

status.⁴⁷³ They are called friends and not servants because of his love for them⁴⁷⁴ and the privilege of the intimate knowledge he shares with them.⁴⁷⁵ Nevertheless, these are not two divergent reasons; his love is the substratum of the intimate knowledge he shares with his friends.⁴⁷⁶ And because it flows from Jesus to his friends (disciples)—not the other way around—the "friendship" is not strictly reciprocal.⁴⁷⁷ Thus, the disciples never referred to Jesus as their friend.⁴⁷⁸

Apart from the unrequited nature of the friendship and contrary to their cultural practice of selecting one's teacher,⁴⁷⁹ Jesus reminds his "friends" that their selection is solely dependent on him (as the emphatic ἐγώ [egō] affirms).⁴⁸⁰ In this way, they become aware of the obligations associated with their elevated status.⁴⁸¹ Their responsibility is that they have been selected and set apart for a particular ministry—to go and bear fruit that will last.⁴⁸² It has been interpreted predominantly as the missionary activity of soul-winning.⁴⁸³ There are good reasons to conclude that the statement aims at the mission as going and the mission as living. The first witness sent from God mirrored both dimensions in his ministry (John 1:28–37). Similarly, Jesus participated in both types of missions. Apart from winning souls, the testimony of the congenitally blind man whom he healed points to the character of the life he lived (John 1:10–13; 5:31). Moreover, looking at the command that precedes this obligation, it is better to agree with Ridderbos that the meaning includes both soul-winning

---

473. Köstenberger, *John*, 459; Schnackenburg, *Gospel*, 110; cf. Esler and Piper, *Lazarus, Mary, and Martha*, 91.

474. Beasley-Murray, *John*, 274; Barrett, *Gospel According to St. John*, 477; Brodie, *Gospel According to John*, 483.

475. Harris, *John*, 270; Barrett, *Gospel According to St. John*, 477; Carson, *John*, 522–23.

476. See Beasley-Murray, *John*, 274; Brodie, *Gospel According to John*, 483.

477. Carson, *John*, 522; Harris, *John*, 270.

478. Carson, *John*, 522; Harris, *John*, 270.

479. Harris, *John*, 270; Köstenberger, *John*, 460.

480. Barrett, *Gospel According to St. John*, 478; cf. Ridderbos, *John*, 521; Vincent, *Word Studies*, 252.

481. Schnackenburg, *Gospel*, 111.

482. Köstenberger, *John*, 460; Carson, *John*, 523; cf. Vincent, *Word Studies*, 252.

483. Carson, *John*, 523; Brodie, *Gospel According to John*, 484; Vincent, *Word Studies*, 252. Ridderbos and Schnackenburg argue that it includes the fruitfulness of Christian life. See Ridderbos, *John*, 522; Schnackenburg, *Gospel*, 112.

and the fruitfulness of Christian life.[484] Finally, as they bear fruit, they have an assurance of answered prayers.[485]

The Commandment to Love (John 15:17)

The command in John 15:12 is repeated as a literary closure.[486] By closing the unit in this manner, John returns to the command in John 15:12 to reinforce the point that the love lavished on the faith community by Jesus must be the paradigm of the reciprocal love expected of them.[487]

In light of the aforementioned context, the discourse shifts towards examining the association of the community with the external world subsequent to focusing on its association with divinity and its constituents.[488]

The World's Hatred for the Believing Community (John 15:18—16:3)

Explanation for the Hatred of the World (John 15:18–21)

Jesus explains the hatred of the world in order to preempt any astonishment and prepare them to cope.[489] Additionally, the purpose is to encourage the community to remain steadfast in its mission to the world as witnesses.[490] Thus, he prepares them to embrace the fact of being bound to be opposed by the world—people opposed to God and the new messianic community.[491] Indeed, the conditional clause denotes the statement of a fact already experienced.[492] Though it is their present reality, the

---

484. Ridderbos, *John*, 522.

485. See Harris, *John*, 270; Vincent, *Word Studies*, 253; Moloney, *Glory Not Dishonor*, 66.

486. Moloney, *Glory Not Dishonor*, 66; Ridderbos, *John*, 522; Keener, *John*, 1004.

487. Moloney, *Glory Not Dishonor*, 66–67; Ridderbos, *John*, 522; Schnackenburg, *Gospel*, 113; Keener, *John*, 1004.

488. See Harris, *John*, 271; Schnackenburg, *Gospel*, 113; Keener, *John*, 1017.

489. Barrett, *Gospel According to St. John*, 480; Carson, *John*, 524–25; Talbert, *Reading John*, 224; Köstenberger, *John*, 463; Harris, *John*, 272.

490. Schnackenburg, *Gospel*, 114.

491. Ridderbos, *John*, 523; Harris, *John*, 272.

492. Schnackenburg, *Gospel*, 114; cf. Vincent, *Word Studies*, 253.

opposition is also futuristic.⁴⁹³ And they stem from the messianic community's union with Jesus.⁴⁹⁴

This union conditions a lifestyle that opposes the world's values.⁴⁹⁵ Since they have been called out of the world to unite with Jesus as his possession and friends, the members of the messianic community do not allow the world to condition their conduct.⁴⁹⁶ As a result, the world hates them.⁴⁹⁷ In many Mediterranean cities, being a friend of one's enemy automatically makes you one's enemy.⁴⁹⁸ Thus, being friends with Jesus means inheriting his enemies and the hatred they have for him. In this regard, they are reminded that a servant is not greater than his lord (John 15:20).⁴⁹⁹

John shows another reason for the opposition from the world: the rejection of Jesus, the one who chose and sent them.⁵⁰⁰ They rejected Jesus because they did not know the sender (cf. John 15:21). The statement elaborates on the theme of the world *told* in the prologue (John 1:10–12), where the idea of the world not knowing Jesus originates (cf. John 1:10). The prologue further clarifies what rejecting and accepting the Word mean. Accepting Jesus is equated with believing in his name (cf. John 1:12).⁵⁰¹ Consequently, those who received him or believed in his name are the believing community. Thus, it is legitimate to label the world (those who rejected Jesus) as the unbelieving community (cf. John 1:12; 5:46–47; 15:21).

---

493. Harris, *John*, 272.

494. Köstenberger, *John*, 464; Ridderbos, *John*, 523; Harris, *John*, 272.

495. See Ridderbos, *John*, 523; Köstenberger, *John*, 464; Carson, *John*, 525; Brodie, *Gospel According to John*, 485.

496. Ridderbos, *John*, 523; Carson, *John*, 525; Keener, *John*, 1019; Moloney, *Glory Not Dishonor*, 68.

497. Carson, *John*, 525; Keener, *John*, 1019; Ridderbos, *John*, 523.

498. Keener, *John*, 1019.

499. Ridderbos, *John*, 523; Carson, *John*, 525–26; Keener, *John*, 1020; Brodie, *Gospel According to John*, 488. Ridderbos, Barrett, and Brodie note that this does not contradict what is stated already (John 15:15) and its latter application (15:20). Ridderbos, *John*, 524, Barrett, *Gospel According to St. John*, 480; Brodie, *Gospel According to John*, 488.

500. Moloney, *Glory Not Dishonor*, 68; Köstenberger, *John*, 465.

501. Köstenberger, *John*, 38; Ridderbos, *John*, 45.

Moreover, because the world—the unbelieving community—knows not the sender, the disciples should expect to be opposed on account of Jesus' name.[502]

The Results of the World's Hatred (John 15:22–25)

John discusses the effects of the world's rejection on the unbelieving community by evoking the theme of light in the prologue to convey a theological truth (cf. John 1:4–5, 7–9). Building on the theme, he indicates that since Jesus (the Logos) came as the Light (John 1:7–10)—divine revelation—rejecting him is tantamount to rejecting God's revelation.[503] It is also an expression of rejection and hatred for the Father who sent him (cf. John 15:23).[504] The rejection was prompted by unbelief.[505] Therefore, it is unexcused because it makes them culpable for rejecting God's revelation.[506]

Jesus strengthens his argument on the inexcusability of their sin and the culpability of the unbelieving community by appealing to his works.[507] Ridderbos affirms that the two "both/and" constructions have a cumulative effect of bringing to expression in a single loaded sentence the guilt of seeing the works and nevertheless hating him and his father.[508] Jesus gave the world visible proofs through the works he performed.[509] The works and words of Jesus provide proofs in an indissoluble relationship as evidence of his divine origin.[510] But in response, they rather hated Jesus and his Father.[511]

---

502. See Ridderbos, *John*, 523; Köstenberger, *John*, 465; Vincent, *Word Studies*, 254; Harris, *John*, 273.

503. Barrett, *Gospel According to St. John*, 481; Harris, *John*, 273.

504. Talbert, *Reading John*, 224; Köstenberger, *John*, 466–67; Moloney, *Glory Not Dishonor*, 69.

505. Harris, *John*, 273; Schnackenburg, *Gospel*, 116; Talbert, *Reading John*, 224; Carson, *John*, 526.

506. Harris, *John*, 273; Schnackenburg, *Gospel*, 116; Talbert, *Reading John*, 224; Carson, *John*, 526.

507. Ridderbos, *John*, 525; cf. Köstenberger, *John*, 466.

508. Ridderbos, *John*, 525.

509. Ridderbos, *John*, 525; Carson, *John*, 527; Moloney, *Glory Not Dishonor*, 69–70; Keener, *John*, 1021.

510. Harris, *John*, 273; Brodie, *Gospel According to John*, 488; Keener, *John*, 1021.

511. Harris, *John*, 273; Beasley-Murray, *John*, 276.

The shift from the encompassing term (the world to they) helps to identify "the Jews" who fail to live up to their Scriptures as the focus.[512] This failure contributes to their inability to grasp what the Son reveals in words and works (cf. John 5:45–47). Thus, their hatred is unfounded;[513] it fulfills what is in their law.[514] The law, consequently, convicts them[515] and heightens their inexcusable culpability.[516]

Witnessing in Times of Hatred (John 15:26—16)

Even though some scholars view the third Paraclete saying (John 15:26-27) as a later insertion that breaks the flow, others disagree.[517] The general position is that it bears a strong mark of unity because of the Paraclete's work after Jesus' departure—bearing witness to vindicate Jesus.[518] As the Spirit of truth, the Paraclete's witness—as Ridderbos succinctly notes—is the assistance that the Spirit will give the disciples in the controversy between the church and the world about the truth concerning Jesus' self-revelation in word and deed as the sent one.[519] Furthermore, in the face of opposition, the companion demonstrates active involvement in their mission, alleviating their apprehensions and bestowing upon them a sense of tranquilly.[520] It produces a single process where the disciples witness about Jesus to the opposing world through the strengthening of

---

512. See Moloney, *Glory Not Dishonor*, 72.

513. Schnackenburg, *Gospel*, 117; Ridderbos, *John*, 256; Keener, *John*, 1021.

514. Ridderbos, *John*, 525; Brodie, *Gospel According to John*, 488; Talbert, *Reading John*, 224.

515. Moloney, *Glory Not Dishonor*, 70; Carson, *John*, 527.

516. See Harris, *John*, 273; Barrett, *Gospel According to St. John*, 482; Carson, *John*, 527.

517. See Carson, *John*, 527; Keener, *John*, 1022; Moloney, *Glory Not Dishonor*, 70–71; Ridderbos, *John*, 526–27.

518. Barrett, *Gospel According to St. John*, 482; Carson, *John*, 528; Ridderbos, *John*, 526; Keene, *John*, 1022.

519. Ridderbos, *John*, 526–27; cf. Keener, *John*, 1022; Talbert, *Reading John*, 224–25.

520. Moloney, *Glory Not Dishonor*, 71; Brodie, *Gospel According to John*, 490.

the Paraclete.[521] Consequently, it is a coherent development of the ideas that preceded it.[522]

Further Explanation for the Hatred of the World (John 16:1–3)

Jesus gives further elucidations on what he has already revealed to his "friends." The purpose is to keep them from apostasy in the face of imminent persecutions.[523] He states clearly that future persecution is both a certainty and an escalation of what they have seen.[524] The rejection of Jesus will necessitate their ejection from the synagogues and execution.[525] However, the irony is that the perpetrators will attach pious motives to these acts and consider them expressions of service to God.[526] But, repeating the thought of John 15:21,[527] Jesus reveals that the root of their conduct is the nonrecognition of God.[528]

The Perlocutionary Effect on the Community Theme

John utilizes the metaphorical representation of the vine to serve as an emblematic representation of the community of believers. In its application, he evokes the metaphor for various reasons. Firstly, it reminds the reader of the unfruitfulness of the old community and the need to anticipate the new fruitful community.[529] As a symbol, it redefines the old concept of community, making the new one an inclusive community,

---

521. Moloney, *Glory Not Dishonor*, 71; Ridderbos, *John*, 527; Brodie, *Gospel According to John*, 490; Keener, *John*, 1022.

522. Schnackenburg, *Gospel*, 117, 119; cf. Brodie, *Gospel According to John*, 489.

523. Carson, *John*, 530; Ridderbos, *John*, 528; Beasley-Murray, *John*, 277; Harris, *John*, 74.

524. Morris, *John*, 615; Ridderbos, *John*, 529.

525. Moloney, *Glory Not Dishonor*, 72–73; Talbert, *Reading John*, 225; Brodie, *Gospel According to John*, 490. Bultmann thinks it is Jewish persecution rather than Roman persecution. Bultmann, *Gospel of John*, 556; cf. Köstenberger, *John*, 469. However, Moloney contends that the expulsion was by "the Jews," but the martyrdom was at the hands of the Romans. Moloney, *Glory Not Dishonor*, 72–73.

526. Köstenberger, *John*, 469; Carson, *John*, 531; Barrett, *Gospel According to St. John*, 485; Talbert, *Reading John*, 226.

527. Ridderbos, *John*, 529.

528. Moloney, *Glory Not Dishonor*, 73; cf. Talbert, *Reading John*, 226.

529. See Isa 5:1–4; Beasley-Murray, *John*, 272; Schnackenburg, *Gospel*, 106.

constituted by both Jews and gentiles.[530] Therefore, it serves as an elaboration on the theme of the family of God in the prologue.[531]

Explaining the cause of the fruitfulness of this community (what distinguishes it from the unfruitful community), John traces it to the union between the vine and the branches. Unlike most religious leaders, whose lives show their unwillingness to receive the Word and thus the absence of the indwelling Word (John 5:38-40), the new community abides in the Vine and vice versa.[532] Consequently, the Father and the message of Jesus prune them to be fruitful.[533]

Apart from nurturing their spiritual communion with Christ, the ground for a fruitful relationship with the vine, the pruning defines and enhances interpersonal relationships among the members.[534] Therefore, they must demonstrate mutually the incessant and sacrificial love experienced in God.[535] By these, the community personifies genuine discipleship because their life and mission culminate in bringing glory to the Father, just as Jesus did.[536]

Therefore, the community is bound to be opposed.[537] However, Jesus promises that the Paraclete, sent by the Father, will allay their fears and strengthen them.[538] Through this divine provision, the Paraclete helps the community participate in and perpetuate the mission of the Logos.[539]

Finally, it is instructive to note that John 17 complements the above narrative by elucidating the Johannine prescription for addressing the character of relationships expected of a believing community. Thus, the community theme in this narrative is explored in the subsequent section.

---

530. Köstenberger, *John*, 449; Ridderbos, *John*, 516; Keener, *John*, 993.

531. See John 1:12-13; Köstenberger, *John*, 449; Ridderbos, *John*, 516; Keener, *John*, 993.

532. Köstenberger, *John*, 451-53; Brodie, *Gospel According to John*, 480; Harris, *John*, 267.

533. Moloney, *Glory Not Dishonor*, 60; Harris, *John*, 267; Keener, *John*, 997.

534. Köstenberger, *John*, 454; Schnackenburg, *Gospel*, 99.

535. Brodie, *Gospel According to John*, 483; Keener, *John*, 1004; Ridderbos, *John*, 520; Moloney, *Glory Not Dishonor*, 64.

536. Köstenberger, *John*, 455; Harris, *John*, 268; Ridderbos, *John*, 518.

537. Morris, *John*, 615.

538. Moloney, *Glory Not Dishonor*, 71; Ridderbos, *John*, 527; Brodie, *Gospel According to John*, 490; Keener, *John*, 1022.

539. See Moloney, *Glory Not Dishonor*, 71; Ridderbos, *John*, 527; Brodie, *Gospel According to John*, 490; Keener, *John*, 1022.

Narrative Analysis of John 17

This narrative augments the previous one in various ways: first, it is the narrative closure to Jesus' exegesis of the community theme (John 17:25–26); second, the reiteration of some of the communal values and their placement in the context of a farewell prayer underscores the significance of these godly traits to the communal life of the believing community; and finally, the rhetoric of the prayer reveals that theocentric communalism is God's plan for the church as a community of God. These factors legitimize the narratological reading of John 17 for its contributions to the community theme.[540]

The Delimitation of John 17

Many Johannine scholars support the delimitation of John 17 as a literary unity. From the writings of these scholars, two reasons can be adduced for this conclusion: the thematic and literary coherence of the narrative.[541] Scholars derive the thematic unity of the narrative from Jesus' prayer, which dominates the narrative.[542] Furthermore, the syntagms "$ταῦτα\ ἐλάλησεν\ Ἰησοῦς$"[543] (John 17:1) and "$ταῦτα\ εἰπὼν\ Ἰησοῦς$"[544] (18:1) affirm the literary unity of John 17:1–26. Just like $μετὰ\ ταῦτα$,[545] they are introductory words that indicate the commencement of new narratives.[546]

The Structure of John 17

Multiple scholars have put forth alternative frameworks for this narrative, but there is a consensus that the prayer can be divided into three distinct petitionary stages or cycles: John 17:1–5, 6–19, and 20–26.[547] It

---

540. Gharbin and Van Eck, "True Vine," 1–9.

541. Haris, *John*, 285; Köstenberger, *John*, 482; Brant, *John*, 224; Talbert, *Reading John*, 231; Keener, *John*, 1050; Ridderbos, *John*, 546; Carson, *John*, 550.

542. See Haris, *John*, 285; Köstenberger, *John*, 482; Brant, *John*, 224; Talbert, *Reading John*, 231.

543. *Tauta elalēsen Iēsous* [After Jesus has said or spoken these things].

544. *Tauta eipōn Iēsous* [After Jesus had said these].

545. *Meta tauta* [After this].

546. See Moloney, *Glory Not Dishonor*, 102; Köstenberge, *John*, 485.

547. For elaborate discussions on the various outlines, see Moloney, *Glory Not Dishonor*, 104–5; Carson, *John*, 553–54.

is important to acknowledge that there are other researchers who endorse the three-stage hypothesis, but with differing frameworks. As an example, Keener provides a categorization of the narrative into three sections: John 17:1–5, 6–24, and 25–26.[548] Talbert also divides the narrative as follows: John 17:1–8, 9–24, and 25–26.[549]

Moreover, the diverse suggested frameworks are formulated based on the portrayal of Jesus' prayer in John 17. This is because the theme of prayer holds significant importance in maintaining the thematic consistency of the narrative. Hence, in accordance with the three-stage theory, a revised framework will be presented for the analysis, taking into consideration the theme of community.

The Analysis of John 17

Given the lack of a community-oriented framework, this section adopts a structure that is derived from a modified version of the three-stage theory.

Jesus Prays for Himself (John 17:1–5)

John establishes the prayer context of the narrative by indicating Jesus' posture and the utterances that accompanied it. The act of lifting one's gaze towards the heavens is recognized as a position for prayer.[550] Furthermore, the address affirms that Jesus, the speaker, was in a state of prayer. The content of Jesus' prayer in the first of the three cycles has two distinctive features: a petition to the Father and an inventory of what the Son has achieved on earth.

In the Gospel of John, "the hour" holds significant importance as it is intricately linked to the glorification of the Son.[551] Thus, Jesus, upon acknowledging the arrival of this pivotal moment, proceeds to implore the Father to bestow glory upon him in order that he would reciprocate and bring glory to the Father as well (John 1:1, 5). Jesus' identification of God as a Father, a repeated term in the narrative, and himself as the Son places the prayer within a familial context. Additionally, the glorification

---

548. Keener, *John*, 1052–64.
549. Talbert, *Reading John*, 232.
550. Köstenberger, *John*, 486; Moloney, *Glory Not Dishonor*, 108; Brant, *John*, 224.
551. Moloney, *Glory Not Dishonor*, 108.

of the Son is "John's shorthand for the cluster of events comprising Jesus' crucifixion, burial, resurrection, ascension, and exaltation with God the Father."[552] The reciprocity of glorification emanates from the idea that, whereas Jesus glorifies his Father by accepting to die on the cross and return to his preincarnate glory, the sustenance he receives from the Father throughout the trying moments allows his death to bring glory to the Father, and glory accrues to him.[553]

In the second feature of the petition, Jesus takes inventory of his ministry in the human community. Again, the glorification theme resurfaces because Jesus makes the completion of the task assigned to him by the Father a sign of honoring or glorifying the Father (John 17:4). In this regard, he reiterates the completion of his task as the one through whom the human community receives eternal life to become members of the community of God, because of the life-giving prerogative given to him by God and the authoritative expositor of the divine community who makes God known (John 17:2).

Against this background of the declaration of his completed ministry, Jesus makes a plea to the Father to glorify him in his presence with his preincarnate glory (John 17:5). This appeal serves to recall the notion of the preincarnate Logos and its inherent connection to the divine community, as expounded upon in the prologue.[554]

Jesus Recounts his Work in the Believing Community (John 17:6–8)

Jesus provides a retrospective account of his ministry, revealing what he has accomplished in the believing community as well as the corresponding responses elicited from the community members towards his work. However, in recounting his accomplishments, he stresses the functional unity between God and the Son, revealing that the outcome is the product of the collaborative effort of the members of the divine community (cf. John 5:19). For instance, though Jesus asserts that he has revealed God's name, a periphrasis or circumlocutory phrase for God's character, to the believers and given them the word he received from the Father, he identifies the believing community as people who belong to God and

---

552. Köstenberger, *Encountering John*, 158; Harris, *John*, 285; Moloney, *Glory Not Dishonor*, 108.

553. Köstenberger, *Encountering John*, 158; Harris, *John*, 285.

554. See Harris, *John*, 287; Köstenberger, *Encountering John*, 162.

were given to him by God (John 17:6, 8).⁵⁵⁵ Through the act of associating the disciples with God as their provider, Jesus establishes God as the instigator, thus positioning God as a vested participant in Jesus' ministry and its resulting outcomes.⁵⁵⁶

The results enumerated by Jesus for the effects of the collaborative effort of the divine community are that the believing community accepted (John 17:8) and kept God's Word (17:6). Moreover, it engendered a profound sense of certainty among the believers that Jesus was divinely commissioned and that all that was bestowed upon him sprang from God (17:7–8).

Jesus Prays for the Believing Community (John 17:9–26)

Jesus prays for the believing community and simultaneously provides justifications for the validity of this intercession. He reveals that the intercession is motivated by the reciprocal ownership of the believers by him and the Father, indicating that whatever belongs to the Father also belongs to him, despite the Father entrusting them to him (John 19:9–10). Furthermore, Jesus is motivated to intercede for them because he will soon depart from the world (John 17:11). While he is still on earth, he keeps them in the Father's name (17:12). His absence will create a void—the lack of a protector—that requires a divine provision (cf. John 17:11–12). Therefore, he prays that the Father will protect them by the power of his name⁵⁵⁷ so that they may replicate the unity in the divine community (17:11).

Jesus clarifies the necessity of the request—the prayer for protection—by elaborating on what he has accomplished through the incarnation and why his absence warrants divine protection. He indicates that he has given the believers his Father's word—the entirety of Jesus' words—and the disciples' acceptance of this word has transformed them into a community of people who do not belong to the world, thereby attracting hatred (John 17:14; cf. 17:8).⁵⁵⁸ Hence, it is imperative to protect the disciples from the threatening nature of the world and the malevolent one

---

555. See Harris, *John*, 288; Moloney, *Glory Not Dishonor*, 111.

556. Moloney, *Glory Not Dishonor*, 111.

557. For elaborate discussions on the various forms of reading, see Harris, *John*, 289; Carson, *John*, 557–58.

558. Harris, *John*, 290.

as they persist in a world that resists God the Sender, Jesus the sent one, and the disciples whom he has likewise sent (John 17:15, 18).[559] To the informed reader, Jesus is simply restating what he has told the disciples already.[560] In John 15, he established a link between the world's hatred and its concomitant persecution of believers and the believing community's decision not to belong to the world (John 15:18-21). He also connected the world's animosity towards the sender with the hostility directed towards the sent (15:23). Therefore, acknowledging the disciples' positive response to his message and affirming that he has also sent them consequently renders them susceptible to persecution and necessitates their protection (cf. John 17:18).

Moreover, Jesus implores his Father to consecrate the disciples by means of his word, which is the embodiment of truth. The suggestion is that the truth, which is God's Word, serves as the method through which the community of believers is sanctified.[561] The petition seems to reference the language used in the prologue, where the terms "word" and "truth" are used to describe the Son as God's revelation (cf. John 1:14-17).[562] The goal of being sanctified by God's Word is for service, or the sacred mission mentioned in the subsequent verse, which involves participating in the mission of sending.[563] This is in line with John's view of sanctification, as it denotes that the individual is set apart for mission.

Further, Jesus turns his attention to the future believing community—the product of the obedience of the disciples to the mission they have been sanctified to accomplish—and includes them in his prayer (cf. John 17:20). He reiterates what he stated earlier in his petition on the unity of the believing community in an emphatic and elaborated form by praying that all members of the believing community, both in the Johannine community and the future ones, will be one, a theologically potent term for unity in John (John 17:21-23).[564] He describes the character of unity redolent of believers as a reflection of the oneness and perichoretic relationship in the divine community.[565] This is corroborated by Jesus'

---

559. See Keener, *John*, 1059; Ridderbos, *John*, 553-55.

560. See Brant, *John*, 226.

561. See Köstenberger, *Encountering John*, 163; Harris, *John*, 290.

562. Brant, *John*, 226.

563. Carson, *John*, 565-66; Harris, *John*, 290; Talbert, *Reading John*, 235; Ridderbos, *John*, 555; Köstenberger, *John*, 495.

564. Keener, *John*, 1061; cf. Bauckham, *Gospel of Glory*, 19.

565. See Talbert, *Reading John*, 23.

application of the reciprocal immanence between him and the Father to Christian unity and the Greek word καθώς (*kathōs*), which possesses both causative and comparative qualities, thereby likening the unity within the divine community to the unity within the believing community and making the former the paradigm and cause for the latter.[566]

Additionally, Jesus reveals that the community's incarnation of this sacred principle, unity, has missiological or evangelistic implications for their mission in the world. The goal of the use of the rhetorical device known as epistrophe, which involves the repeating of words, is to emphasize its significance (John 17:21, 23). The oneness of the believing community serves as a testimony to the validity of the gospel,[567] a persuasive testimony that can culminate in the world's belief in Jesus, God's authoritative expositor of the divine community sent from the Father (17:21).[568] Another potential result is the world's recognition of that fact and of God's love for Jesus and the disciples (17:23).

Furthermore, the prayer moves to its final culmination as Jesus petitions the Father for a future union with the believing community, a time where the believers would be where Jesus is going and behold his unveiled glory (John 17:24), something more than what the community experienced during his earthly life (cf. John 1:14).[569] Though Jesus presents this as his will for the believing community, the request is expected to be granted for two reasons: first, in John, the Father's will and the Son's will are congruent with each other, and secondly, identifying the Father as righteous implies the inclination to grant Jesus' request (John 17:24-25).[570]

Finally, Jesus reiterates the effect of what he has done and will continue; that is, he has made known the Father's name and will continue to make it known (John 17:26). Harris rightly notes that "the use of the aorist and future of the same verb stresses the continuity."[571] This implies that Jesus will continue the work of revealing God's character. However, this would be done presumably through the Spirit.[572] The goal of this work

---

566. Harris, *John*, 292; Ridderbos, *John*, 560.
567. Carson, *John*, 568; Harris, *John*, 292.
568. Carson, *John*, 568; Talbert, *Reading John*, 236.
569. Ridderbos, *John*, 564-65; Köstenberger, *John*, 500; Carson, *John*, 569-70.
570. Köstenberger, *John*, 500.
571. Harris, *John*, 293.
572. Carson, *John*, 570; Köstenberge, *John*, 500; Talbert, *Reading John*, 238.

is that the disciples will become a loving community that replicates the loving relationship found among the members of the divine community (17:26).[573]

The Perlocutionary Effect on the Community Theme

This narrative serves to enhance the previous one in several ways. Firstly, it concludes Jesus' explanation of the community theme (John 17:25–26). Secondly, by restating certain communal values within a farewell prayer, it emphasizes the importance of these divine qualities to the communal life of the believing community. Lastly, the language used in the prayer demonstrates that a God-centered sense of community is God's intention for the church. The presence of these characteristics justifies the use of narratological analysis when interpreting John 17, due to its valuable insights into the concept of community.

The story portrays the embodiment of the divine community as a joint effort of the divine and human communities. Jesus exposes the Father's role by explaining that the Father gave him the authority to give life and the members of the believing community (John 17:2, 6). The Son is the authoritative expositor who reveals God and through whom the believing community gains eternal life to join the community of God. The Spirit is responsible for revealing God in the physical absence of Jesus (17:26).[574]

Furthermore, the narrative reveals the character and participatory role of the believing community. The believers are characterized as a group of people who have received eternal life, know the Father as the only true God, and Jesus as the sent one (John 17:2–3, 8). Additionally, they are those who are not of the world (17:16), having received and kept God's word (17:7–8), thereby attracting hatred and its concomitant persecution from the world (17:14).

Their role as members of the community of God is binary in nature: mission as *going* and *living*. The two are not divergent; rather, they are convergent in the sense that they serve the missional aim of the community. One of these is that they are required to participate in the divine activity of sending (John 17:18). The other is to live a communal life redolent of a community of God. This entails replicating the perichoretic relationship of the divine community by being united (17:21–23),

---

573. See Carson, *John*, 570.
574. Carson, *John*, 570.

a divine communalistic value that demonstrates the truth of the gospel, which can lead to the world believing in Jesus, the authorized interpreter of the divine community. Another possible outcome is the acknowledgment of this truth by the world and of God's affection for Jesus and the disciples (17:23).

Concluding Remarks

The selected narratives enable the reader to delineate the progression of the communal motif in John, from the prologue to the Book of Glory. The prologue helps to establish that the concept of community in John is a divine intention and not a human invention. John opens with some interrelated concepts to this effect: 1. he presents God as a community;[575] and 2. community as a starting point.[576] The relationship between these propositions is that community is a starting point because John begins with the concept of an eternal community, constituted by God and the Logos. On this foundation, John presents creation as a collaborative work and an extension of the divine relationship. Humanity, therefore, exists to participate in the community of God.[577]

However, this divine purpose cannot be fulfilled without God; a world that does not know God is oblivious to the purpose of God (cf. John 1:10). Consequently, a genuine relationship with God is necessary for the revelation and manifestation of the divine intentions for humanity. Therefore, God sends John the Baptist, the witness who has experienced this relationship, to testify about the revelation of God to humanity—the Light (or the Logos).[578]

Mediated through the incarnation, the Logos assumes a community of nature with humankind and exegetes his community to the world,[579] thereby granting the members of the believing community the authorization to become the community of God.[580]

To give the community a paradigm for imitation, Jesus' exegesis of his eternal community exposes the problems in the community.

575. See Borchert, *John 12—21*, 106; Harris, *John*, 68.
576. Kunene, *Communal Holiness*, 188; Kanagaraj, *John*, 2.
577. Grenz, *Community of God*, 112.
578. Brant, *John*, 31; Keener, *John*, 392.
579. Vincent, *Word Studies*, 61; Brant, *John*, 37; Morris, *John*, 101; Köstenberger, *John*, 50.
580. Vincent, *Word Studies*, 49; Watt, *Family of the King*, 182; Keener, *John*, 403.

First, it brings to light the enormous cultural and religious failure in the Bethesda community.[581] Additionally, it discloses the exacerbated nature of the problem: the custodians of the Law are neither willing to accept the incarnate Logos nor have the word of God abiding in them (John 4:38–40). Thus, a suitable replacement is necessary—a new community that imitates the eternal community.[582]

John 15–16:3 begins with expositions on the theme of abiding to demonstrate how the new community fits into the purpose of God (what the former failed to fulfill). Employing the vine metaphor, John elaborates on the concept of the constitution of a new believing community in the prologue (cf. John 1:12–13). It is an inclusive community where both Jews and gentiles are united in Christ, the Vine.[583] The community (unlike the Jewish leaders) abides in the Vine, and vice versa.[584] Consequently, the message of Jesus prunes them to be fruitful.[585] And their fruitfulness glorifies God.[586] Furthermore, their relationship with the Vine prescribes a pattern of life that must be visible in the community. They must demonstrate mutually the incessant and sacrificial love experienced in God.[587]

Just like Jesus, people who fulfill the divine purpose for the community are bound to be opposed.[588] Thus, Jesus promises that the Paraclete, sent by the Father, will allay their fears.[589] He will also strengthen them.[590] Through this divine provision, the Paraclete will be actively involved in their mission to testify about Jesus.[591]

Finally, John 17 is a continuation of the community ideation in John 15, as it reiterates some of the themes discussed there and other preceding narratives on the mode of life of the community of God in the form of a prayer. After mentioning the completion of his earthly mission in his

---

581. Pilch, *Healing*, 13.

582. Grenz, *Community of God*, 112; Kunene, *Communal Holiness*, 103.

583. Köstenberger, *John*, 449; Ridderbos, *John*, 516; Keener, *John*, 993.

584. Köstenberger, *John*, 451–53; Brodie, *Gospel According to John*, 480; Harris, *John*, 267.

585. Moloney, *Glory Not Dishonor*, 60; Harris, *John*, 267; Keener, *John*, 997.

586. Harris, *John*, 266; Talbert, *Reading John*, 220; Watt, *Family of the King*, 44.

587. Brodie, *Gospel According to John*, 483; Keener, *John*, 1004; Ridderbos, *John*, 520; Moloney, *Glory Not Dishonor*, 64.

588. Morris, *John*, 615.

589. Moloney, *Glory Not Dishonor*, 71.

590. Moloney, *Glory Not Dishonor*, 71; Ridderbos, *John*, 527; Keener, *John*, 1022.

591. Moloney, *Glory Not Dishonor*, 71; Brodie, *Gospel According to John*, 490.

prayer, Jesus recounts exactly what these accomplishments are. One of them is his declaration of making God's character known, authenticating the claim in the Johannine prologue that he exegetes the Father (cf. John 1:18; 17:6–7, 26). This makes John 17 a narrative closure on the community theme. Additionally, his prayer for the believers harks back to his previous message on the *modus vivendi* of a believing community: living as a missional community. It involves modeling a community that participates in the missionary activity of sending and replicating the paradigm of unity and love demonstrated among the members of the divine community. This is a repetition of mission as *going* and *living* in the narrative of the vine metaphor. However, the difference is that Jesus attaches evangelistic ramifications to how the believers incarnate the united and loving nature of the divine community, thereby adding new perspectives to his expositions on the theme in the previous narrative.

From the above discussions, it is becoming increasingly clear that although these narratives provide a panoramic view of the community theme in the Fourth Gospel, John is replete with materials that reflect the interests and experiences of a group of people.[592] Some of these are outside the parameters of the above-discussed narratives. Therefore, a narrative development of the theme is discussed in the next section to make the portrait even more perspicuous.

---

592. Martyn, *History* and *Gospel*, 145. See Aune, *Cultic Setting*, 73–84.

3

Narrative Development of the Community Theme

CHAPTER 2 ESTABLISHES THE legitimacy of the community theme in the prologue and its perlocutionary effect on the narrative, demonstrates the community's struggle with incarnating its religious-cultural values (John 5), and explicates how Jesus teaches the believing community to incarnate the divine concept of community in response to these challenges (John 15—16:3). Elaborating on the pattern employed in that analysis, chapter 3 attempts to trace the narrative development of the theme, concentrating on narratives that develop the foundation and formation of the ideal (divine) community, expose the sociocultural maladies, and reveal the proposed remedy—the model Jesus established in response to the lacuna created by the community's immense religious-cultural failure.

The Foundation of Community

The Divine Community (John 1:1–5)

The impact of the prologue on John makes it a hermeneutical key for every academic autopsy on its themes: it *tells* what the narrative *shows*.[1] Therefore, the narrative develops the enigmatic constructs mentioned in the prologue.[2] One of these is the concept of community.

---

1. See Moloney, *Belief in the Word*, 24; Carson, Carson, *John*, 111.
2. See Moloney, *Belief in the Word*, 24; Köstenberger, *Encountering John*, 44.

In John, the community is a starting point.³ It opens with the community of God as the source and ideal paradigm of a community.⁴ John establishes the divinity of the community members and the eternalness of the quality relationship demonstrated by the eternal distinctions (cf. John 1:1). In an effort to elucidate the perpetual existence and divine essence of the society, the author ascribes divine qualities to it by situating the discourse within the framework of eternity. First, John evokes Genesis 1 to argue in favor of the eternality of the Logos and God (the Father).⁵ Further, describing the existence of the Logos, John employs the imperfect tense that expresses the continuous state of existence to strengthen the argument for the pre-existence of the Logos before creation.⁶ And he guides the reader with a third statement that culminates in the conclusion that the eternal Logos enjoys ontological equality with God, thereby cementing the deity of the Logos (John 1:1c).⁷

However, since the attribution of traits of deity to the Logos alone does not satisfactorily warrant the designation of the Logos' relationship with God as a community, John legitimizes the description. First, what John depicts in the prologue bears the mark of a community.⁸ It manifests the relational dimension of the community concept exhibited by the Logos and God in these expressions: καὶ ὁ λόγος ἦν πρὸς τὸν θεόν (John 1:1b) and οὗτος ἦν ἐν ἀρχῇ πρὸς τὸν θεόν (John 1:2).⁹ These statements connect the relationship to ἐν ἀρχῇ (en archē, which depicts eternity in this context), thereby establishing its eternality.¹⁰ Furthermore, the Greek preposition πρὸς (pros), which John employs to describe the relationship that the Word enjoys with God, reveals its qualitative nature as an intimate union or communion between two distinct persons.¹¹ Therefore,

---

3. Kunene, *Communal Holiness*, 188; Kanagaraj, *John*, 2.

4. Grenz, *Community of God*, 112; cf. Kanagaraj, *John*, 2.

5. See Chennattu, "Scripture," 172.

6. Ngewa, *John*, 11; Vincent, *Word Studies*, 24; Keener, *John*, 267; Borchert, *John 12—21*, 104; cf. Skinner, "Characterization," 124.

7. Mounce, *Biblical Greek Grammar*, 27; Vincent, *Word Studies*, 34–35; Harris, *John*, 19; Borchert, *John 12—21*, 103–4; Tenney, *John*, 65.

8. See Gusfield, *Community*, xv-xvi; Cohen, *Symbolic Construction*, 12; Klink, *Sheep of the Fold*, 52.

9. *Kai ho Logos ēn pros ton Theon* and *Houtos ēn en archē pros ton Theon*.

10. Ngewa, *John*, 11; Tenney, *John*, 64; Moloney, *Belief in the Word*, 28.

11. Vincent, *Word Studies*, 34; Morris, *John*, 70; Borchert, *John 12—21*, 103; Tenney, *John*, 64.

the paradigm epitomized in this relationship is that the coexistence of distinct persons and the quality of relationship demonstrated between them define a community.[12]

Most importantly, the expression of community is rooted in God's nature.[13] As Borchert concisely observes, community and unity are two compatible sides of the eternal God.[14] Thus, the conspicuous mark of community exemplified in the prologue is traceable to God's nature. God and the Logos enjoy communal coexistence eternally because the community is compatible with their nature.[15] In cognisance of the ontological equality and the character of the eternal relationship that the Logos enjoys with God, one is not wrong to surmise that John postulates the concept of a community of God in John 1:1–2.[16]

Nonetheless, the idea that God and the Logos constitute a community is not limited to their intimate relationship but includes a community of action. Consequently, John depicts creation—another community-oriented subject[17]—as the outcome of the collaborative work of the Logos and God (John 1:3–4).[18] In this regard, the Father, who is the source of all that exists,[19] cocreates all things through the Logos as its life-giver and light-giver (John 1:4).[20] Consequently, creation outflows from a community of action, a collaboration between the Father and the Logos.[21]

The notion that creation outflows from the eternal relationship requires it to participate in the community.[22] Moltmann affirms that the community of God is an open, inviting, and integrating unity within

---

12. See Gusfield, *Community*, xv–xvi.

13. Borchert, *John 12—21*, 106.

14. Borchert, *John 12—21*, 106; cf. Grenz, *Community of God*, 112.

15. See Borchert, *John 12—21*, 106.

16. Kunene, *Communal Holiness*, 188; Borchert, *John 12—21*, 106; Kanagaraj, *John*, 2.

17. Kanagaraj, *John*, 2.

18. Morris, *John*, 71; Harris, *John*, 22; Vincent, *Word Studies*, 37; Ngewa, *John*, 13.

19. Morris, *John*, 71; Harris, *John*, 22; Grenz, *Community of God*, 102.

20. See Harris, *John*, 23; Köstenberger, *John*, 30; Carson, *John*, 119; Morris, *John*, 73. Kanagaraj argues that God created "all things" as families according to their kinds (Gen 1:21, 24–25) and, therefore, John is disclosing the community motif embedded in creation. Kanagaraj, *John*, 2.

21. Morris, *John*, 71; Harris, *John*, 22; Grenz, *Community of God*, 104.

22. Grenz, *Community of God*, 112; cf. Kanagaraj, *John*, 2; Bauckham, *Gospel of Glory*, 48.

which the whole world can find room.²³ Nevertheless, humankind cannot participate in this relationship without divine assistance and invitation. For this purpose, God sends John the Baptist to partake of this mission (cf. John 1:6–8).

The Preparations for the New Community (John 1:6–9, 15)

The introduction of John the Baptist is the bridge between the community of God, the incarnation, and the contextualization of the ideal society. In the role of a witness, he assumes the unique distinction of being the initial human participant in the divine endeavor of *sending*, as recounted in John 1:6. Thus, in introducing him, John changes the tense from imperfect (which stresses the eternality of the Logos) to aorist²⁴ and describes him as ἄνθρωπος—to denote the humanity of John and the historicity of his assignment.²⁵

John distinguishes the Baptist from the ramifications of the generic term, identifying him as a witness (John 1:6–8). This characterization helps the reader recognize that the Baptist *knows* God (unlike the world, John 1:10). It is characteristic of John to portray genuine witnesses as people who testify after experiencing God.²⁶ Thus, John introduces him as a man sent from God (John 1:6).²⁷ Most importantly, this labeling serves to mark his unique place in salvation history as the one who pointed to the coming of the Light.²⁸ Through the privilege of the divine assignment, he participates in God's mission for creation—the social life of the community of God.²⁹

23. Moltmann, "God," 375.
24. Ngewa, *John*, 11; Keener, *John*, 267; Borchert, *John 12—21*, 104.
25. Köstenberger, *John*, 32; cf. Morris, *John*, 79.
26. Brant, *John*, 31; Keener, *John*, 392; cf. John 1:6; 3:32; 15:26–27. Morris lists seven who bear witness to Jesus in John: each of the three Persons of the Trinity, Scripture, the Baptist, and a variety of human witnesses. Morris, *John*, 80; cf. Köstenberger, *John*, 32–33; Barrett, *Gospel According to St. John*, 159; Brant, *John*, 31. Apart from Scripture and Jesus, all these witnesses have experienced the Logos in one way or another. Jesus' statements attest to this (John 15:26–27). He tells his disciples to testify about him because they have been with (experienced) him from the beginning (John 15:27). He instructed them to testify after telling them that he would send the Holy Spirit (who has coexisted with him eternally) to witness about him (John 15:26).
27. See Carson, *John*, 120.
28. Ridderbos, *John*, 42.
29. Grenz, *Community of God*, 112.

As significant as his role is, it warrants the expectation of the emergence of the Light, a higher-ranking person whose pre-existence and pre-eminence are indisputable.[30] Moreover, the appearance of the Light is a prerequisite for the exegesis of God (cf. John 1:14). The task assigned to John the Baptist, which is to testify about the Light, and the superior status of the Light, precludes him from exegeting the community of God (cf. John 1:6–9, 14–15). Therefore, John introduces the incarnation to establish the framework within which the exegesis occurs.

The Incarnation of the Divine Community (John 1:10–18)

The incarnation explicates the community of God as the divine purpose of community and provides a perfect paradigm to emulate. In John, creation emanates from the eternal relationship and is intended to mirror it through participating in a sense of communal existence.[31] Consequently, it requires a paradigm because the human community did not have the ideal portrait before the incarnation. The prologue reveals the reasons that account for this. First, it states that apart from the theanthropic Jesus,[32] no human being has seen God, not even Moses.[33] Moreover, it establishes that, being God uniquely begotten,[34] the Son enjoys an unprecedented and perpetual intimacy with the Father.[35] John attributes this peculiar relationship only to the Logos, the Son (John 1:1–2, 18). These attributions of quintessential properties of deity to the Son culminate in his authorization as the only authoritative expositor of the Father and the community he represents.[36]

Furthermore, the exegesis of God within the context of the human community materialized through the instrumentality of the

---

30. John 1:15; Harris, *John*, 36; Tenney, *John*, 74; Ridderbos, *John*, 55; Köstenberger, *John*, 45; Ngewa, *John*, 15.

31. Grenz, *Community of God*, 112; cf. Kanagaraj, *John*, 2.

32. Harris, *John*, 35; Vincent, *Word Studies*, 51; Morris, *John*, 91; Westcott, *Gospel According to John*, 19–20.

33. John 1:18a; Ridderbos, *John*, 58–59; Köstenberger, *John*, 48.

34. Carson, *John*, 139; Morris, *John*, 100; Voorwinde, "John's Prologue," 31.

35. Köstenberger, *John*, 49; Voorwinde, "John's Prologue," 32; Vincent, *Word Studies*, 60.

36. John 1:18; Voorwinde, "John's Prologue," 32; Vincent, *Word Studies*, 61; Brant, *John*, 37; Morris, *John*, 101.

incarnation.³⁷ By "assuming a community of nature with humankind," Jesus allows the human community to respond to the will of God concerning its existence.³⁸ Thus, the prologue unearths two different reactions that characterized the reception of the exegesis of God during the incarnation: the negative (John 1:10–11) and the positive (1:12–13). The negative response is evident in the rejection of the divine relationship or appropriate response to Jesus by the *kosmos* and some members of his own home, Israel.³⁹ The world's and certain individuals within the ancient covenant community's inappropriate reaction to the incarnation serves as evidence of the human community's tendency to deviate from the intended purpose of God, which is to actively engage in the social principles that define the community of God.⁴⁰ Conversely, the positive or appropriate response manifests in the reception given the incarnate Word by remnants within the above groups.⁴¹ Given that *the name* is a circumlocution for God,⁴² John equates accepting or receiving the Word with believing in his name to indicate the means through which they received the incarnate Word.⁴³ Unlike those who refused to be partakers of God's purpose for creating the human community through their inappropriate response to God's revelation, the remnants, by responding positively, participate in the social life of the community of God.⁴⁴ They constitute the community that mirrors the community of God on earth.

However, their appropriate response to this divine invitation is not the only criterion that allows them to participate in the social life of God's community and the mission of the Logos. Receiving the Son of God helps individuals obtain what guarantees their incorporation into this community.⁴⁵ The term τέκνα θεοῦ (*tekna theou*) implies a change of status⁴⁶ or

---

37. Vincent, *Word Studies*, 61; Wuest, *New Testament*, 210.

38. See Vincent, *Word Studies*, 51.

39. See Carson, *John*, 122; Morris, *John*, 85–86; Köstenberger, *John*, 37; Ridderbos, *John*, 44.

40. Grenz, *Community of God*, 112; cf. Kanagaraj, *John*, 2.

41. Ridderbos, *John*, 45; Tenney, *John*, 69; cf. Morri, *John*, 85.

42. Brant, *John*, 33.

43. Köstenberger, *John*, 38; Harris, *John*, 31; Ridderbos, *John*, 45.

44. See Morris, *John*, 87; Grenz, *Community of God*, 112; Kanagaraj, *John*, 2.

45. Morris, *John*, 87; Köstenberger, *John*, 39; Ridderbos, *John*, 45; McHugh, *Commentary on John*, 45.

46. Morris, *John*, 87.

identity[47] that warrants participation in the divine nature.[48] Partaking in the divine nature also symbolizes their incorporation into the family of God, thereby enjoying an intimate familial relationship with God and sharing in the community life of God.[49]

Participating in the familial relationship of the community of God, the believers (the "we" in John 1:14) transformed into a community of witnesses and supported the μαρτυρία (*marturia*) of John with theirs—the glory of the pre-eminent Son.[50] It is glory "revealed under human limitations both in Himself and in those who beheld Him"[51] and manifested through his works or signs,[52] death, and resurrection.[53] Thus, the testimony is genuine because it is evidence-based.[54]

Moreover, the privilege of partaking in the life of God's community and assuming the role of a community of witnesses extends beyond John's community (the "we"). It includes all believing communities after John.[55] The Johannine criteria for the characterization of the group as the family of God support the above conclusion. Employing three different expressions, John demonstrates that natural procreation is not the criterion for membership in the family of God.[56] The qualification is by divine procreation, in which God changes the identity of individuals to warrant their incorporation into the new community (John 1:13).[57] And this is not limited to the members of the community of John.[58]

Finally, John interprets the work of the incarnate Word towards the establishment of the new covenant community as exegeting the Father (cf. John 1:14). The incarnation is the vehicle through which Jesus explains God within the context of the human community.[59] Harris rightly

---

47. Watt, *Family of the King*, 182.
48. See Vincent, *Word Studies*, 49; Morris, *John*, 87.
49. Watt, *Family of the King*, 166, 182; cf. Keener, *John*, 403.
50. Keener, *John*, 416; Ridderbos, *John*, 53; Morris, *John*, 93.
51. Vincent, *Word Studies*, 52.
52. Carson, *John*, 128; Morris, *John*, 93; Harris, *John*, 35.
53. Morris, *John*, 93; Carson, *John*, 128.
54. See Brant, *John*, 31; Keener, *John*, 392.
55. See Ngewa, *John*, 17.
56. John 1:13; Watt, *Family of the King*, 183; Brant, *John*, 33–34; Tenney, *John*, 69; McHugh, *Commentary on John*, 47.
57. See Watt, *Family of the King*, 183; Köstenberger, *John*, 39; Brant, *John*, 33–34.
58. See Ngewa, *John*, 17.
59. Vincent, *Word Studies*, 61; Harris, *John*, 39.

concurs that the term ἐξηγήσατο (exēgēsato) comprises the whole span of the earthly life of Christ.⁶⁰ Therefore, the entire gospel, the compendium of inestimable information about Christ's life in the flesh, must be read as *telling* what the prologue *shows* about the incarnation of the ideal concept of community.⁶¹ As a result, what follows traces how John develops the contextualization of the community concept, beginning with and concentrating on relevant narratives in the Book of Signs.

The Conception and Mission of the Community

Preparing for the Conception of the Community (John 1:19–34)

The prologue reports that the ministry of John the Baptist is a precursor to the establishment of the new covenant community.⁶² Consequently, to unpack the theme, the narrative begins with the ministry of John the Baptist to determine the reverberations of the "voice crying in the wilderness" on the formation of the new community of God.⁶³

Given that the prologue defines his mission as one sent from God to testify to the Light so that all might believe through him, the narrative presents his *modus vivendi* and *modus operandi* as a witness (cf. John 1:6–8). John orders the character of the ministry of the Baptist and its concomitant impact according to days (John 1:29, 35) to place the service of John within a historical timeframe and context.⁶⁴ Perhaps John is also seeking to announce the commencement of something new—the dawning of a new day (John 1:29, 35).⁶⁵ Ridderbos asserts that it allows the narrative to acquire a clear salvation-historical meaning, marking an epoch in the history of the human community.⁶⁶

---

60. Harris, *John*, 39.
61. See Köstenberger, *John*, 50; Moloney, *Belief in the Word*, 24.
62. See John 1:6–8, 15; Talbert, *Reading John*, 83–87; Ridderbos, *John*, 61.
63. See Moloney, *Belief in the Word*, 24; Köstenberger, *Encountering John*, 44; Robinson, "Relation of the Prologue," 122.
64. Borchert, *John 12—21*, 104; McHugh, *Commentary on John*, 6; Moloney, *Belief in the Word*, 31.
65. Given that the narrative marks the beginning of the gospel and groups what transpired under days, Köstenberger asserts that John is probably developing a "new creation" motif just like Genesis 1. Köstenberger, *John*, 53.
66. Ridderbos, *John*, 78.

In unpacking the events that culminate in the new era, the narrative gives prominence to John's testimony to the delegation of interrogators sent by the Jewish ecclesiastical leaders because it is an established dictum that John the Baptist is the precursor to the formation of the community of God (John 1:7, 19–28). Thus, the narrative must begin with John's testimony, given that it focuses on the commencement of the believing community.[67] Moreover, the religious character of the community, coupled with its significance to the mission of the incarnate Word, makes the encounter a great opportunity; it allows him to testify to the religious leaders and Israel about the emergence of a new order. Additionally, the content of the testimony impacts the witnesses and the theme of community, given that it transpired publicly (John 1:28).[68] How does John employ the testimony to sustain the narrative development of the community theme?

John sustains it through the questions posed to the Baptist and his corresponding response (John 1:19). The question accomplishes two goals: 1. it allows John to clarify the misconceptions of the religious leaders about his identity by defining who he is not (neither Christ nor Elijah nor the prophet) and who he is (the precursor, one crying out in the wilderness, make straight the way of the Lord); and 2. it provides an opportunity for a subliminal introduction of a discussion on the Messiah into the narrative by the emphatic negative response (ἐγώ οὐκ εἰμὶ ὁ Χριστός).[69] His explicit refusal of messiahship takes the focus away from him and draws attention to the ἐγώ εἰμί (*egō eimi*)—Jesus (the Messiah).[70] To advance his argument, he also equates Christ to the Hebrew Messiah by introducing the term Χριστός (*Christos*) and identifying him as the expected messianic precursor whom Isaiah prophesied to create anticipation for the emergence of the Messiah in the community and narrative.[71]

---

67. See Talbert, *Reading John*, 83.

68. See Keener, *John*, 439.

69. "I am not the Christ (translation mine)." John 1:19–23; cf. Moloney, *Belief in the Word*, 61; Talbert, *Reading John*, 83–84; Ridderbos, *John*, 64; Morris, *John*, 117.

70. Morris classifies this emphatic pronoun as an expression constantly employed by the Baptist whenever he contrasts himself with Jesus and takes the subordinate position. Morris, *John*, 117.

71. See John 1:23; Carson, *John*, 143. See also Isa 40:3. Whereas all the Gospels apply Isaiah to the text, only John places the citation on the lips of the Baptist. Keener, *John*, 438; cf. Carson, *John*, 143.

Furthermore, the delegation asks a question that helps advance the argument for John's messianic expectations: Why are you baptizing?[72] John the Baptist employs the answer to advance his messianic beliefs, positing that the one who is coming after him is standing among them but unknown to them (John 1:26; cf. 1:10). His response tells us that John held him in high regard.[73] Essentially, the statement exalts Jesus, the Coming One, in divine terms,[74] allowing the reader to immediately recognize the reiteration of the testimony of John encapsulated in the prologue: the pre-eminence of the incarnate Word, the Messiah.[75] The narrative closes the testimony for the day with the commentary that the event transpired publicly in Bethany (John 1:28). The geographical reference marks a structural break in the narrative and prepares the reader for the climax of the testimony.[76]

Given that the Baptist's testimony has not culminated in the establishment of the community of God, John presents the second part of the witness.[77] It iterates and elaborates on what he said the previous "day." The reader recognizes the reiteration of a familiar affirmation by simply observing what the Baptist says.[78] He reminds his audience of his previous testimony about someone who is coming after him—a repetition of his testimonies in the prologue and to the delegation (John 1:30; cf. 1:15, 27).[79] By so doing, the narrative harks back to his testimony concerning his role as the precursor and elaborates on it. John clarifies that the purpose of baptizing with water is to reveal the Coming One to Israel (John 1:31, 33).[80] However, without the assistance of God, his ministry would be fruitless in becoming the conduit to introduce Jesus. Consequently,

---

72. To explain the possible background of the question, Keener has copiously discussed the significance of baptism in John. Keener, *John*, 440–48. Moloney affirms that "whatever one makes of this question from the Jerusalem authorities, the reader is following a discussion between Judaism and the Baptist, which presupposes the context of messianic expectation." Moloney, *Belief in the Word*, 61.

73. Köstenberger, *John*, 64; Keener, *John*, 448; cf. Ridderbos, *John*, 67.

74. Keener, *John*, 448.

75. See John 1:15; Harris, *John*, 36; Tenney, *John*, 74; Köstenberger, *John*, 45; Ngewa, *John*, 15.

76. Ridderbos, *John*, 68.

77. See Ridderbos, *John*, 69.

78. See Ridderbos, *John*, 75.

79. Ridderbos, *John*, 75; Carson, *John*, 151.

80. See Carson, *John*, 151; Talbert, *Reading John*, 85.

he receives divine indicators through a revelation,[81] and God confirmed that the features mark Jesus as the Coming One to help John the Baptist identify Jesus.[82]

The testimony about the content of the revelational event suggests that the goal of establishing the new community and its implementation remain the products of the collaborative works of the social Trinity; all members of the Godhead play essential participatory roles towards its realization. Thus, as the narrative unfolds, the reader must expect a community of action from the Godhead, culminating in the creation of the new believing community. These actions begin with the Father sending and guiding the precursor (through the Spirit's act of descending and remaining and the declaration from the Father) to identify the Coming One, testify about him, and introduce him to the community (John 1:19–34).[83]

Additionally, the act of remaining upon him aims to help the community differentiate him from anyone who received divine enablement for a task and review its messianic expectations.[84] The Spirit descended on people to empower them temporarily to accomplish a task.[85] However, the Spirit descends upon him and remains.[86] The implication is that the Spirit permanently abides and equips him.[87] Therefore, throughout his ministry, the Spirit remained upon him, so that the accomplishment of his mission was not without the participation of the Spirit.[88]

---

81. Morris and Carson opine that the Spirit descended in bodily form. Morris, *John*, 133; Carson, *John*, 152. Probably they are appealing to the events in the Synoptic Gospels (Matt 3:16; Mark 1:10; Luke 3:22).

82. Ridderbos, *John*, 76; Köstenberger, *John*, 70; Carson, *John*, 151.

83. Talbert cites passages from deuterocanonical books to support the claim that some in Jewish circles believed that the identity of the Messiah remained hidden to people until another revealed it. Talbert, *Reading John*, 85. Consequently, the various roles that culminate in identifying the Messiah are critical to creating a believing community because both are inextricably linked.

84. See Harris, *John*, 46; Keener, *John*, 460.

85. See Ridderbos, *John*, 76; Harris, *John*, 46; Keener, *John*, 460.

86. See Harris, *John*, 46; Keener, *John*, 460; Köstenberger, *John*, 70.

87. Ridderbos, *John*, 76; Harris, *John*, 46; Keener, *John*, 460; Carson, *John*, 152. Elsewhere in the narrative, John employs the term for mutual abiding elsewhere. Keener, *John*, 460.

88. See Morris, *John*, 133; Köstenberger, *John*, 70; Keener, *John*, 461; Barrett, *Gospel According to St. John*, 178. The participation of the Spirit in creating the new community is evident from the commencement of the ministry of Jesus, throughout his entire earthly ministry, and the ministry of the disciples (John 15:26—16:3).

Furthermore, it marks him as the expected Messiah. The Old Testament prophets anticipated that the Spirit would fully and permanently rest upon the Messiah.[89] They prophesied a messianic period where God would pour his Spirit upon all.[90] Jesus fulfills both expectations as the person upon whom the Spirit rests permanently without measure and as one who baptizes with or "dispenses" the Spirit.[91] Through the establishment of connections between Jesus and messianic occurrences and functions, John effectively proclaims the commencement of the messianic age and signifies Jesus as the Messiah.[92]

Within this particular context, John the Baptist testifies that Jesus is the Son of God[93] and identifies him as the Lamb of God[94] who takes away the world's sin. Two alternating explanations have characterized the reading of the phrase the Lamb of God: the genitive of source (the origin of the Lamb) and the genitive of possession (the Lamb belongs to God).[95] These positions are complementary and not contradictory: Jesus is the

---

89. Köstenberger, *John*, 70; Moloney, *Belief in the Word*, 66.

90. Carson, *John*, 152; Köstenberge, *John*, 71.

91. Ridderbos, *John*, 76; Keener, *John*, 460; Carson, *John*, 152.

92. Carson, *John*, 152.

93. Other authorities read "the Chosen One of God," arguing that it has significant textual support. Carson, *John*, 152-53; Morris, *John*, 134-35. According to them, it is quite intelligible to think of altering an original "Chosen One of God" into a "Son of God" rather than the reverse. Morris, *John*, 134-35; Carson, *John*, 152-53; Barret, *Gospel*, 178. However, there is sufficient and diverse evidence for the above reading. Metzger, *Textual Commentary*, 200; Harris, *John*, 46; Keener, *John*, 464. As Metzger explains, most of the committee members preferred the reading (Son of God) based on age, and diversity of witnesses, and the fact that it agrees with the theological terminology of John. Metzger, *Textual Commentary*, 200. Moreover, the messianic nature of the alternative (The Chosen One of God) is disputed. Köstenberger, *John*, 71. Consequently, this work follows the first reading, considering the messianic context of the discourse between John and the delegation that resulted in his answers, the theological significance of the term "Son of God" in John, and the community theme.

94. Ridderbos considers the first part (the Lamb of God) the most characteristic of the witness of John. Ridderbos, *John*, 69.

95. Köstenberger, *John*, 66; cf. Harris, *John*, 45; Moloney, *Belief in the Word*, 65.

Lamb from God and was provided by God to take away the world's sin.[96] The completeness or breath of the atonement is implied.[97]

Concerning the significance of the Son of God title to the narrative, the prologue defines it (cf. John 1:18, 34). In the context of the theme, the prologue ties it to the incarnation and formation of the community (cf. John 1:18). The basis of this connection is that being the Son of God makes him the exclusively authoritative exegete of the community of God.[98] Therefore, by applying the term, John reminds the reader to anticipate the narratological manifestation of the exegesis of the community of God.[99] The introduction of the exegete—the incarnate Word—necessitates the expectation of the *exegetical process*: the narrative development of the creation of the community of God. Therefore, the narrative discusses the effect of the climax of John's testimony on the commencement of the new believing community.

Incarnating the Community of God (John 1:35–42)

John expounds upon the previous testimonies, presenting what transpired on the "next day" (John 1:35). Though dividing the witness by days allows it to acquire a clear salvation-historical meaning, the events recorded on this day are especially significant because they bring finality to the salvation-historical significance of the testimony to the narrative—the creation of the community of God.[100] The day marks a critical epoch because John identifies Jesus as the one who is to engage in the activity of creating a new community.[101]

---

96. Harris, *John*, 45; Köstenberger, *John*, 66; Carson, *John*, 151. The narrative regards sin as one entity, or generic singular. Harris, *John*, 45; cf. Morris, *John*, 130. Many scholars have attempted to explain the background of John's statement. For an extensive discussion on the various views, see Ridderbos, *John*, 69–75; Keener, *John*, 452–56.

97. Morris, *John*, 130.

98. Harris, *John*, 35; Vincent, *Word Studies*, 51; Morris, *John*, 91.

99. Vincent, *Word Studies*, 61; Brant, *John*, 37; Morris, *John*, 101.

100. See Ridderbos, *John*, 78.

101. See Morris, *John*, 114; Köstenberger, *John*, 53. The one-week events presumably parallel the creation narrative in the first week of Genesis. Morris, *John*, 114; Köstenberger, *John*, 53. Whereas in Genesis, God created *ex nihilo*, John borrows the concept of creation as a framework to suggest that Jesus engages in a different type of creative activity during this week. Morris, *John*, 114.

Despite their criticality, the events cannot be separated from the previous narrative because they place it in the proper context.[102] "The Lamb of God" is a link phrase that connects both.[103] Employing the title "the Lamb of God," John harks back to his earlier testimony.[104] Having received previous instructions, the two disciples of John the Baptist were not oblivious to the appropriate response expected of them.[105] Hence, the reminder necessitated the movement *away* from John *towards* Jesus.[106] Consequently, the resolution to follow Jesus resulted from the past and present testimonies of John.[107] John fulfills his mission by bearing witness to the Light and becoming the conduit through which people believe in him (John 1:6–7).

Many describe this act as a precursor to discipleship.[108] This is because the narrative has not yet indicated that they are following the teachings of Jesus. Therefore, John develops the culmination of the encounter, employing a probing question from Jesus to elicit a response from the potential disciples and clarify their motive.[109] Their answer focuses on identifying where Jesus dwells (John 1:38). Considering the discussions on the messianic expectations that precede this encounter, some scholars have raised questions about the title (Rabbi) and the answer entirely (cf. John 1:19–34). For instance, Moloney argues that the response does not meet the earlier messianic expectations because the disciples approached Jesus solely as a teacher.[110]

Contrary to this view, there are sufficient reasons to believe otherwise. The narrative makes the testimony of John, including his

---

102. See Talbert, *Reading John*, 85; Ridderbos, *John*, 78–79.

103. Talbert, *Reading John*, 85; Mooney, *Belief in the Word*, 67.

104. John 1:29; Talbert, *Reading John*, 85; Köstenberger, *John*, 72.

105. Morris, *John*, 137; Carson, *John*, 154.

106. Moloney, *Belief in the Word*, 67; Morris, *John*, 137; Carson, *John*, 154; John 1:37.

107. Morris, *John*, 137; Moloney, *John*, 67; Ridderbos, *John*, 79.

108. Keener, *John*, 467–68; Carson, *John*, 154. It resonates with the verb, which means to follow as a disciple. Carson, *John*, 154. The language of following is also the conventional Jewish locution for discipleship. Keener, *John*, 468. Though generally, disciples follow their teacher literally, the progressive use of the term in John suggests following the teachings of Jesus. Köstenberger, *John*, 73. Thus, the actions of the two disciples indicate a decision to follow Jesus and his instructions.

109. See Keener, *John*, 468.

110. Moloney, *Belief in the Word*, 67; cf. Keener, *John*, 469.

identification of Jesus as the Lamb of God, the basis of their decision.[111] It employs the title to link the earlier testimony with the latter.[112] Additionally, it makes the pronouncement of the title the ultimate pointer that necessitated the step towards discipleship (John 1:37).[113] Therefore, the motivation to follow emanates from encountering the Lamb (and Son) of God. They referred to him as a Rabbi simply because it was appropriate in a status-conscious culture.[114] The narrative indicates that he was more than a Rabbi to them.[115]

Brodie sees in their response (ποῦ μένεις;)[116] a quest for God.[117] His claim is legitimate because it considers the symbolic significance of the verb μένω (menō) in Johannine theology.[118] As Brodie succinctly states, "the richness of the word has passed from the Spirit (John 1:32–33), to Jesus (John 1:38–39), to the disciples (John 1:39)."[119] The events Brodie mentions indicate that John employs the verb to hark back to the past and forecast the future. First, the word is applied in the narrative to establish the abiding relationship between the Spirit and Jesus.[120] John employs it later to describe the character of the relationship—mutual indwelling and intimacy—that exists between the divine and human communities

---

111. Talbert, *Reading John*, 85; Morris, *John*, 137; Carson, *John*, 154.

112. Talbert, *Reading John*, 85; Mooney, *Belief in the Word*, 67.

113. See Barret, *Gospel*, 180.

114. See Keener, *John*, 468.

115. See John 1:41; 6:25; 9:2. Since Moloney avows that the disciples approached Jesus solely as a teacher and failed to identify him by what the Baptist indicated, he treats their confession as a development. Moloney, *Belief in the Word*, 68; cf. John 1:41. If the disciples were addressing Jesus on both occasions, this claim would be legitimate. However, the narrative indicates otherwise. Thus, that scenario may represent a confirmation of the testimony of John and not progress or sudden discovery. See Keener, *John*, 475; Ridderbos, *John*, 85; Beasley-Murray, *John*, 26. This explanation is possible because their question triggered an invitation to go and ascertain what they wanted to know about him. Ridderbos, *John*, 82. They were introduced to the Messiah, not a Rabbi. And beyond what John instructed, the narrative gives no information about what Jesus shared with them to warrant that sort of development. As a result, the confession did not result from discovery; Andrew was only interpreting John's testimony through the eyes of his personal experience. Ridderbos, *John*, 85; Keener, *John*, 475.

116. *Pou meneis?*

117. Brodie, *Gospel According to John*, 160.

118. See Carson, *John*, 155; Köstenberger, *John*, 74–75; Barret, *Gospel*, 180.

119. Brodie, *Gospel According to John*, 160.

120. Ridderbos, *John*, 76; Keener, *John*, 460; Carson, *John*, 152.

NARRATIVE DEVELOPMENT OF THE COMMUNITY THEME 107

(John 15:1–17).[121] This symbolic meaning of the verb, characteristic of Johannine theology, is presumably intended.[122] Thus, the disciples' answer indicates a quest for an abiding relationship with God or the community of God.[123] The reader recognizes this in Jesus' invitation and how they honored it. Accepting the invitation and dwelling with Jesus that day transforms them into the first humans to dwell in or participate in the community of God.[124] We can, therefore, conclude that the narrative indicates the beginning of the fulfillment of God's purpose for the human community.[125] The reader identifies the commencement of the gathering of those who constitute the community of God as revealed in the prologue.[126]

The gospel is focused first on the individual and progresses to the community, suggesting that believing leads to becoming part of the community.[127] In addition, the foundational principle of Christian expansion is a repeated process of witnessing, whereby new disciples testify about Jesus to others.[128] Thus, this encounter prepares the reader for the narrative development of the gathering of the community. Consequently, a chain of events is narrated to this effect, beginning with Andrew. As a community member,[129] Andrew participates in its mission by becoming a witness who replicates the invitation that he received from Jesus by first[130] bringing his brother Simon to the Messiah[131] to become a member (John

---

121. Brodie, *Gospel According to John*, 160; Keener, *John*, 472; Barret, *Gospel*, 181.
122. Carson, *John*, 155; Barret, *John*, 180–81.
123. See Brodie, *Gospel According to John*, 160.
124. John 1:39; Brodie, *Gospel According to John*, 160–61.
125. See Brodie, *Gospel According to John*, 160; Bultmann, *Gospel of John*, 100.
126. John 1:14; Ridderbos, *John*, 79–80.
127. Brodie, *Gospel According to John*, 37.
128. Carson, *John*, 159; cf. Talbert, *Reading John*, 86.

129. It is critical to note that though he took a step towards discipleship based on John's testimony, the personal encounter with Jesus transformed him into a true disciple. Keener, *John*, 475.

130. There are three textual variants. However, the above reading—that the first thing Andrew did was finding his brother—has received support because it is well attested. Carson, *John*, 157; Ridderbos, *John*, 84; Brodie, *Gospel According to John*, 161; Metzger, *Textual Commentary*, 200. For more information on the three textual variants, see Harris, *John*, 50; Carson, *John*, 157; Metzger, *Textual Commentary*, 200; Barret, *Gospel*, 181–82.

131. John is the only New Testament writer who employs the term Messiah. Ridderbos, *John*, 85; Köstenberger, *John*, 76; Barret, *Gospel*, 182. Andrew's proclamation

1:40–41).¹³² The implication is that an encounter with Jesus transforms individuals into members of the community of God, a community of witnesses. Additionally, it demonstrates the archetypal character of the Baptist's literary function as a witness, making witnessing a duty incumbent upon every member of the community of God, regardless of the length of time their affiliation with this community has existed.¹³³

Therefore, the narrative presents Philip as a witness who participates in the mission of the community after Jesus finds him (John 1:43–51).¹³⁴ However, Philip's case is unique in the sense that Jesus took the initiative to summon him to discipleship.¹³⁵ Thus, in John, Philip is the only true example of a *call*.¹³⁶ Nevertheless, it parallels the first account (of Andrew and Simon) in several ways. For instance, the narrative repeats the identification (we have found, John 1:41, 45) and invitational phrases (come and see, John 1:39, 46). Though articulated distinctly, their testimony demonstrates an understanding of Jewish messianic expectations and the messiahship of Jesus.¹³⁷ Most importantly, they performed their responsibilities as fruitful witnesses, adding to the community (John 1:41–46).¹³⁸ Finally, the repeated phrase (we have found) harks back to the community of God in the prologue (we) that beheld his glory (John 1:14). Therefore, by employing the plural (we), Philip identifies with this community in the prologue that is now fledgling in the narrative.¹³⁹

Having identified the genesis of the community, John begins to define its role in its social and cultural context. Employing some of the signs, he develops narratives linked to community identity, casting them

---

stems from his interpretation of John's testimony through the prism of his encounter. Keener, *John*, 475.

132. See Ridderbos, *John*, 79. Though the narrative does not name the other disciple, most Johannine scholars affirm that the unidentified person is John, the Evangelist. Ridderbos, *John*, 83; Köstenberger, *John*, 76; Harris, *John*, 50; Witherington, *John's Wisdom*, 70; Beasley-Murray, *John*, 26.

133. See Keener, *John*, 475.

134. See Keener, *John*, 480.

135. Talbert, *Reading John*, 86; Morris, *John*, 142.

136. Köstenberger, *John*, 78.

137. Ridderbos, *John*, 88. Whereas Andrew employs the title Messiah, Philip speaks of the same person by referring to the testimony of Moses concerning him in the Law. John 1:45; Ridderbos, *John*, 88; cf. John 5:39, 45–47.

138. See Ridderbos, *John*, 87. John anticipates the future expectations of fruit-bearing required of the believing community. See John 15:1–5.

139. See Morris, *John*, 143; Köstenberger, *John*, 74.

in a religious-cultural context to guide the reader to discover how the disciples grew in a community plagued by sociocultural maladies.[140] Finally, he presents the community of God as the remedy to these societal maladies. The first symbol of community identity that John employs for this purpose is the Jewish ceremonial ritual.[141]

Defining the Community's Sociocultural Role (John 2:1–11)

To explicate the character and mission of the new community, John begins with a narrative containing elements that symbolize Jewish community identity (cf. John 2:1–11). It evokes a plethora of Jewish religious-cultural symbolism, employing marriage, wine, and jars for purification rites.[142] By situating the narrative plot within the context of a Jewish wedding, John gives the event a religious-cultural context (John 2:1).[143]

To unpack the religious and cultural significance of the narrative, John identifies a problem with religious and cultural impact: a scarcity of wine. Wedding celebrations are typically held within a span of seven days, as supported by scholarly sources.[144] Therefore, experiencing a shortage of wine was not improbable. The only problem is that lacking wine on a wedding day in a *shame* culture is tantamount to embarrassment.[145] First-century Mediterranean culture views marriage as a fusion of the honor of two extended families.[146] Wine is also indispensable to any well-organized public celebration because it symbolizes joy and celebration in Jewish thought.[147] Its absence on a day of communal celebration consequently raises questions about the organization of the wedding and casts aspersions on the bride and groom, a social *faux pas*

---

140. See Köstenberger, *John*, 102.
141. See John 2:1–11; Köstenberger, *John*, 102.
142. See Moloney, *Belief in the Word*, 79.
143. Marriage is a traditional symbol that evokes Jewish messianic expectations. Moloney, *Belief in the Word*, 80. The nuptial rituals that mark the initiation of the union between the bride and groom also draw the participation of their respective kin and the wider society. Köstenberger, *John*, 91; Keener, *John*, 499. The wedding, therefore, places the *sign* within the sphere of religious, family, and community life.
144. Köstenberger, *John*, 91; Harris, *John*, 57; Carson, *John*, 169.
145. Carson, *John*, 169; Keener, *John*, 502; Köstenberger, *John*, 93.
146. Campbell, *Kinship Relations*, 127.
147. Keener, *John*, 502; Köstenberger, *John*, 93.

that could make the wedding the talk of the guests for many years.¹⁴⁸ The Jews also associate wine with the messianic banquet and age as a period of the superabundance of wine in their theological reflections.¹⁴⁹ So, the wedding and wine, which are traditional symbols of the messianic time and the messianic fullness, and the lack of wine, which suggests a sociocultural crisis, show that John puts Jesus in a religious-cultural situation, preparing the reader for Jesus' solution to this social problem with religious implications.¹⁵⁰

In this context, the mother of Jesus reports the problem to Jesus (John 2:3). Given the sociocultural implications of the crisis, she may have acted to save the family from dishonor.¹⁵¹ It is also possible that she was only expressing her confidence in the resourcefulness of Jesus¹⁵² or acting on the presumption that her request would be granted.¹⁵³

Jesus responds with a question in the form of a rebuke, indicating that even biological family ties are subservient to his divine mission.¹⁵⁴ However, this is not the absence of filial affection for his mother but an indication that his position as the Son of God (and Mary) and mission

---

148. Keener, *John*, 502.

149. Köstenberger, *John*, 93; Keener, *John*, 494.

150. See Moloney, *Belief in the Word*, 80.

151. Köstenberger, *John*, 93; Carson, *John*, 169; Keener, *John*, 502; cf. Morris, *John*, 158. Morris opines that Mary reported the incident to Jesus because she expected a public demonstration of his messiahship. His conclusions rest on questionable assumptions because he relies on the infant narratives, an event John never mentions. The first appearance of Mary in the Gospel of John is in this narrative. John excludes her from the conversation between Jesus and the burgeoning community, where Jesus gives a hint about these signs (John 1:51). Furthermore, since John indicates that this is the first sign of Jesus, it may be arduous to justify the above position. Campbell, *Kinship Relations*, 121–22. Consequently, it is doubtful if that was her motivation. See Carson, *John*, 169–70; Morris, *John*, 158; Keener, *John*, 503; Köstenberger, *John*, 94; Campbell, *Kinship Relations*, 121–22.

152. Carson, *John*, 169–70; Morris, *John*, 158; cf. Köstenberger, *John*, 94.

153. Keener, *John*, 503.

154. Carson, *John*, 171; cf. Morris, *John*, 159–60. The reply from Jesus has divided scholars (John 2:4). The debate focuses on the vocative he employs to address Mary and the question he poses. Most Johannine scholars argue that though the vocative may not be an endearing term, Jesus is acting courteously by referring to Mary simply as a woman. Carson, *John*, 171; Morris, *John*, 158; Köstenberger, *John*, 94; Ridderbos, *John*, 105; Beasley-Murray, *John*, 34. It also appears that by using the vocative expression, Jesus is politely establishing a distance between himself and his mother. Köstenberger, *John*, 94; Carson, *John*, 171; Ridderbos, *John*, 105.

require obedience from the Father who sent him.[155] Consequently, his actions will be dependent on something other than the wishes of Mary.[156] Since Mary stands outside a mysterious and unknown "hour," the timing must be determined by a person who is part of the unknowable union between the Father and the Son.[157]

With the response of Jesus, the narrative introduces a prominent theme in John: the hour. John employs the term to allude to the glorification of Jesus.[158] So, how does it address the concerns of his mother? Carson avers that Jesus typically identifies more symbolism in the utterances than the speaker envisions.[159] Hence, whereas Mary wanted to save the wedding from embarrassment, Jesus was looking at the messianic age, a period when he supplies "wine" for the banquet.[160] Consequently, the reader recognizes that the response of Jesus, though it may address mundane issues, has messianic ramifications and will, therefore, be done within the parameters of divine direction and timing.[161]

Having evoked Jewish messianic expectations, John identifies symbols of Jewish religious rites: six water jars for purification (John 2:6). He provides vital information to set the narrative within the context of Jewish messianic expectations. He states the capacity of the jars as possibly indicative of the abundance of the messianic provision that is about to happen.[162] Also, the goal of stating the purpose of these jars is to indicate the impending replacement of the old order of Jewish religious practices with something better.[163] Additionally, some scholars interpret the number six as symbolizing incompleteness and suggest that it signifies the imperfectness of Jewish religious practices.[164] The qualities attributed to the jars, their inseparable connection to Judaism, and the

---

155. Köstenberger, *John*, 94; cf. Morris, *John*, 159.

156. Moloney, *Belief in the Word*, 82; Köstenberger, *John*, 95; Harris, *John*, 58.

157. Moloney, *Belief in the Word*, 81.

158. It includes his suffering, death, resurrection, and exaltation. Carson, *John*, 171; Ridderbos, *John*, 105; Barrett, *Gospel According to St. John*, 191.

159. Carson, *John*, 172.

160. Carson, *John*, 172–73.

161. Harris, *John*, 58; cf. Ridderbos, *John*, 106.

162. Ridderbos, *John*, 107; Morris, *John*, 162; Köstenberger, *John*, 97; Carson, *John*, 174.

163. Carson, *John*, 173; Painter, *Gospel of John*, 5.

164. Köstenberger, *John*, 96; Barrett, *Gospel According to St. John*, 191; cf. Carson, *John*, 174; Morris, *John*, 160.

religious-cultural crisis linked to the absence of wine at the wedding create gaps that prepare the reader for something different and better.

Jesus' response to the request fills the cultural and religious lacunae. At the cultural level, the provision of wine averts a potential social crisis.[165] Religiously, both the process and the provision point to the inauguration of a messianic community. For instance, filling the jars to the brim highlights the messianic age, displaying that what will transpire is a lavish provision of wine, a portrait akin to the messianic time.[166] Additionally, the superiority of the wine validates its connection to the new, messianic age Jesus is introducing.[167] It is congruent with John's comment about the *sign*: Jesus did the first of his signs in Cana of Galilee and revealed his glory (John 1:10). Jesus has kept the manifestation until now. The hour, that is, the time of this lavish provision of wine, marks the epoch when the presence of Jesus as glory manifests.[168] John labels it a sign because it is both what Jesus is doing and what it says about him.[169] The Jewish symbolism evoked throughout the narrative only points to the Messiah and a messianic age.[170] Incidentally, the Jews consider the messianic age a time of the manifestation of the glory of God.[171] Thus, by manifesting his glory through this sign, Jesus is inaugurating a new (messianic) era or order.[172]

The remedy to the scarcity of wine has spiritual and cultural ramifications for the growing community (cf. John 2:11). The manifestation of glory occasioned spiritual growth in the disciples,[173] suggesting that

165. Carson, *John*, 169; Keener, *John*, 502; Köstenberger, *John*, 93.

166. Harris, *John*, 59; Carson, *John*, 174.

167. Carson, *John*, 174.

168. See Moloney, *Belief in the Word*, 88.

169. Moloney, *Belief in the Word*, 88; Carson, *John*, 175; cf. Köstenberger, *John*, 99.

170. See Moloney, *Belief in the Word*, 80; Harris, *John*, 59; Carson, *John*, 174; Köstenberger, *John*, 99.

171. Köstenberger, *John*, 99.

172. Harris, *John*, 60; Carson, *John*, 175.

173. Moloney and like-minded scholars interpret the statement as the beginning of true faith. According to Moloney, the implied reader traces the disciples' journey through failure into acceptance of the glory of God in this sign. Moloney, *Belief in the Word*, 88. However, the context of the symbolism evoked in the narrative and the previous encounters between Jesus and the disciples indicate something contrary. The plethora of images (as discussed earlier) point to the messiahship of Jesus. Aside from John the Baptist, all messianic titles attributed to Jesus came from the disciples (cf. John 1:35–51). Apart from Nathanael, whose testimony resulted from a personal experience, the messianic testimonies of Andrew and Philip were products of encounters given after abiding with Jesus, a sign of being part of the community of God. Cf. John

NARRATIVE DEVELOPMENT OF THE COMMUNITY THEME   113

they either put their faith in Jesus[174] or learned to understand him more and more after seeing his glory.[175] Stating that the disciples witnessed the messianic glory harks back to some ideas in the prologue. The prologue indicates that remnants of the covenant community became part of the messianic community who beheld the glory of the Son during the incarnation.[176] John is intimating that despite the general failure of the Jewish community to grasp the significance of the sign, there are remnants who recognize it. Their presence at the time of the manifestation of the glory makes them part of the community in the prologue (cf. John 1:14). Thus, John is not suggesting the inception of true faith, as Moloney annotates.[177] As Ridderbos affirms, the narrative presents their faith earlier in their encounter with Jesus.[178] John is thus indicating that witnessing the glory led to the spiritual growth of the disciples or caused them to learn to understand Jesus more.[179]

Given the narrative context, we cannot limit it exclusively to understanding his identity; it includes recognizing the significance of this act for the group's community identity. By tying the inauguration of the messianic community to wine, something that symbolizes the messianic era and whose absence is tantamount to shame (a sociocultural problem), Jesus is establishing a relationship between the community and its response to its sociocultural challenges. He is redefining community identity and the character of a covenant community. With his sign, he characterizes the messianic community as a group whose social presence must curtail sociocultural challenges. The implication is that its absence also creates a necessitating environment for societal maladies, akin to the lack of wine at the wedding ceremony.

Finally, employing it as the first sign, John publicizes the anticipation of religious-cultural problems and the divine response through the

---

1:37–51; Brodie, *Gospel According to John*, 160–61. Furthermore, the act of witnessing means that the encounter transformed them into a community of witnesses. Cf. Keener, *John*, 475. Therefore, John may be portraying something other than the beginning of true faith. As Harris rightly avows, the expression is more likely constative (put their faith), though it could be ingressive (began to believe). See Harris, *John*, 61.

174. Harris, *John*, 61; Carson, *John*, 175.
175. Ridderbos, *John*, 113.
176. See John 1:12–14; Ridderbos, *John*, 45.
177. Moloney, *Belief in the Word*, 88.
178. Ridderbos, *John*, 113; cf. John 1:50–51.
179. See Harris, *John*, 61; Carson, *John*, 175; Ridderbos, *John*, 113.

messianic community. Consequently, he introduces the cleansing of the Jerusalem temple, another symbol of Jewish religious and community identity.[180]

Redefining Community Identity (John 2:13–22)

In the preceding section, it was established that the first sign resulted in deepening the messianic community's faith in Jesus or enabling them to learn to understand him more.[181] It also necessitates recognizing Jesus' response to the problem as characterizing the messianic community as the remedy to society's religious-cultural quandaries. In what follows, John tracks the religious and cultural plights and how the messianic community fills the lacuna created by these challenges.

John marks the beginning of the narrative by placing it within a religious context. Specifically, he cites the proximity of Passover as the rationale for Jesus' pilgrimage to Jerusalem (John 2:13). While in Jerusalem, Jesus goes to the court of the Gentiles.[182] He identifies a religious-cultural problem: the abuse of the court of the Gentiles (2:14). Discovering the happenings at the court, he drove out the moneychangers and merchants, together with the sacrificial animals.[183] Jesus speaks for the first time in the narrative.[184] He commands the pigeon sellers: Take these things out of here![185] John explains the reason for his actions with another imperative: Stop making my Father's house a marketplace (2:16)! The presence of the present imperative forbids the continuation of an act.[186] Thus, some

---

180. See Köstenberger, *John*, 102.

181. See Harris, *John*, 61; Carson, *John*, 175; Ridderbos, *John*, 113.

182. See Moloney, *Belief in the Word*, 96; Carson, *John*, 178; Brodie, *Gospel According to John*, 179. The events that follow could have happened only at the outward court of the temple: merchants selling sacrificial animals and moneychangers seated at their tables. Moloney, *Belief in the Word*, 96; Köstenberger, *John*, 103; Carson, *John*, 178. The availability of sacrificial animals and currency exchange facilities for the half-shekel temple tax payment was convenient for temple visitors. Harris, *John*, 63; cf. Köstenberger, *John*, 105; Carson, *John*, 178.

183. Harris, *John*, 63. Some scholars assert that the act implies that the emergence of the Lamb of God renders these practices redundant. Barrett, *Gospel According to St. John*, 198.

184. John records this speech with the Greek imperatives (John 2:16).

185. Though Jesus addresses the pigeon sellers directly, it extends to all merchants because it is within the context of the temple cleansing. Harris, *John*, 63.

186. Harris, *John*, 63; Köstenberger, *John*, 107; cf. Morris, *John*, 171.

scholars maintain that John employs the prohibition to teach that the emergence of the Lamb of God necessitates the abrogation or discontinuation of Jewish religious sacrifices.[187] Though this is possible, it appears that Jesus is not objecting to animal sacrifices or taxes but to their impacts on Gentile worship.[188] Conducting these activities at the outer court disrupts Gentile worship.[189] Designating a court for Gentiles to worship in a symbol of Jewish community identity, despite its location, shows that the divine purpose for the community of God is an interracial community serving one God.[190] Thus, obstructing Gentile worship defeats its divine purpose (cf. John 2:16).

Considering the zealous response from Jesus, his disciples remembered the righteous sufferer in the Psalms (Ps 69:9). John does not clarify if it transpired on the spur of the moment or after the resurrection.[191] However, the memory of the righteous sufferer achieves two things in the narrative. It gives the disciples a teachable moment to understand Jesus more and deepen their faith, aside from the impact of the first sign.[192] The event develops their previous knowledge about Jesus, thereby contributing to their spiritual growth.

Additionally, the narrative changes the tense of the quotation from the LXX to the future tense: "Zeal for your house will consume me."[193] The purpose of the change of tense is to proclaim the prophetic or proleptic ramifications of the cleansing of the temple in the narrative.[194] His zeal for unadulterated worship and relationship with God, demonstrated in the cleansing of the temple, will consume him and culminate in his death.[195]

John introduces new characters: the Jewish religious leaders (John 2:18). Ironically, the disciples readily found in the Old Testament

---

187. Barrett, *Gospel According to St. John*, 198.
188. Köstenberger, *John*, 106; Keener, *John*, 524; Harris, *John*, 64.
189. Köstenberger, *John*, 106; Keener, *John*, 524.
190. See Köstenberger, *John*, 102.
191. Carson, *John*, 180.
192. See Ridderbos, *John*, 113.
193. Carson, *John*, 180; Harris, *John*, 64.
194. Carson, *John*, 180; Köstenberger, *John*, 107; Ridderbos, *John*, 111; cf. Harris, *John*, 64. Harris acknowledges that the future tense could be prophetic (My jealous ardour for temple purity will lead to my death), but it is more probably gnomic (My intense eagerness for the sanctity of the temple and purity of worship always eats me up).
195. Carson, *John*, 180; Brant, *John*, 71; Köstenberger, *John*, 107.

Scriptures a justification for Jesus' actions and accepted it, but those who search the Tanakh rigorously ask for a sign.[196] The religious leaders are spiritually blind to discern, through the prism of the Old Testament, the significance of the act.[197] Therefore, in line with their expectations that the Messiah will perform signs, they ask for one.[198] Jesus provides a messianic proof as legitimation: the destruction and reconstruction of the temple (of his body).[199] Nevertheless, he purposely expresses it ambiguously or cryptically, making it difficult for the leaders to grasp the importance of the answer.[200] However, the purpose is to generate discussions on Jewish messianic expectations and demonstrate how he fulfills them. The notion of reconstructing the temple of God is a prominent recurring theme in early religious literature.[201] This concept is found in both the Old Testament and Second Temple texts, where there is a shared anticipation of constructing a new temple during the messianic era.[202] Despite the scriptural evidence, the interlocutors of Jesus focus on their temple, a sign that they have still not grasped the communicative force of his enigmatic statement (cf. John 2:20). Even the disciples who discerned the connection between the zeal of Jesus and the righteous sufferer (Ps 69:9) did not understand the cryptic message either (John 2:22).[203] Thus, John clarifies that Jesus was referring to his body as the temple (cf. John 2:21).

The explanation guides the reader to understand the significance of the enigmatic sayings of Jesus for the messianic community. John is redefining the community of God and sacred spaces through the lens of the death and resurrection of Jesus (cf. John 2:22). The temple symbolizes a national and religious identity.[204] It is the locality of the divine presence where the community serves God.[205] The shift from the cleansing of the temple to his body announces a new season where the religious and (inter)national identity of the community of God will be this new

---

196. Carson, *John*, 180; Köstenberger, *John*, 108; Ridderbos, *John*, 117; cf. John 5:39.

197. Carson, *John*, 181.

198. Morris, *John*, 173–74; cf. Köstenberger, *John*, 108.

199. John 2:19; cf. Köstenberger, *John*, 102.

200. Harris notes that τοῦτον (*touton*) could refer either to the actual temple or the body of Jesus. Harris, *John*, 66.

201. Watt, *Family of the King*, 105.

202. Köstenberger, *John*, 102; cf. Keener, *John*, 530.

203. See Carson, *John*, 182; Ridderbos, *John*, 121.

204. Köstenberger, *John*, 105.

205. Watt, *Family of the King*, 106.

temple—Jesus.[206] The intimate familial relationship between Jesus and the Father makes him the living abode of God on earth; therefore, he is the fulfillment of all that the Jewish temple meant.[207] Therefore, faith in Jesus (the Messiah) replaces Jewish temple worship.[208] Thus, Barrett rightly avers that "the human body of Jesus was where a unique manifestation of God took place and consequently became the only true temple and centre of true worship."[209] In his body, the original intention of the religious and national identity of the temple finds expression. The universal dimension of God's purpose for community life and identity, which had been displaced by the narrowly based worship in the temple, manifests in Jesus.[210] The death and resurrection of Jesus destroy the temple wall that divides worshippers into Jews and Gentiles, bringing them together as a new community of God.[211]

Additionally, it culminates in strengthening the disciples' or the existing messianic community's faith in the Scripture and the word that Jesus spoke. The general view is that Scripture refers to the Old Testament passages that focus on the righteous sufferer.[212] Most likely, the word that Jesus spoke is the message about the destruction and resurrection of his body.[213] Since Jesus fulfills the Old Testament Scripture on the righteous sufferer and his prediction about his death and resurrection, we can surmise that the expression (faith in Scripture and the word) ultimately points to faith in Jesus.

Unlike the disciples, who kept progressing in their faith in Jesus, the community members who upheld the Jewish faith in general responded differently. Many believed in his name because of the signs he performed. Their penchant for seeking signs is akin to that of their religious leaders

---

206. See Köstenberger, *John*, 108; cf. Harris, *John*, 67.

207. Carson, *John*, 182; Watt, *Family of the King*, 106; cf. Moloney, *Belief in the Word*, 101.

208. Köstenberger, *John*, 108; cf. Harris, *John*, 67; Watt, *Family of the King*, 106; Brodie, *Gospel According to John*, 179.

209. Barrett, *Gospel According to St. John*, 201.

210. Köstenberger, *John*, 105; Brodie, *Gospel According to John*, 179; Barrett, *Gospel According to St. John*, 195.

211. Barrett, *Gospel According to St. John*, 195; Brodie, *Gospel According to John*, 179; Köstenberger, *John*, 105.

212. Harris, *John*, 67; Morris, *John*, 179–80; Carson, *John*, 183; cf. Ps 16:10; 69:9; Isa 53:12.

213. John 2:19; Köstenberger, *John*, 110.

(cf. John 2:18). Thus, the reader is cautioned not to infer a demonstration of genuine faith from their attitude because it bears the mark of spurious faith.[214] It is evident in the comments about the response of Jesus: on his part, he would not entrust himself to them because he knew all people and needed no one to testify about anyone (John 2:24). Jesus reacted based on the foreknowledge of their character.[215] The narrative does not also furnish us with evidence that they followed Jesus after the encounter. Consequently, even if they desired to become part of the community, they approached it wrongly and, therefore, needed divine guidance.

Against the background of the demonstration of spurious faith, the subsequent narratives address the divinely ordained entry requirements and the community identity of the messianic community, employing two personal encounters with Jesus: Nicodemus (John 3:1–21) and the Samaritan woman (John 4:1–39).

Entering the Community of God (John 3:1–21)

Nicodemus's introduction to the narrative is critical because he enters the story immediately after John has cast the Jewish religious authorities and community in a bad light. Nevertheless, John's failure to particularize the aim of his visit has occasioned varying interpretations because it transpires at night. Some argue that he opted for the night visit to have a conducive atmosphere for discussions akin to rabbinic practice.[216] Considering his position as a Pharisee, others propose that he feared being identified by the public.[217] However, predominantly, scholars interpret this symbolically.[218] Considering the narratological application of the

214. Köstenberger, *John*, 116; cf. Carson, *John*, 184; Köstenberger, *John*, 115; Keener, *John*, 531. Ridderbos contends that the people displayed genuine faith. Based on how the prologue applies the expression (believed in his name), he concludes that John does not indicate any pretence in their attitude. Ridderbos, *John*, 122. Even though the prologue employs the expression as genuine faith, it is problematic to accept that it applies to this context (cf. John 1:12). The reason is that Jesus connects the faith of Nathanael to what he saw, but he promised him more extraordinary things than he had seen (John 1:50–51). The future promise makes Nathanael part of Jesus' journey. However, no such commitment exists in this case. Consequently, it seems more accurate to assert that it was dubious faith. Carson, *John*, 184; Köstenberger, *John*, 115.

215. Keener, *John*, 531.

216. See Carson, *John*, 186; Morris, *John*, 187.

217. Keener, *John*, 536; cf. Ridderbos, *John*, 124; Morris, *John*, 187.

218. Morris, *John*, 187; Moloney, *Belief in the Word*, 108; Carson, *John*, 186; Brant, *John*, 74.

word "night" in John, many opine that Nicodemus's action symbolizes a movement from darkness towards the Light.[219]

Such a transition is possible if he acts on his own volition. Some have inferred that the first-person plural verb οἴδαμεν (oidamen) suggests that Nicodemus is speaking for like-minded religious leaders.[220] However, it is pertinent to note that John does not state it explicitly, unlike in the case of the delegation sent to interrogate John the Baptist (cf. John 1:19). Additionally, the narrative gives no indication of Nicodemus eliciting the response for any sender, unlike the above (cf. John 1:22). It does appear that it was for personal gain. However, considering how John develops the idea of Jesus fulfilling and replacing what Judaism represents, the message of Jesus has far-reaching implications.

Nicodemus initiates the conversation by addressing Jesus as Rabbi (John 3:2). Carson suggests that the application of the term by Nicodemus is worth more than the utterance of "the two untaught disciples of John the Baptist" (cf. John 1:38). Nevertheless, placing both within their narrative contexts does not favor this interpretation. The disciples followed because John introduced Jesus to them after a series of messianic testimonies. Their question and the corresponding response of Jesus also affirm that they went to abide with the community of God.[221] Carson admits that Nicodemus's question implies that he went to verify the identity of Jesus.[222] He acknowledges in the latter part of his analysis of the questions that Nicodemus had not even begun to appreciate who Jesus is.[223] Therefore, his reference to Jesus as Rabbi is not weightier than that of the disciples, who were convinced through the testimonies of the divinely ordained precursor and followed.

Addressing the narratological impact of the title, Morris conversely opines that Nicodemus sees Jesus simply as a teacher.[224] His explanation rests on questionable assumptions; it suggests that Nicodemus regards signs as prevalent among Rabbis. If this is true, Nicodemus should equally perform Jesus' miracles, given his position as a Rabbi (cf. John 3:10).

---

219. Moloney, *Belief in the Word*, 108; Morris, *John*, 187; Keener, *John*, 536; Brant, *John*, 74. Köstenberger argues that the timing depicts the flatness of this character in John. Köstenberger, *John*, 108.

220. See Carson, *John*, 187.

221. See John 1:38–40; Brodie, *Gospel According to John*, 160–61.

222. Carson, *John*, 199; cf. Köstenberger, *John*, 122.

223. Carson, *John*, 199.

224. Morris, *John*, 187.

Additionally, he would not have visited Jesus at night over the demonstration of signs (cf. John 3:2). Contrarily, his comment proves that he regards Jesus as more than a teacher.[225] For instance, unlike the religious leaders who failed to recognize the significance of the signs, Nicodemus at least emphasizes that they point to his divine calling (from God) and backing.[226] Judaism holds that miracles attest to God's presence.[227] Consequently, recognizing that the signs point to God's presence distinguishes him from the other religious authorities as a leader who considers Jesus more than a teacher.

However, this is not enough for a transition from darkness to Light. His credentials are also inadequate to enable him to understand the nature of Jesus' identity without the influence of spiritual birth.[228] Thus, focusing on his thoughts, Jesus rejects the approach by which Nicodemus seeks to know him, introducing him to the divine entry requirement.[229] Employing the double amen, he establishes the emphatic and authoritative nature of spiritual rebirth as the only means to see the kingdom or community of God.[230] The word ἄνωθεν (anōthen) has a dual meaning: again and from above.[231] Nicodemus understands the statement primarily as denoting rebirth (John 3:4). The perlocutionary effect indicates that he missed the illocutionary force: from above.[232] As a result, Jesus restates the earlier sentence with two substitutions. He replaces ἄνωθεν with "*water and the Spirit*" and the word "*see*" with "*enter*" (John 3:5).[233] The Greek construction suggests that John employs *water and Spirit* as a conceptual unity.[234] Jesus is intimating a new birth produced by the

---

225. See Carson, *John*, 186; Moloney, *Belief in the Word*, 109.

226. Carson, *John*, 186; cf. Barrett, *Gospel According to St. John*, 205; Köstenberger, *John*, 121.

227. Köstenberger, *John*, 121.

228. Keener, *John*, 537.

229. See Köstenberger, *John*, 121–22.

230. See Ridderbos, *John*, 192; Brodie, *Gospel According to John*, 280.

231. Brant, *John*, 31; Carson, *John*, 189; Morris, *John*, 188; Keener, *John*, 538; Moloney, *Belief in the Word*, 110. Scholars appeal to the interpretation of Nicodemus, John's testimony of the Spirit descending on Jesus, and the origin of Jesus as the basis for the dual meaning (cf. John 1:31–36; 3:31; Ridderbos, *John*, 125).

232. Keener, *John*, 538; Moloney, *Belief in the Word*, 110.

233. See Carson, *John*, 191; Moloney, *John*, 110.

234. Carson, *John*, 194; Harris, *John*, 73; Keener, *John*, 550; Talbert, *Reading John*, 103; cf. Moloney, *Belief in the Word*, 111. For the summary of various interpretations on the verse, see Carson, *John*, 191–95; Morris, *John*, 191–93.

Spirit, a transition from natural to spiritual birth, harking back to the entry requirement of the community of God in the prologue.[235] Thus, John parallels the expression *from above* to the spiritual birth to clarify its source and extend its application and necessity for entering the kingdom of God (John 3:7).[236] Since Nicodemus is a member of the Jewish religious authorities and community, the plural (you) denotes the inclusion of these groups.[237] It also includes humanity, given that this experience is a prerequisite for humankind.[238]

John illustrates the impact of this spiritual truth by employing a simile in which Jesus compares the movement of the wind to the activity of the Spirit during the process of spiritual rebirth.[239] The analogy serves to demonstrate the mysterious and sovereign will of the Spirit in effecting rebirth.[240] The indication is that the spiritually reborn, the regenerated community, experiences the divine activity even though it is invisible.[241]

Unlike the wind, the effect or experience of spiritual rebirth is not temporary but marks the beginning of a new life. The state of being reborn from above is a means to an end, not the end. The expression (see or enter the kingdom of God) implies that this birth ushers anyone who experiences it into a different state, given that Jesus makes it the prerequisite for seeing or entering the kingdom of God (cf. John 3:5).[242] The word "*see*" means to experience, encounter, or participate.[243] Therefore, the rebirth allows individuals who have been reborn to participate in the experience of being members of the community or family of God.[244]

---

235. Harris, *John*, 72; Moloney, *Belief in the Word*, 111; John 3:6.

236. Morris, *John*, 194; Köstenberger, *John*, 124; Harris, *John*, 73. In John, the word δει (*dei*) gives the impression of a divine necessity.

237. Morris, *John*, 194; Köstenberger, *John*, 124.

238. Harris, *John*, 73.

239. John 3:7; cf. Carson, *John*, 194; Köstenberger, *John*, 124.

240. Ridderbos, *John*, 129; Harris, *John*, 73; Carson, *John*, 197.

241. John 3:8; Carson, *John*, 197; Harris, *John*, 74; Ridderbos, *John*, 129.

242. Metzger indicates that though a wide range of patristic authors and a few manuscripts substitute τοῦ θεοῦ (*tou theou*) with τῶν οὐρανῶν (*tōn ouranōn*), the committee was impressed with the age and diversity of witnesses in favour of τοῦ θεοῦ and the possibility that copyists introduced τῶν οὐρανῶν in imitation of the recurrent expression in Mathew. Metzger, *Textual Commentary*, 203.

243. Harris, *John*, 72; Carson, *John*, 188; cf. Keener, *John*, 537.

244. Moloney, *Belief in the Word*, 113; Harris, *John*, 77.

Though a recognized and established teacher, Nicodemus cannot discern the communicative force of Jesus' message.[245] In the narrative, he moves from misunderstanding Jesus (John 3:4) to being surprised at his sayings (3:7) and expressing a growing exasperation and lack of understanding.[246] His inability to grasp these realities occasioned further elucidations from Jesus, focusing on the foundation for spiritual rebirth (cf. John 3:11–21).

Jesus repeats the double amen to reestablish the authoritative and emphatic character of the testimony.[247] However, on this occasion, he speaks in the first-person plural (*oidamen*). Consequently, whereas some hold that Jesus was referring to himself and his disciples, or John the Baptist,[248] others include his future disciples.[249] However, Carson sees a sardonic expression.[250] Since Jesus replicates Nicodemus by using the expression "we know," it is reasonable to think of the plural as including the disciples, given that Nicodemus applied it in a collective sense.

Replicating the opening statement of Nicodemus, Jesus addresses the root of his problem.[251] It is not his inability to intellectually comprehend the testimony of Jesus but his willingness to accept it.[252] He addresses Nicodemus by employing the plural you, suggesting that the unwillingness to accept the testimony is ubiquitous and not an idiosyncratic problem.[253] It justifies why he speaks to Nicodemus in the plural in his message on the necessity of spiritual rebirth (cf. John 3:7). The source of the testimony legitimizes the comments Jesus made about their unwillingness to accept the testimony: it proceeds from witnesses who testify to what they have seen and speak of what they know.[254] Jesus refers

---

245. See Ridderbos, *John*, 132; Morris, *John*, 195; Barrett, *Gospel According to St. John*, 211; Köstenberger, *John*, 122.

246. Köstenberger, *John*, 125.

247. Köstenberger, *John*, 125; Ridderbos, *John*, 133; cf. Brodie, *Gospel According to John*, 280.

248. See Carson, *John*, 198; Ridderbos, *John*, 133.

249. Harris, *John*, 74.

250. Carson, *John*, 199.

251. See Carson, *John*, 199; Köstenberger, *John*, 125–26.

252. Carson, *John*, 199; Köstenberger, *John*, 125–26.

253. John 3:11; Moloney, *Belief in the Word*, 115; cf. John 3:7; Beasley-Murray, *John*, 49.

254. John 3:11; Moloney, *Belief in the Word*, 116–17; cf. John 3:31–32.

to the witnesses in the first-person plural: himself and his disciples.[255] Alternatively, other scholars include the church as part of the community of witnesses.[256] He gives a portrait of the Jewish community's unwillingness to accept the testimony of the community of God.

Employing the above as the basis, Jesus develops the foundation for spiritual rebirth. Before advancing his argument, he prepares the mind of Nicodemus for "heavenly things" (John 3:12). The announcement is necessary because Jesus is moving from elementary to higher discourse.[257] Given that John records no interaction between Jesus and Nicodemus before this narrative, earthly and heavenly things refer to the previous and present discussions.[258]

The promulgation of these higher spiritual realities requires a qualified expositor. Thus, Jesus positions himself as the authority on this enigmatic discourse by explicating the basis of his authorization as the authoritative expositor of the message.[259] The phrase "no one has ascended into heaven except the one who descended from heaven" harks back to the prologue.[260] He appeals to his origin, relationship with the Father, participation in divine glory, incarnation, and mission as legitimation for being the qualified expositor of heavenly things.[261]

Jesus commences his expositions on heavenly things by evoking the story of Moses and the bronze serpent to illustrate his point.[262] Thus, the reader must explore the import of his message through the prism of the

---

255. Morris, *John*, 196; Ridderbos, *John*, 134; Kysar, *Voyages with John*, 188; Harris, *John*, 74; cf. Carson, *John*, 198–99; Keener, *John*, 558. Carson excludes the disciples because he argues that it is too early. Carson, *John*, 198–99. The first members of the community of God started witnessing immediately after dwelling with Jesus. Cf. John 1:39–42. The encounter transformed into a community of witnesses, thereby demonstrating the paradigmatic nature of the literary role of John as a witness and making witnessing the responsibility of the community of God. Keener, *John*, 475. Therefore, it is not too early to consider them witnesses. Alternatively, Keener also argues in favor of Jesus and the Father. Keener, *John*, 558.

256. Beasley-Murray, *John*, 49; Harris, *John*, 74.

257. Carson, *John*, 199; Harris, *John*, 74.

258. Carson, *John*, 199; Harris, *John*, 74; Morris, *John*, 197.

259. See Harris, *John*, 75; Morris, *John*, 197; Carson, *John*, 199; John 3:31–32.

260. See John 1:18; Köstenberger, *John*, 127. The shorter reading (without the words, who is in heaven) has quality external attestations. Metzger, *Textual Commentary*, 203–4; Harris, *John*, 75; Carson, *John*, 203.

261. John 1:1–2, 18; Köstenberger, *John*, 127; Carson, *John*, 201.

262. Num 21:8–9; cf. John 3:14–15.

story. In the Old Testament, God intended the event as a way of salvation; looking at the bronze serpent results in restoring physical lives.[263] Similarly, God has ordained that looking to Jesus through faith leads to eternal life.[264] However, in this instance, the source of salvation is Jesus, the object of faith, not the individual.[265] Moreover, unlike Moses, who lifted the bronze serpent as a means, Jesus will accomplish it through his crucifixion.[266] But the benefit of his salvation, the life of the age to come (eternal life), is neither restricted to Nicodemus nor his community but to everyone, striking a universal note (John 3:15).[267] The universal implication of the invitation to faith in Jesus as the substratum of eternal life is consistent with John's theological and soteriological perspective since the author posits that the Son was sent with the purpose of providing eternal life to all who have faith in him (3:16).

Jesus explains the purpose of the divine provision of eternal life: the character of the love of the Father.[268] The intensity of love necessitated the provision of the greatest gift, the unique and beloved Son, for the redemption of humankind.[269] Once again, Jesus expands the communicative force of the message beyond Nicodemus and the theological reflections of the Jews by extending God's love beyond the Jewish race.[270] Nevertheless, the appropriation of the divine provision is contingent on the human response, positive or otherwise (John 3:17–18). Thus, John distinguishes between believers and unbelievers and the repercussions of

263. Köstenberger, *John*, 128; Carson, *John*, 202; cf. Harris, *John*, 75.

264. Köstenberger, *John*, 128; Carson, *John*, 202; Keener, *John*, 563; Harris, *John*, 75; Moloney, *Belief in the Word*, 117.

265. Köstenberger, *John*, 128.

266. Carson, *John*, 201; Köstenberger, *John*, 128; Harris, *John*, 75; Ridderbos, *John*, 136–37; Morris, *John*, 199. The term (lifted) has a double meaning in John, namely crucifixion and exaltation. Carson, *John*, 201; Köstenberger, *John*, 128; Harris, *John*, 75; Keener, *John*, 565; Moloney, *Belief in the Word*, 117.

267. Carson, *John*, 202; Harris, *John*, 75; Köstenberger, *John*, 128; Morris, *John*, 201. Throughout the conversation, Jesus extends his message beyond Nicodemus, employing the second person plural (John 3:7, 12). Though he changes the word here, the import is the same.

268. John 3:16; Brant, *John*, 77; Köstenberger, *John*, 128; Carson, *John*, 204.

269. See Köstenberger, *John*, 128–29; Carson, *John*, 204. The verb (gave) encapsulates both incarnation and crucifixion. Beasley-Murray, *John*, 51; Harris, *John*, 78; Brodie, *Gospel According to John*, 106; cf. Ridderbos, *John*, 138; Keener, *John*, 566, who restrict it to the crucifixion.

270. Carson, *John*, 205.

their response as two sides of the same coin, where salvation for believers implies a judgment on unbelievers.[271] Whereas God does not condemn the believer, the unbeliever stands condemned.[272] The ground for condemnation is their response to the incarnation: lack of faith in the name of the only Son of God (John 3:19–21; cf. 3:36).

In summary, the narrative develops the idea initiated in the preceding chapter. In the previous chapter, the abuse of the Gentiles' court, an emblem of the universal dimension of the community of God, served as a teachable moment to introduce the new symbol of community identity. In Jesus, God's purpose for the human community—the interracial community of worshippers—materializes. Since the Jewish authorities fail to recognize the ramifications of the new thing Jesus inaugurates and many demonstrate spurious faith, Jesus develops the theme in his interactions with Nicodemus, revealing the entry requirements for participating in the messianic community. Nicodemus's lack of response to the invitation creates a pause in the narrative plot and anticipation for the reception of the new universal community identity. John fills the narrative gap with two narratives in chapter 4.

Universalizing the Community of God (John 4)

The narrative is structured by John with the intention of directing the informed reader to uncover the universalization of the community of God. This is achieved through the emphasis on the themes of the universalization of sacred space, witnesses, and the community of God.

To demonstrate the universalization of holy space, John maintains the Gentile context of the earlier narrative, albeit with a different setting. He announces Jesus' decision to move from Judea to Galilee to avoid the polarization of his ministry and that of the Baptist (John 4:1–3),[273] and in consequence, Jesus must go through Samaria. Given the location from Judea to Galilee, the shortness of the distance is a reason to consider this path (John 4:4).[274] Most importantly, however, Jesus chose that route

---

271. Morris, *John*, 205; Köstenberger, *John*, 129.
272. Harris, *John*, 79; Carson, *John*, 207; cf. John 3:36.
273. See Carson, *John*, 215; Harris, *John*, 88.
274. See Carson, *John*, 215; Köstenberger, *John*, 146; cf. Harris, *John*, 89; Ridderbos, *John*, 153; Moloney, *Belief in the Word*, 137, who argue that it is not geographically necessary because travellers could go north by crossing the river Jordan to the east and then crossing it again north of Samaria. Though this is undisputable, it was a longer

because of the necessity of accomplishing a divine mission.[275] This divine mission leads Jesus to Sychar, a non-Jewish region.[276] Even though the Samaritans viewed themselves as Jews, the Jews considered them mixed-race or Gentiles.[277] A Samaritan woman enters the narrative as a representative of the race inhabiting that territory.[278] Additionally, going to the well alone at that time portrays her as ostracized and marginalized by the community she embodies.[279]

Reading the encounter through the prism of the above characteristics and the fact that it follows a narrative where Jesus deals with a Pharisee, the reader discovers that the mission transcends racial, religious, and social boundaries. John justifies the above with a conversation between Jesus and a Samaritan woman.[280] The woman's response affirms her knowledge of the existing barriers (cf. John 4:9).[281] Instead of engaging her along that tangent, he follows a different trajectory because these walls of segregation are irrelevant to the new reality that Jesus is

---

route. Köstenberger, *John*, 146; Carson, *John*, 215–16; Keener, *John*, 589; Moloney, *Belief in the Word*, 137. Therefore, going through Samaria seemed more appropriate. Cf. Carson, *John*, 215; Köstenberger, *John*, 146.

275. See Ridderbos, *John*, 153; Harris, *John*, 89; Carson, *John*, 216. John employs the Greek word δει (*dei*) ten times in the entire Gospel and trice in this narrative (John 3:7, 14, 30; 4:4, 20, 24; 9:4; 10:16; 12:32; 20:9). Predominantly, it expresses the performance of an act that is a divine imperative. Similarly, in this narrative, it denotes a divine necessity. Köstenberger, *John*, 146; Carson, *John*, 216; Moloney, *Belief in the Word*, 137; Keener, *John*, 590.

276. Moloney, *Belief in the Word*, 132.

277. Carson, *John*, 216; Witherington, *John's Wisdom*, 117; Keener, *John*, 599–600.

278. Morris, *John*, 227; cf. Köstenberger, *John*, 148.

279. Keener, *John*, 606; Witherington, *John's Wisdom*, 120.

280. See Keener, *John*, 591–98; Carson, *John*, 218; Brant, *John*, 84. For a thorough discussion on social, gender, moral and ethnic barriers, see Keener, *John*, 591–98.

281. Several witnesses omit the explanatory comment. Metzger, *Textual Commentary*, 206; cf. Barrett, *Gospel According to St. John*, 232. Metzger writes: The omission, if not accidental, may reflect the scribe's opinion that the statement is not exact and therefore should be deleted. Metzger, *Textual Commentary*, 206. The majority of scholars who include it opine that the comment refers to sharing drinking vessels because the alternative reading is difficult to sustain since the disciples had gone to the Samaritan village to buy food. Harris, *John*, 90; Morris, *John*, 229; Carson, *John*, 218; Barrett, *Gospel According to St. John*, 232. However, others think it goes beyond this. For instance, Ridderbos refers to the deep-rooted hostility that Jews felt for Samaritans as the interpretation of the comment. Ridderbos, *John*, 154.

initiating, introducing her to the living water.²⁸² Metaphorically, Jesus is speaking of something better, the water of life.²⁸³

At this point, the reasons for breaking the racial, social, and gender barriers are unfolding gradually. He is there to universalize the community by offering satisfaction to the deepest thirst of Samaritans.²⁸⁴ Thus, he declares the greatness of his gift by contrasting it with the well. He reveals that unlike the water from Jacob's well, what Jesus provides is perpetually refreshing and produces eternal life.²⁸⁵ It also transcends racial boundaries; he gives to everyone and whoever.²⁸⁶ Finally, through a request for water, the narrative demonstrates the Samaritan's inability to grasp the metaphorical import of what Jesus is offering.²⁸⁷

Jesus suddenly shifts the conversation and commands her to go and call her husband (John 4:16).²⁸⁸ She answers deceitfully, knowing the dual sense of the word translated as a husband.²⁸⁹ But Jesus demonstrates that he knows the woman's circumstances, culminating in her acknowledgement that he is a prophet (John 4:18-19).²⁹⁰ The informed reader recognizes that the question is serving its purpose; the woman is gradually changing her view on the identity of the Jewish stranger.²⁹¹ However, besides this change, she redirects the conversation from discussing her relationships with different men to debating the issue of worship (John 4:20-26). The question seeks to elicit Jesus' clarification on the subject. However, it introduces the symbol of community identity and allows Jesus to clarify the universalization of the community of God.

---

282. See Ridderbos, *John*, 154-55; Köstenberger, *John*, 150.

283. Keener, *John*, 604.

284. See Ridderbos, *John*, 157-58; Köstenberger, *John*, 151-52.

285. John 4:14; Harris, *John*, 91-92; Ridderbos, *John*, 156.

286. See Moloney, *Belief in the Word*, 140.

287. John 4:15; Carson, *John*, 220; Ridderbos, *John*, 158; Keener, *John*, 605.

288. It appears that the purpose is to let her come to terms with the identity of Jesus and the nature of the gift he is offering. Cf. Carson, *John*, 221. The goal of demonstrating supernatural knowledge of her past and present lives is to produce an aha moment. Ridderbos, *John*, 159. Thus, Jesus is defining the course of the conversation. Keener, *John*, 605. For a summary of the various interpretations of the command, see Ridderbos, *John*, 158-59.

289. Köstenberger, *John*, 152-53; Harris, *John*, 92; Keener, *John*, 605.

290. The woman was not referring to the prophet in Deuteronomy 18:15-18. See Harris, *John*, 92; Köstenberger, *John*, 153; cf. Keener, *John*, 609, who suggests otherwise.

291. See Carson, *John*, 221; Ridderbos, *John*, 161; Keener, *John*, 609.

Standing at the foot of Mount Gerizim, the woman raises a contentious topic: the locus of true worship (John 4:20). The Samaritans associated the site with many events in the patriarchal period.[292] They later constructed a temple on the mountain, which the Jews considered an illegitimate competitor to the Jerusalem temple and thus razed it.[293] The expressions "our ancestors" and you (plural) reflect the opposing views of the two communities on sacred space and worship.[294] The use of the second-person plural verb "you say" suggests an inference that the woman is interested in understanding Jesus' perspective on the aforementioned tension. This inference is drawn based on the assumption that the verb choice reflects the viewpoint of the community to which Jesus belongs, namely Israel, regarding the subject matter.

In response, Jesus offers new perspectives that circumvent the significance of two sacred spaces (John 4:21). Her statement indicates that she is oblivious to what Jesus has already communicated through the conversion of water for Jewish purification rites to wine (John 2:1–11) and the cleansing of the Jerusalem temple (2:13–25). Thus, he reiterates that he fulfills and replaces what the temple symbolizes.[295] His ministry, crucifixion, and resurrection, that is, the coming hour that is also here now, will occasion or have occasioned a new season where Jesus replaces the temple as the center of worship for the community of God.[296] In this new temple, racial barriers do not exist because the believing community will worship one Father, God.[297] Additionally, the new era does not focus on geographical locations; it focuses on genuine worship, where people give the Father what he seeks: worship in spirit and truth (John 4:23–24).[298] Thus, Jesus concludes with an explanation for bypassing both religious spaces: God is Spirit.[299]

---

292. Köstenberger, *John*, 153–54.

293. Morris, *John*, 237; Witherington, *John's Wisdom*, 117.

294. See Köstenberger, *John*, 154; Harris, *John*, 92–93; Ridderbos, *John*, 161.

295. See John 2:18–22; Köstenberger, *John*, 155.

296. Carson, *John*, 224; Köstenberger, *John*, 155; cf. Watt, *Family of the King*, 106; Witherington, *John's Wisdom*, 120.

297. Morris, *John*, 238; Köstenberger, *John*, 155. The racial proclivities (our fathers) give way to the universalized (the Father).

298. See Morris, *John*, 239; Harris, *John*, 93; cf. Talbert, *Reading John*, 121; Keener, *John*, 615, who intimate that John is talking about worship in the Holy Spirit or worship empowered by the Holy Spirit, respectively.

299. Köstenberger, *John*, 157; Carson, *John*, 226; Brant, *John*, 86.

Though the woman does not respond specifically to Jesus' statement, she comes closer to his thinking, introducing a discussion on messianic expectations (John 4:25).³⁰⁰ The theological reflections of the Samaritans make provision for an eschatological figure, a "Restorer" (*Taheb*), expected to be a teacher and lawgiver like Moses, who will reveal all things.³⁰¹ In response, Jesus openly discloses his messiahship, affirming that he is the expected Messiah.³⁰²

While awaiting her response, the disciples return to the well in a state of bewilderment because Jesus is breaking cultural values (John 4:26).³⁰³ The reader becomes aware that although Jews have a Gentile court as a religious symbol of communal identification, their interactions with their neighbors contradict its principles. Instead of assuming the role of a symbol of optimism, the disciples, who are tasked with addressing religious and cultural issues, inadvertently contribute to this mindset by interpreting the event from their own cultural perspective rather than aligning with their divine mission (cf. John 2:1–11). While contemplating the cultural implications of the conversation, the woman leaves her water jar and returns to the city (John 4:28–29). Is her attitude tacitly intimating the reception of the living water?³⁰⁴ Though John is not explicit on that, her action warrants interrogation. The informed reader is aware that Jesus is here to fulfill a divine obligation. Yet the disciples offer what is not Jesus' priority now (4:34).³⁰⁵ Thus, he admonishes them to realign their priorities and participate in the harvest (4:35–36).³⁰⁶ However, the Samaritan woman participates in the harvest as a witness.³⁰⁷

300. Ridderbos, *John*, 164.

301. Keener, *John*, 619; Brant, *John*, 83; Harris, *John*, 94; Köstenberger, *John*, 157; Ridderbos, *John*, 164.

302. Köstenberger, *John*, 157; Talbert, *Reading John*, 122; Harris, *John*, 94.

303. Keener, *John*, 621. The Jews held that Rabbis should not talk to women publicly. Harris, *John*, 96; Köstenberger, *John*, 159; Morris, *John*, 242; Barrett, *Gospel According to St. John*, 240. By the conventions of the day, talking to a (Samaritan) woman alone at the well was also immoral. Ridderbos, *John*, 166; cf. Brant, *John*, 83; Witherington, *John's Wisdom*, 120.

304. See John 4:15; Talbert, *Reading John*, 122.

305. See Keener, *John*, 623; Witherington, *John's Wisdom*, 122–23.

306. Ridderbos, *John*, 168; Witherington, *John's Wisdom*, 122.

307. Brant, *John*, 31; Talbert, *Reading John*, 124. Her response to the message of Jesus is noteworthy because it transformed her into a member of the community of witnesses, a reflection of the action of the first disciples after encountering Jesus. Cf. John 1:35–42; Keener, *John*, 475. Her invitation (come and see) also reflects what Jesus

Now the reader is beginning to understand that Jesus broke barriers to engaging the Samaritans because of this woman's role in the universalization of the community of God.[308] John clarifies it explicitly, stating what her testimony occasioned. First, she participates in the universalization of the community of God because her testimony stimulated faith in many Samaritans to believe in Jesus (John 4:39).[309]

The believing Samaritans also accompanied her to Jesus and asked him to abide with them (John 4:40). Given the theological significance of the verb "to remain," the reaction of Jesus, and the confession that follows, one has no reason to cast doubt on their inclusion into the community of God. The Samaritans responded to testimony about Jesus and not the signs.[310] The narrative also reflects the conversion of the first disciples, who remained in the company of Jesus and acknowledged his messiahship subsequent to the events described in John 1:35–42. The invitation to abide with Jesus is indicative of their willingness to serve God or to be part of the community of God.[311] Jesus' response to their request validates the genuineness of their faith.[312] It further settles the conviction of the Samaritans and contributes to an inundation of Samaritan believers, a harvest of more souls, and thereby universalizing the community of God (John 4:41).[313] Finally, the testimony of the people after abiding with Jesus attests to the universalization of the community. They confessed him as the Savior of the world (John 4:42; cf. 3:16–17). Given that the confession proceeds from the Samaritans, a mixed-race community, it reveals the universalization of the believing community.[314] In Christ, the community of God is accessible to a "mixed-race" and not only Jews.[315]

---

demonstrated. See John 1:39; Köstenberger, *John*, 159. Thus, if the disciples demonstrate the paradigmatic nature of the Baptist's literary role as a witness through witnessing, she embodies the universalization of witnesses by testifying. Cf. John 1:35–42; Keener, *John*, 475. Thus, the universalization of sacred space in Christ culminates in the universalization of witnesses.

308. See Keener, *John*, 606; Carson, *John*, 217.
309. Köstenberger, *John*, 164; Ridderbos, *John*, 171; Morris, *John*, 250.
310. Witherington, *John's Wisdom*, 119.
311. See Brodie, *Gospel According to John*, 160.
312. See John 2:23–25; Talbert, *Reading John*, 124.
313. See Köstenberger, *John*, 164; Keener, *John*, 626.
314. Witherington, *John's Wisdom*, 125; Keener, *John*, 626.
315. Witherington, *John's Wisdom*, 125.

Further, John develops the theme by employing the second sign to explicate how Jesus is the Savior of the world (John 2:46-54). To prepare the reader for the development of the theme, he indicates a geographical change from Sychar to Galilee, an abbreviation of a Hebrew phrase that means the region of the Gentiles.[316] In this context, John announces the return of Jesus and his disciples to Cana, where he performed the first sign. A Gentile official in Capernaum whose son is ill receives a message about the return of Jesus to Cana and comes to beg for his healing.[317] Responding to the man, Jesus rebukes him and extends it to the Galileans in general for insisting on signs before believing, employing the second-person plural.[318] Nevertheless, the man persists in asking Jesus to follow him to Capernaum to heal his son (John 4:49). However, Jesus assures him of healing without traveling with him (4:50). And without any sign, the man believes the spoken word of Jesus, a proof of one who is demonstrating or progressing in his faith in Jesus.[319] However, his servants confirm the healing on his way to Capernaum (4:51). The information he receives establishes a connection between the word of Jesus and the recovery: it happened just after Jesus spoke (4:52-53). The voyage translates into a faith journey: the man and his household become part of the believing community because of the healing (4:53).

John concludes the narrative, stating that it is a sign (John 4:54). Why does John describe it as such? Jesus saved the official's son from

---

316. Talbert, *Reading John*, 125; cf. Isa 8:23.

317. Talbert, *Reading John*, 124-25; cf. Köstenberger, *John*, 169. Other scholars have expressed different opinions on the identity of the official. Since John does not state it explicitly, scholars can only speculate. Beasley-Murray suggests that the official was probably a Jew. Beasley-Murray, *John*, 288. Others take no sides because the narrative does not state it explicitly. Cf. Carson, *John*, 234; Brant, *John*, 90. Köstenberger intimates that, though it is unspecified, the official was probably a Gentile. See Köstenberger, *John*, 169. Barrett's acceptance of the Gentile identity of the official stems from the similarities existing between this narrative and the synoptic incidents. Barrett, *Gospel According to St. John*, 245. Talbert also draws such conclusions. Besides that, he develops this position by placing it within its narrative context. He argues that this narrative illustrates the confession of the Samaritans: The Savior of the world. Talbert, *Reading John*, 124-25. According to him, Galilee is the region of Gentiles, a culture that concentrates on non-Jews. The logic of his argument is that since the Samaritans declared Jesus as the Savior of the world and he is in a Gentile region, John is employing a Gentile character to illustrate the theme. Cf. Talbert, *Reading John*, 125.

318. Köstenberger, *John*, 170; Carson, *John*, 238.

319. Harris, *John*, 102; Moloney, *Belief in the Word*, 186.

death, confirming that he is the Savior of the world.[320] Further, it culminates in the salvation of the Gentile official and his family from eternal death, a confirmation that Jesus is the world's Savior (cf. John 4:54).

Finally, the analysis shows that John presents the universalization of the community as a response to the relationship problems that existed between the Jews and the Samaritans. The Jews have a court that allows Gentiles to participate in their communal worship, but they are hostile to the Samaritans, who are their neighboring community. These belligerent actions undermine the theological significance of the Gentile Court because it exists as a sign that God is interested in a universalized religious society. Additionally, the existence of the Gentile court in the Jewish symbol of community identity vis-à-vis the conflict between the Jews and the Samaritans indicates the failure of the Jewish community to incarnate its religious tenets in concrete sociocultural issues.

However, this is not peculiar to their relationship with the Samaritans. The problem of relationships exists within the Jewish community. The healings at Bethesda also characterize the community as a group that fails to contextualize its religious and cultural values. Thus, John employs the narrative to address the relationship flaws at Bethesda—the microcosm of the community—and unveil the believing community's religious-cultural obligation in a society grappling with the inability to incarnate its communal values.[321]

Identifying the Problems of the Community (John 5—12)

The Implications of the Healing at Bethesda (John 5)

John casts the narrative in a religious-cultural context, announcing that Jesus traveled to Jerusalem for a Jewish religious feast.[322] He heightens it by identifying the setting as a house where God expresses mercy through healings, thus attracting a multitudinous community of sick and marginalized groups.[323] Given that they belong to one house with a common goal, the reader expects them to operate as members worthy of their communal identity. However, it is a house divided. Therefore, the narrative

---

320. Talbert, *Reading John*, 125.
321. See Pilch, *Healing*, 13.
322. See John 5:1; Yee, *Jewish Feasts*, 16.
323. See Köstenberger, *John*, 178; Yee, *Jewish Feasts*, 16.

unveils the problems in this microcosmic community, focusing on a peculiar case.

John concentrates on a man with a multifarious condition that exposes the religious and cultural problems of the community. His identification denotes an impoverished man without status in his society.[324] His sickness, a long-term debilitation, indicates the severity and hopelessness of his condition, preparing the reader for the community's response.[325] In this context, the narrative introduces Jesus, whose question makes the reason for the community's response perspicuous—the inability to incarnate its religious-cultural values.

The man's answer indicates that the cause of his prolonged sickness is the privation of help caused by individualism, manifesting in the competitive spirit that characterized the search for healing.[326] This characterization is antithetical to the tenets of a collectivistic society.[327] A collectivistic culture promotes seeking the neighbor's good over pursuing individualistic goals.[328] Therefore, it does not countenance competition because it disrupts social harmony.[329] However, Bethesda became a house of competition.[330] Their attitude also uncovers the absence of cultural values such as cooperativeness, family-centeredness and friendship.[331]

Apart from these reasons, the Bethesda community should have responded appropriately on religious grounds. It lives in expectation of the omnibenevolence of God and, therefore, must replicate it. The religious context warrants the demonstration of justice, which reminds them to treat each other as they expect from God and manifests special care for the marginalized.[332] But this does not happen. The absence of these religious-cultural values indicates that the microcosmic community failed immensely, both culturally and religiously.[333]

---

324. Köstenberger, *John*, 180; Porter, *John*, 54; Keener, *John*, 640.

325. See Ridderbos, *John*, 185; Tenney, *John*, 104.

326. See John 5:6–7; Witherington, *John's Wisdom*, 137.

327. Neyrey, "Group Orientation," 89.

328. Neyrey, "Group Orientation," 89.

329. Malina, "Collectivism," 22.

330. Witherington, *John's Wisdom*, 137.

331. Pilch, "Cooperativeness," 33; *Healing*, 13; Moxnes, *Economy of the Kingdom*, 62.

332. Keenan, "Justice," 121–22, 126; Harrington, "Biblical Perspectives," 126.

333. See Pilch, *Healing*, 13.

Consequently, apart from exposing these problems, the reason for Jesus' presence is to provide the solution to these societal maladies by evoking the community's religious-cultural values to illustrate how they must respond to these challenges. The first action he takes targets the community's view of lameness. Instead of contempt, he views the man through the eyes of pity.[334] Addressing their view is critical because it encourages the community to evaluate human conditions through God's eyes, given that pity is a theological value and a quality of God.[335] Furthermore, looking at the community through God's lens influences the human response to societal problems because of the inseparable link between perception and action. The Mediterranean culture establishes a connection between an individual's views and actions.[336] They affirm that the quality of pity inheres in a person's eyes or heart and is revealed by what a person does on behalf of others in need.[337] Looking through the eyes of pity provokes honorable, compassionate, or merciful acts towards the needy.[338] The narrative establishes this connection through Jesus' action towards eradicating the problem.[339] By this approach, he becomes the Merciful One missing in the house of mercy.

Moreover, Jesus demonstrates that looking at the community from God's perspective allows the members to actualize their religious-cultural values. For instance, through the Sabbath healing, the narrative portrays Jesus as the agent of liberation who incarnates the cultural significance of the Sabbath, emancipating a man from servitude irrespective of his social classification.[340] Thus, the attitude of Jesus and the healing challenge the community to reflect its religious-cultural values.

Furthermore, the narrative closes, revealing the exacerbated nature of the problem and the need for a new community: the unimaginable and short-sighted behavior of the religious authorities.[341] They jettisoned the weightier matters of the law, such as justice, mercy, and faithfulness, but promoted strict adherence to the law.[342] Like Bethesda, the reader

---

334. John 5:6; Ridderbos, *John*, 185.
335. Malina, "Pity," 139.
336. Malina, "Pity," 139.
337. Malina, "Pity," 139.
338. Malina, "Pity," 139.
339. See Ridderbos, *John*, 185; Malina, "Pity," 139.
340. See Nelson, *Deuteronomy*, 83; Hasel, "Sabbath," 32.
341. Köstenberger, *Encountering John*, 79; cf. Beasley-Murray, *John*, 74.
342. See Matt 23:23; Köstenberger, *Encountering John*, 96.

discovers the absence of religious-cultural values in the religious community. Even when Jesus employs the family metaphor to explicate the community of God, the religious authorities are unable to grasp it because they study the Scriptures for self-aggrandisement.[343] Their response to the teachings of Jesus exposes their failures and inability to fill the lacunae in the Bethesda community. These challenges pervade the subsequent narratives and demonstrate the exacerbated nature of the problem.

The Root of the Lacunae: A Journey of the Reader (John 6—12)

These narratives elaborate on the root of their inability to reflect their religious-cultural values. They depart from the microcosmic community of Bethesda and focus on the Jewish religious leaders and community. It is instructive to note that the recurrent expression "the Jews" is a Johannine characterization of the Jewish religious leaders and the community.[344] In the Johannine use of the word to explicate the two communities' delinquency to reflect their mandate, the narrative focuses on one group or both. Therefore, it records the response of the Jewish community, religious leaders, or both to the mission of Jesus.

In both instances, however, the leaders dominate and influence the actions of the populace. John portrays the response of the religious authorities generally as the greatest obstacle to the mission of incarnating the community of God. The unfruitfulness of their studies in leading them to faith in Christ becomes even more conspicuous with the narrative development of the theme. The problem Jesus catalogues in John 5—the leaders' inability to recognize him despite their rigorous scrutiny of the Old Testament Scriptures—recurs (cf. John 5:39-47). It manifests in various ways in the interactions between Jesus and the Jews. One of these is their view of the source of the authority of Jesus (John 7:15; cf. 5:17-18).

The religious leaders grapple with the source of Jesus' authority (John 7:15; cf. 5:17-18). Belonging to the rabbinic schools, the leaders assume that a teacher derives his authority only through this medium (cf. John 7:15). Given that, without any rabbinic training, Jesus employs the rabbinic hermeneutical approach in his authoritative interpretation

---

343. Köstenberger, *John*, 194-95; cf. Ridderbos, *John*, 207; Harris, *John*, 120.

344. See Brown, *Community*, 41; Martyn, *History and Theology*, 41; Köstenberger, *Encountering John*, 26; Dunn, *Evidence*, 41; Morris, *John*, 357; Moloney, *John*, 97; Boer, "Jews," 148; Wheaton, *Jewish Feasts*, 41.

of the Scriptures, they questioned the legitimacy of that authority (John 7:15).[345] Their distorted view of the source of his power emanates from continuously evaluating Jesus through the prism of their misguided study instead of the Scriptures, the compendium of testimonies about him (cf. John 5:39–47).

Moreover, questioning the messenger's authority affects their reception of the message. John portrays the religious leaders as people who are unreceptive to the teachings of Jesus. They constantly grapple with grasping the communicative force of the message of Jesus (cf. John 2:18–21; 5:17–18; 6:41–52; 8:34–36). Even when they ask questions, they mostly do not approach it as sincere inquirers but as those seeking to challenge his legitimacy and doubt his message (cf. John 2:18–21; 5:17–18; 6:41–52; 8:12–19). In some instances, the leaders register their disbelief in his character and the content of his message (cf. John 7:45–52; 9:28–29).

Due to their resistant attitude towards Jesus' teachings, which serve as a primary source of pertinent information regarding his status, they grapple with embracing his assertions concerning his identity. Their question concerning the identity of Jesus and its corresponding response affirms the above: they sought answers on a subject he had discussed from the beginning (John 8:25). Through referencing previous encounters, Jesus prompts the Jews to recall the proclamation of his identity, proving that the leaders are either struggling to grasp or refusing to accept his claims (cf. John 2:13–22; 5:19–45; 8:25).[346]

The religious leaders' misunderstanding of the message and identity of Jesus, with its concomitant nonacceptance of the messianic claims, pervades the subsequent narratives. It is evident in the reactions of the Jewish community to his teachings. These reactions are binary: the antagonistic attitude towards people who believe in the messianic proclamations and the object of messianic claims (cf. John 9:22; 6:34–42, 60; 8:34–42). The antagonism is apparent in the punishment meted out to individuals for believing in Jesus or confessing him as the Messiah: excommunication (John 9:22). Further, the Jews opposed Jesus' testimony in various ways. They met his message on his identity as the Bread of Life with mistrust, incomprehension, and grumbling (John 6:34–42, 60).

---

345. Carson, *John*, 311; Harris, *John*, 153–54.

346. Moloney sees an honest question and not a rejection of Jesus. However, even if we assume that the question bears a mark of honesty, their behavior after this encounter betrays this explanation, just like the earlier ones. Moloney, *Signs and Shadows*, 99; cf. John 9:22; 10:19–20, 31–33.

They also challenged the testimony about his self-identification as the Light of the World (John 8:34-42). The narrative also makes the Jews' misunderstanding and rejection of his identity the principal grounds for the accusations of demon possession leveled against Jesus (John 8:48-52; 10:20). It also ties the two attempts at stoning Jesus to these factors (John 8:58-59; 10:30-33; cf. 8:58-59). These attempts reveal a deep-seated antagonism towards Jesus and a quest to annihilate him for his claims, culminating in their participatory role in the crucifixion of Jesus (John 18-19). The narrative makes Jesus' exegesis on his identity the preponderant stimulant for their fixation with exterminating him (cf. John 5:16, 18; 7:1, 11, 30; 10:39).

Beyond these challenges, John's characterization of discipleship also exposes the root of the community's failure. The narrative reveals that many Jews believed in Jesus apart from his disciples—both the laity and leaders (John 2:23; 7:31; 8:30-31; 10:42; 11:45; 12:11, 45). Nevertheless, the majority believed because of the miracles they witnessed Jesus perform (cf. John 2:23; 7:31; 11:45; 12:11, 45). The leaders who believed through signs were also afraid to confess it due to the trepidation of the Pharisees (John 12:45). Additionally, the faith of many who followed Jesus was spurious (John 8:30-31).[347] This is evident from the disparity between their profession of faith and their actual conduct; they became indifferent to his word, liars, people who did not know his Father, doubted the identity of the Son, children of the devil, and guilty of participating in attempted murder.[348] These people who were once with Jesus turned away from him and became hostile to him.[349]

Their response to the teachings and mission of Jesus indicates that the community struggles with false discipleship: the inability to abide

---

347. Ridderbos, *John*, 306; Köstenberger, *John*, 261; Carson, *John*, 346-48. Given that the narrative asserts that many believed in Jesus but concludes with rebukes about behavior uncharacteristic of believers, Harris and like-minded scholars categorize the people into believers (John 8:30-31) and Jewish opponents (John 8:33) to reconcile the anomaly. Harris, *John*, 174; Carson, *John*, 346. Harris, for example, opines that the concluding part deals with an interaction between Jesus and the Jewish opponents, not the believers. Harris, *John*, 174. His explanation overlooks other instances of demonstrations of spurious faith in John where disciples turned back due to the teachings of Jesus. John 2:23; 6:60-66; cf. Carson, *John*, 346-47; Köstenberger, *John*, 261; Ridderbos, *John*, 306. For further explanations of this distinction and rebuttals to this view, see Carson, *John*, 346-48.

348. John 8:37-59; Carson, *John*, 346; cf. Köstenberger, *John*, 261.

349. Ridderbos, *John*, 306; Köstenberger, *John*, 261.

in Christ or his teachings.[350] Therefore, Jesus instructs them to continue in his word, given that remaining in the teachings of Jesus is a mark of true discipleship.[351] Obedience to this instruction is the panacea for unfruitfulness and the only way the community can incarnate the divine concept of community. Thus, its absence implies that the community cannot be fruitful in fulfilling its mandate (cf. John 15:1–17). Against this background, Jesus teaches his genuine disciples in the farewell discourse the remedy for spurious discipleship and the participatory role of the believer in incarnating the community of God. Therefore, the reader analyzes the community theme in the farewell discourse to ascertain the proposed Johannine response to these societal issues.

The Community that Imitates God (John 13—17)

Various reasons support the criticality of examining the farewell discourse for solutions to sociocultural maladies. One of them is the prevalence of topics related to the relational dimension of community, such as the character of relationships in the divine community, the participatory role of the members of the divine community in the incarnation of the principles of the divine community, and the role of the believing community in participating in this mission. Furthermore, it defines how members of the believing community must replicate this paradigm in their relationships with each other and the world. Finally, it explains how these relationships function to remedy the enormous religious and cultural failures exposed in this milieu. Therefore, the study analyzes the discourse thematically for an informed understanding of the Johannine response to the community challenges in John.

The Portrait of the Divine Community

A predominant theme in the farewell discourse is community—the nature of the relationships that the members of the eternal community enjoy. Whereas the prologue creates anticipation for elaborations on the subject, the farewell discourse brings the exegesis and development of the community theme to finality. In the farewell discourse, Jesus indicates the culmination of his mission as the uniquely authoritative expounder

---

350. See John 8:31; Carson, *John*, 348.
351. Carson, *John*, 348; Ridderbos, *John*, 306.

of the Father (and the perfect community), announcing that he has made his name known to the disciples (John 17:25; cf. 1:18).³⁵² The criticality of this revelation stems from its effect on the theme. Johannine narratives expounding traits that affirm the characterization of the relationship between the eternal distinctions as a community concentrate preponderantly on Jesus' relationship with his Father (cf. John 13:3; 14:7–11; 15:9; 16:15). The Johannine Jesus customarily speaks of himself through the prism of his relationship with his Father.³⁵³ Therefore, analyzing it provides elucidations on this community. Understanding the character of the Father also helps the various communities evaluate their own character as members of a community.³⁵⁴ How does Jesus characterize the Father? What is its impact on their relationship and the human community?

One of the ideas that Jesus develops from the prologue is the depiction of the Father as inherently relational (community).³⁵⁵ The divine self-differentiation at the opening and end of the prologue portrays the Father as relational in his divine essence (John 1:1–2, 18). Whereas the self-differentiation marker at the beginning describes an eternal communion with God (1:1–2), the end depicts him as the Son in the bosom of the Father (1:18). The commonality between both is the emphasis on quality relationship—the relational dimension of community. Developing this thought, the farewell discourse and the narrative present another dimension. Jesus substitutes the idea of the Logos being *with* God with a perichoretic relationship, employing the reciprocal immanence formula (John 10:38; 14:10–11, 20; 17:21).³⁵⁶ In various instances, he describes his relationship with the Father as being in-one-another—mutual

---

352. See Harris, *John*, 293.

353. The "I am" sayings express his divine identity without explicitly linking it to the Father. Bauckham, *Beloved Disciple*, 251.

354. For instance, whereas the struggle for healing at Bethesda reveals the presence of individualism, Jesus identifies the absence of the love of God as a motivation for the response from the religious leaders (John 5:42). Thus, an informed view of this character—the foundation of community—positions the disciples to replicate the community of God. Therefore, discussions on love feature prominently in what Jesus presents about the character of the Father. Elaborating on the relationship between Jesus and the Father and its role in their relationship in the farewell discourse, he describes the Father primarily as loving. John 15:9, 10; 17:23, 24, 26; cf. John 3:35; 5:20; 10:17.

355. Borchert affirms that the expression of community is rooted in God's nature. Borchert, *John 12—21*, 106.

356. Ridderbos, *John*, 495; Harris, *John*, 258.

interpenetration (John 10:38; 14:10–11, 20; 17:21).[357] A perichoretic relationship denotes unity of being.[358] Akin to the prologue, the union between the ontological co-equals, the Father and Son, is intimate.[359] It also affirms community status, describing a *community of being* that allows the individuality of the eternal distinctions to be maintained while sharing in the lives of each other.[360]

Furthermore, Jesus makes the relationship of mutual interpenetration the cause of a community of action. Regarding this, he identifies two areas: works and words (John 10:38; 14:10). He attributes his operations to this *circumincession,* making them the outcome of a divine partnership (John 10:38; 14:10; cf. 5:17–20). The idea that their relationship produces functional unity originates from the prologue (cf. John 1:3–4). However, the distinctive feature is that the prologue associates it with the Logos being *with* God, not mutual indwelling. The concept of coinherence appears only in the narrative, identifying Jesus' works as the works of the Father (the Sender) or the product of the Father working through him (John 9:4; 10:37). Even when John does not suggest interpenetration explicitly, it is implicit in the narrative. For instance, Jesus appeals to his ontological equality with the Father as the ground for his work (John 5:17–20).[361] It implies a *circumincession* because the perichoretic relationship in the Godhead requires ontological equality or unity.[362] Jesus further attributes his words to the perichoretic union, revealing that they do not originate from himself but rather from his Father (John 15:15).[363] He asserts that these words are what he has heard from the Father (15:15).

The community of being and actions demonstrated by the Father and Son define the kind of community represented in the farewell discourse. It is a collectivistic community, not an individualistic one. The functional unity expressed in this community portrays it as one characterized by communal values such as unity, cooperation, and love (John 14:10, 31; 15:9; 17:11, 21; 9:4; 10:37; cf. 5:17–20).

---

357. See McGrath, *Christian Theology,* 325.

358. Köstenberger, *John,* 431; cf. McGrath, *Christian Theology,* 325.

359. See Bauckham, *Beloved Disciple,* 251.

360. See McGrath, *Christian Theology,* 325; Carson, *John,* 494; Bauckham, *Beloved Disciple,* 251.

361. See Ridderbos, *John,* 191; Köstenberger, *John,* 185; Moloney, *John,* 174; Harris, *John,* 110.

362. See Köstenberger, *John,* 431; McGrath, *Christian Theology,* 325.

363. See John 14:10; Carson, *John,* 494.

Additionally, elucidating reciprocal indwelling as the cause of the community of actions, John casts the relationship in a family context.[364] As the authorized expositor of God, another thing Jesus reveals about the character of God is that God *consists in* the communion between Father and Son.[365] Bauckham aptly and succinctly writes: The Father is Father only because Jesus is his Son, and Jesus is Son only because he is the Son of the divine Father. Each is essential to the identity of the other.[366] Jesus appeals to the family bond to interpret the unity and collaboration in works and words within this community as products of familial relationships (John 14:10; 17:11, 21; cf. 9:4; 10:37; 5:17–20).

Another way John expresses the import of the perichoretic relationship is through the divine partnership that sustains the incarnation of the concept of community. Therefore, what follows analyzes the participatory roles of the members of the eternal community in incarnating the community of God.

The Participatory Roles of the Members of the Divine Community

Even though the materials on the participatory roles that the members of the eternal community play in its mission for the human community pervade John, the farewell discourse makes the individual functions perspicuous by defining them, thereby making it the narrative where the reader encounters more of the participatory roles of the members of the eternal and human communities in the incarnation of the divine concept.

THE ROLE OF THE FATHER

His role in the contextualization of the community of God is critical because everything revolves around it. The narrative ties it to the incarnation of the Logos, a medium through which the divine concept of society became concrete in the human community. Jesus, the expositor of the community, makes the Father the beginning and end of the process of contextualizing the divine concept, stating that he proceeds from and returns to the Father after his earthly mission (John 13:1, 3; 14:12, 28; 16:16, 28). Within this timeframe, the Father also participates in the

---

364. See John 17:25; Köstenberger, *John*, 500.
365. Bauckham, *Gospel of Glory*, 28–29.
366. Bauckham, *Beloved Disciple*, 251.

mission of the Son. First, the Father sent the Son, putting all things under his power (John 13:3; 14:24; 15:21). In the incarnation, the Father is present with the Son and is the subject that the Son exegetes (John 17:25; 16:32; cf. 1:18). And he accomplishes it through a community of action—collaborating with the Father in works and words (John 14:10; cf. 10:38; 5:17–20).

Furthermore, John connects the Father's role to the work of the Spirit in the establishment of a society that imitates God (cf. John 15:26). He presents the Father as the one who sent the Spirit to participate in the mission of incarnating the community of God (cf. John 14:26; 15:26–27; 16:7–14). Given that, in Johannine theology, the Spirit proceeds from the Father, he is primary in these relations.[367]

Finally, the disciples cannot imitate God without the Father's participation. The Father is the vinedresser of the vine, the symbol of the community (John 15:1).[368] In this context, the narrative assigns two roles to the Father, describing them negatively and positively.[369] The negative aspect describes how he deals with unproductive branches. John states it using the pronoun in the first statement to point to the Father as the one who removes them (John 15:2) and the passive voice in the detailed description of the fate of the unfruitful branches to attribute their destruction to the Father (John 15:6).[370]

Conversely, the Father prunes the fruitful branches to fulfill the purpose of the vineyard—fruit-bearing (John 15:1).[371] Scholars adduce several factors to explain the meaning of fruitfulness in this context. Some approach it from John's primary usage: the "missionary" activity of leading others to Christ.[372] Others opine that it means expressing the life of a Christian disciple.[373] However, it would seem to include love, Christian character, and outreach.[374] These interpretations suggest that

367. See John 15:26; Ridderbos, *John*, 526.
368. Keener, *John*, 993; Köstenberger, *John*, 449.
369. See Harris, *John*, 266–67; Köstenberger, *John*, 448–49; Carson, *John*, 514.
370. Moloney, *Glory Not Dishonor*, 62; Schnackenburg, *Gospel*, 101; Watt, *Family of the King*, 46.
371. Harris, *John*, 266; Talbert, *Reading John*, 220.
372. Köstenberger, *John*, 453; Schnackenburg, *Gospel*, 100; cf. Keener, *John*, 997; Talbert, *Reading John*, 220.
373. Barrett, *Gospel According to St. John*, 474; Beasley-Murray, *John*, 273; Brodie, *Gospel According to John*, 480.
374. Moloney, *John*, 420–21; Morris, *John*, 595; Schnackenburg, *Gospel*, 100.

the divine work expands the family and helps to incarnate God's purpose for the human community. Whereas missionary activities populate the community because they aim at leading others to Christ, demonstrating Christian character and love are natural constituent elements of the community of God.[375] The implication is that the community performs these activities—critical components of the mission to imitate the community of God—through the pruning of the Father.

The Role of the Son

As the expositor of the community of God, the Son defines his role in the incarnation of the community, employing the I am statements (John 14:6; 15:1–7). The first statement identifies Jesus as the bridge connecting the divine and human societies, stressing that he is the way to the Father (John 14:6). Jesus accentuates his declaration, stating it positively and negatively.[376] By this declaration, Jesus claims more than showing the way or being one of the ways in a religiously pluralistic setting: he positions himself as the only means of access to the Father, the community of God.[377] On what grounds is Jesus the way?

Two views attempt to explain why Jesus is the Way. One explains the verse with the principle that the first noun governs the other two, thereby considering "the Truth and the Life" simply as explanatory or clarification of the Way.[378] Consequently, they translate the sentence in a manner that absorbs the force of the two nouns. For instance, I am the true and living Way, or the true Way of life.[379] This approach weakens the supporting and illocutionary functions of the two nouns.[380] It also fails to explain why, in some narratives in John, three terms linked with conjunctions remain distinct.[381]

Conversely, though many Johannine scholars agree that "way" gains emphasis over "truth" and "life," they do not subsume the import of the

375. See John 15:9, 12; Köstenberger, *John*, 453; Schnackenburg, *Gospel*, 100.
376. John 14:6; Talbert, *Reading John*, 212.
377. See Ridderbos, *John*, 493; Köstenberger, *John*, 430; Morris, *John*, 640–41.
378. Keener, *John*, 943; cf. Carson, *John*, 490–91; Moloney, *Glory Not Dishonor*, 35–36.
379. Carson, *John*, 490–91; Ridderbos, *John*, 429.
380. Morris, *John*, 569; Carson, *John*, 490; Harris, *John*, 256; Talbert, *Reading John*, 212.
381. See Köstenberger, *John*, 429.

last two nouns into the first like the minority view but recognize their supporting role in justifying why Jesus is the Way to the Father.[382] How do these nouns support the claim that Jesus is the Way to the Father? On the role of the first noun (ἡ ἀλήθεια or hē alētheia) in affirming the claim of being the Way, the principal thing to note is that Jesus is truth in his very essence.[383] Additionally, as the incarnate Word, he anthropomorphizes God's truth as the supreme revelation.[384] It implies that knowing him as the ultimate revelation—God's truth—is tantamount to knowing the Father, corroborating the claim of Jesus.[385] Jesus also embodies God's life and gives life.[386] Thus, appealing to his essence as life substantiates his claim as the only door to the Father. Therefore, the exclusivity that Jesus enjoys as the only access to the Father and the community of God originates from being the Truth and the Life.[387]

Furthermore, the work of the Son extends beyond being the Way to the Father and the community of God. Jesus identifies himself as the true Vine, a description of a community symbol (John 15:1).[388] Thus, one of the goals of this symbolic depiction is to remind the reader of Israel's failure to reflect its intended purpose as a covenant community. This reminder makes possible the anticipation of something that reflects the divine intentions for choosing Israel as the vineyard of God.[389] Avowing to be the true Vine, Jesus "replaces" Israel as the one through whom the blessings of God flow, thereby demystifying the idea of tying the community of faith to a territory.[390] He becomes the ideal design of the community concept, epitomizing the territorial dimension through the demystification of the idea of the holy land[391] and the relational aspect through the character of relationships expressed in the vine metaphor.[392]

382. See Morris, *John*, 569; Carson, *John*, 490; Harris, *John*, 256; Talbert, *Reading John*, 212; Ridderbos, *John*, 493.

383. Köstenberger, *John*, 430.

384. Carson, *John*, 490–91; Harris, *John*, 256.

385. See John 14:7–11; Talbert, *Reading John*, 212.

386. See John 1:4; 5:26; Harris, *John*, 256; Morris, *John*, 569.

387. Köstenberger, *John*, 430; Carson, *John*, 490–91; cf. Harris, *John*, 256.

388. See Keener, *John*, 993.

389. See Isa 5:1–4; Beasley-Murray, *John*, 272; Schnackenburg, *Gospel*, 106.

390. See Köstenberger, *John*, 15; Carson, *John*, 514; Burge, *Jesus and the Land*, 54; Watt, *Family of the King*, 52; Whitacre, *John*, 372.

391. Whitacre, *John*, 372; Burge, *Jesus and the Land*, 54; Köstenberger, *John*, 449.

392. Brant, *John*, 217.

Thus, the vine image denotes the universalized community of God constituted by both gentiles and believing Jews.[393] The ramification is that aside from being the only means of access to the Father (community of God), Jesus is also the *community* in which the believers dwell—the true Vine. Thus, having access to the Father leads to the Son; it culminates in union with Jesus.

The union with Christ, the true Vine, introduces another role of the Son in the incarnation of the divine concept of community: to initiate the process of fruitfulness of the branches—the believing community (John 15:2, 4-5). The farewell discourse explains fruitfulness as resulting from two interconnected theological concepts: mutual abiding and the pruning of the Father. Jesus employs the vine metaphor to juxtapose the fruitfulness of the believing community with a vine and its branches (15:4-5). The juxtaposition aims to demonstrate the impossibility of pursuing fruitfulness outside the parameters of the community's relationship with Christ (15:4-5).[394] Thus, the narrative positions the Son as the cause or source of fruitfulness, his contribution to the mission of the believing community.[395]

Furthermore, the second reason Jesus gives for fruitfulness justifies the above: divine pruning. Jesus attributes fruitfulness to the pruning activity of the vinedresser, the Father (John 15:1-2). Nevertheless, the narrative indicates that the Father does not initiate fruitfulness but develops his Son's work (cf. John 15:2). His responsibility is to prune fruitful branches to be exceedingly fructuous, thereby fulfilling the purpose of the vineyard (John 15:2).[396] Given that the Father only prunes branches that bear fruits because of their connection to the Vine, we could attribute the outcome also to the participatory role of the Son, who initiates fruitfulness.

The Role of the Spirit

The Spirit's role in the mission of the divine community is binary in nature; it involves the participatory roles of the Son and the disciples

---

393. Köstenberger, *John*, 449; Ridderbos, *John*, 516; Keener, *John*, 993.

394. See Köstenberger, *John*, 451-53; Brodie, *Gospel According to John*, 480; Keener, *John*, 998; Harris, *John*, 267.

395. See Keener, *John*, 998.

396. Harris, *John*, 266; Talbert, *Reading John*, 220; cf. Carson, *John*, 514.

in embodying the principles of the community of God within human society. John ties the understanding of the first function to Jesus' characterization of the Holy Spirit as the Spirit of Truth (John 14:17; 15:26; 16:13).[397] In this capacity, he testifies about Jesus, the truth, to vindicate him (John 15:26; 14:6).[398] Furthermore, he glorifies Jesus, revealing him to the disciples after his departure (16:14).[399]

Additionally, the Spirit plays various roles in the believing community and its mission to imitate God, such as being a helper, comforter, teacher, and witness. The first two are intertwined and could be deduced from the title Jesus links to the functions of the Spirit to reflect his mission: the Paraclete, a label that presents him as the Helper and Comforter of the believing community (John 14:16-19, 26; 14:26; 15:26; 16:7). The exclusive occurrence of these labels just inside the farewell discourse might be attributed to a multitude of factors. One notable aspect is the recurring proclamation made by Jesus on his impending departure (cf. John 13:1-3; 14:2-3, 19, 28; 6:28; 7:13). His absence necessitates the advent and crucial work of the Paraclete. The arrival is necessary because the Paraclete fills the vacuum created by Jesus' departure, preventing the believing community from being orphaned (cf. John 14:18). To be orphaned includes a state of fatherlessness but encompasses other forms of bereavement like friendlessness and helplessness.[400] Therefore, it is unsurprising that secular Greeks applied the word to disciples bereft of a teacher or master.[401] Arguing along this trajectory, Keener interprets the "fatherless" image as a teacher-disciple relationship, asserting that the culture sometimes compares teachers to fathers.[402] It is pertinent to note that John does not treat the relationship between Jesus and the disciples through the prism of a father-son relationship. The prevalent and predominant characterization in the Johannine narrative is the Lord-servant relationship, followed by the Teacher-disciples relationship, with these depictions appearing forty-three and eleven times consecutively. Moreover, Jesus describes the relationship as friendship (John 15:13-15). Thus,

---

397. See Carson, *John*, 500.
398. See Carson, *John*, 528; Ridderbos, *John*, 526; Keener, *John*, 1022.
399. See Harris, *John*, 278.
400. See Harris, *John*, 261; Carson, *John*, 501; Keener, *John*, 973.
401. Carson, *John*, 501; Harris, *John*, 261.
402. Keener, *John*, 973.

his departure deprives the disciples of their Lord, friend, and teacher, necessitating a suitable replacement to fill the brief hiatus.

Therefore, the Comforter title accurately describes the work of a person coming after the deprivation of a friend. The Spirit is another Comforter who succeeds Jesus as the friend of the disciples (John 15:13–15; cf. 14:16). The ramification of this statement from Jesus is that he is the first Comforter, thus legitimizing one of the interpretations of the word (orphan): a friendless state.[403] It further presents the Spirit as the Comforter to a community in need of assistance. The narrative context defines the type of help that necessitates the presence of the Comforter. The thought of Jesus' departure occasioned fear in the believing community. Jesus, therefore, reminds them repetitively not to let their hearts be troubled nor to fear (John 14:1, 27; 16:20–22). He also speaks about imminent opposition and persecutions, aggravating the already troubling and heart-throbbing condition (John 15:20–21; 16:2–3). Amidst these conditions, the community has a mission to fulfill that requires divine assistance. Thus, the Companion fills the gap by being actively involved in their mission,[404] taking away their fears, and granting them peace.[405] His help produces a single process where the disciples witness about Jesus to the opposing world through the strengthening of the Paraclete.[406]

Furthermore, the teaching role of the Paraclete is one of the topics Jesus elucidates to the disciples before departing. It is one of the reasons he identifies the Paraclete as the Spirit of Truth (cf. John 15:26; 16:13). In this capacity, the Paraclete teaches the disciples all things, bringing to their remembrance all that Jesus taught (John 14:26). Jesus restates this idea, indicating that the Spirit will guide the believing community in all truth and show them things to come (cf. John 16:13). The former denotes two successive events in which the Spirit expounds the teachings of Jesus for the disciples to grasp the communicative intent.[407] The latter reinforces what Jesus said earlier, revealing the mode through which the Spirit teaches the messianic community. In this regard, the Spirit will

---

403. See Harris, *John*, 261.

404. Brodie, *Gospel According to John*, 490.

405. Moloney, *Glory Not Dishonor*, 71; cf. Ridderbos, *John*, 526–27.

406. Moloney, *Glory Not Dishonor*, 71; Ridderbos, *John*, 527; Brodie, *Gospel According to John*, 490; Keener, *John*, 1022.

407. See Ridderbos, *John*, 511; Keener, *John*, 977; Carson, *John*, 505; Harris, *John*, 263.

guide the community to explore and understand the truth already unveiled by Jesus without revealing new things.[408]

Aside from these, the Spirit functions as a witness. As the Spirit of truth, his witness vindicates Jesus as the truth (John 14:6; 15:26; 16:13).[409] This witness, as Ridderbos succinctly notes, is the assistance the disciples receive from the Spirit in the controversy between the believing community and the world about the truth concerning Jesus' self-revelation in word and deed as the sent one.[410]

Finally, the incarnation of the concept of community demonstrated in the community of God is a product of a divine-human partnership. Just as the members of the community of God perform various roles, both corporately and idiosyncratically, the believing community has a role to play. In the following session, the work discusses these responsibilities.

The Participatory Role of the Believing Community

As partners with God in incarnating the ideal community concept, the disciples are responsible for continuing God's mission of anthropomorphizing the divine purpose through the explications Jesus provides. To manifest this, they must act in cooperation with God. Thus, Jesus reveals what their assignment prescribes and proscribes as members of the believing community, focusing on their relationship with God, themselves, their role as partners in God, and the associated problems of inevitable persecution.

Their role begins with maintaining their participation in the community of God. Given that they are part of the community, the farewell discourse addresses them as people who have already entered it and accentuates the need to perpetuate their union with Christ. In this regard, Jesus commands them to abide in the Vine (John 15:4), that is, to continue to believe.[411] It also denotes remaining in their union with Jesus, maintaining a vibrant and intimate spiritual fellowship,[412] or nurturing their spiritual communion with Christ.[413]

---

408. See Ridderbos, *John*, 536; Carson, *John*, 539; Harris, *John*, 278.

409. See Carson, *John*, 528; Ridderbos, *John*, 526; Keener, *John*, 1022.

410. Ridderbos, *John*, 526–27; cf. Keener, *John*, 1022; Talbert, *Reading John*, 224–25.

411. Harris, *John*, 267; Beasley-Murray, *John*, 272.

412. See Harris, *John*, 267; Beasley-Murray, *John*, 272.

413. Köstenberger, *John*, 454; cf. Carson, *John*, 516–17.

Remaining in the Vine is the divine requirement for the believing community's response to Christ's indwelling; it establishes a relationship of reciprocal indwelling, necessary to implement the divine mission.[414] Akin to the vine-branch relationship, they can do nothing without Christ (John 15:4–5). The narrative context suggests that fruitfulness is in view.[415] This depends on remaining in the relationship of reciprocal indwelling— abiding in the Vine and vice versa.[416] Fruitfulness in this context hinges on two areas of Christian mission: *going* and *living*. While the former culminates in community expansion through Christian outreaches,[417] the latter emphasizes the disciples' interpersonal relationships as people whose mission is to imitate God's concept of community. Some of the attributes they must characterize as a believing community are godly character,[418] discipline,[419] moral fruit,[420] love,[421] and serving each other (John 13:14–15). Given that these attributes flow from this relationship, it is impossible to fulfill their mission without it. Jesus restates this idea, applying the metaphor to his relationship with the Father to produce a perlocutionary effect: fruitfulness flows naturally from mutual abiding, just as Jesus' works outflow from his union and communion with the Father.[422]

The second imperative Jesus ties to fruitfulness—the goal of the disciples—is to abide in his love.[423] Jesus juxtaposes his relationship with the Father with that of the disciples to clarify the import of the divine imperative (cf. John 15:9–10). In the eternal relationship, love and commands are inseparable because they are mutually dependent. The love of the Father flows from the obedience of the Son, and the obedience of the Son flows from love (John 15:10).[424] Since the Father loves the obedient

---

414. See John 15:4; Köstenberger, *John*, 451; Ridderbos, *John*, 517; Harris, *John*, 267.

415. Harris, *John*, 267; cf. Ridderbos, *John*, 517.

416. Köstenberger, *John*, 451–53; Brodie, *Gospel According to John*, 480; Harris, *John*, 267; Schnackenburg, *Gospel*, 99.

417. Köstenberger, *John*, 453; Keener, *John*, 997; Talbert, *Reading John*, 220.

418. Morris, *John*, 595.

419. Barrett, *Gospel According to St. John*, 474; Beasley-Murray, *John*, 273; Brodie, *Gospel According to John*, 480.

420. Keener, *John*, 997.

421. Moloney, *John*, 420–21; Talbert, *Reading John*, 220.

422. John 15:5; Beasley-Murray, *John*, 273; Keener, *John*, 998.

423. See John 15:9–10; Carson, *John*, 510.

424. Barrett, *Gospel According to St. John*, 476.

Son, he reciprocates it by keeping the commandments of the Father out of love.[425] As Harris notes, obedience is evidence of love and reinforces love. Jesus, in a similar fashion, requires the believing community to remain in his love by adhering to his commands.[426] And reflecting the character of its paradigm, obedience should outflow from love, not compulsion.[427]

Like the first imperative to remain in the Vine, the love command extends to the quality of relationships expected within the believing community (cf. John 13:34–35). Jesus requires the disciples to incarnate this theological value within the believing community (cf. John 13:34–35; 15:12). Members must demonstrate reciprocal love, thereby creating a chain of love uniting the divine and the human community.[428] Being obedient to this command identifies them as disciples of Jesus.[429]

Finally, the disciples have a role as a community of witnesses (John 15:27). In John, testifying about Jesus is an integral part of the incarnation of the divine concept of community because it sustains the mission. It started with John the Baptist, whose testimony had a pivotal role in heralding the arrival of the Messiah (John 1:6–7). Then the earliest disciples also began as witnesses (John 1:40–41). Additionally, Jesus and the Father provide a further testimony about the Son (John 8:18). To participate in this mission, the disciples must witness. This is because advancing the work requires a collective body of individuals who bear testimony concerning Christ, given that the foundational principle of Christian expansion is a repeated process of witnessing whereby disciples testify about Jesus to others.[430] Consequently, Jesus commands them to testify as people who have been with him from the beginning (cf. John 15:27).

Performing their role as witnesses brings antagonism from the world (John 15:18–25; 16:1–4). Jesus enumerates the causes of the opposition. Their union with Christ conditions a lifestyle that triggers hatred because it is antithetical to the world.[431] John establishes a relationship between the sender and the sent, such that honoring or dishonoring the sent is tantamount to honoring or dishonoring the sender, and vice versa

---

425. Köstenberger, *John*, 456; cf. Harris, *John*, 269; Keener, *John*, 1003.
426. Harris, *John*, 269.
427. Ridderbos, *John*, 519; Carson, *John*, 520; Köstenberger, *John*, 453.
428. Köstenberger, *John*, 457; Carson, *John*, 521; Ridderbos, *John*, 520.
429. Harris, *John*, 269; Carson, *John*, 522.
430. Carson, *John*, 159; cf. Talbert, *Reading John*, 86.
431. See Ridderbos, *John*, 523; Köstenberger, *John*, 464; Carson, *John*, 525; Brodie, *Gospel According to John*, 485.

(John 18:20–23; 5:22–23). Thus, a world that does not recognize the Father automatically rejects the Son and opposes his disciples because he sent them (John 15:18–20). Since the world rejects Jesus, the community of witnesses (the sent) will face ejection from the synagogues and execution.[432] However, the community performs its functions with the assistance of the Paraclete.

The above indicates the impossibility of incarnating the concept of community without the involvement of all partners—God and the believing community. Since the community is God's idea, its explanation belongs to God. Nevertheless, its incarnation requires a community of witnesses who receive guidance and empowerment from the Paraclete to testify about the Son, thereby uniting the divine and human communities.

Finally, whereas the farewell discourse allows the reader to see the participatory roles of the divine and human communities in the incarnation of God's purpose, the words of Jesus to the community at the foot cross and the corresponding reaction from the hearers practically demonstrate the theological construct in the farewell address. Therefore, the work discusses this event and its ramifications for the community theme.

Jesus' Final Moments with the Community

After Jesus' farewell discourse with the disciples, there are two momentous events worth noting because of their criticality to the narrative development of the community theme, constituted by the disciples' encounter with the crucified and the resurrected Lord. The discussion, therefore, assesses the contributions of these events to the development of the theme.

The Community at the Foot of the Cross (John 19:25–30)

Having taught the disciples about living as the community of God, the events at the crucifixion scene give a practical application of some community-centered teachings. In this narrative, the abiding theme finds expression through the actions of these disciples (cf. John 15:1–5). John mentions that not all twelve disciples are present because of their state of petrification (cf. John 9:25–27). Peter's attitude towards Jesus—denial

---

432. Moloney, *Glory Not Dishonor*, 72–73; Talbert, *Reading John*, 225; Brodie, *Gospel According to John*, 490.

during the trial—reveals the intensity of fear that had gripped the believing community, a situation predicted before the arrest (cf. John 14:1, 27; 16:20–22; 18:17, 27). Therefore, the indication is that these were the only ones to have followed him to this point, portraying them as the personification of true discipleship. In a narrative replete with spurious disciples who become hostile to Jesus upon teaching what they deem hard, following Jesus to the cross demonstrates genuine discipleship—continuing in Christ.[433]

Moreover, John ties the abiding theme to life in the new relationships in Christ (cf. John 19:26–27). In unpacking the vine metaphor, Jesus reveals that abiding in him implies allowing his words to remain in the community members, that is, governing their lives and practices by his teachings.[434] The reaction of the beloved disciple exemplifies the relationship between the community's union with Christ and living by his word. At the foot of the cross, Jesus commits his mother into the hands of the beloved disciple, introducing her simply as "mother" (John 19:27).[435] Employing the term, Jesus establishes a new familial relationship at the foot of the cross, defining how the community must live.[436] In response to Jesus' instructions, the beloved disciple took her to his own house at that hour (19:27). His actions demonstrate his subservience to the word, allowing it to govern his life. It also implies that he understood the communicative force of the word of Jesus—to take care of her (19:27).[437] The perlocutionary effect of the narrative is that it presents a paradigm requiring the believing community to demonstrate stronger bonds than biological or familial relationships.[438] It also characterizes the members of the community of God as people living in a family-oriented or collectivistic society in praxis, not just theoretically. Consequently, they demonstrate their union with Christ and the influence of his word on the community by caring for the members.[439] Such is the crux of

---

433. See John 2:23; 6:60–66; 8:30–31; Ridderbos, *John*, 306; Köstenberger, *John*, 261; Carson, *John*, 346–48.

434. See John 19:27; Harris, *John*, 268; Köstenberger, *John*, 455; Carson, *John*, 518.

435. See Harris, *John*, 317.

436. See Moloney, *Glory Not Dishonor*, 146; Ridderbos, *John*, 613; Keener, *John*, 1145.

437. Harris, *John*, 316; Ridderbos, *John*, 613; cf. Brodie, *Gospel According to John*, 547.

438. Keener, *John*, 1145.

439. See John 19:27; Brodie, *Gospel According to John*, 547.

the narrative—a portrait of profound care, even under nightmarish or adverse conditions.[440]

Finally, another momentous event John mentions is Jesus' post-resurrection appearance to the disciples on the evening of the first day of the week, where he commissions and empowers the community to fulfill its mandate (John 20:19-23).

The Commissioned and Empowered Community (John 20:19-23)

Due to the Jewish religious leaders' role as the architects of Jesus' crucifixion, they became the believing community's object of trepidation.[441] Therefore, the disciples congregated in a room and locked themselves up after the burial of Jesus (John 20:19). Nevertheless, Jesus appeared and stood among them in those moments of fear.[442] More importantly, the reunion and the joy it evokes in the petrified community mark the fulfillment of his promise to the disciples.[443]

Most importantly, what Jesus shows and says to his disciples is noteworthy, given his standing posture and what transpired. He stood in their middle, the appropriate place for revelations, before showing them his wounds (John 20:19).[444] These lacerations on the hands and sides of his resurrected body serve a dual function. First, they serve as tangible proof of his suffering and demise, establishing his identity as the individual who was crucified, deceased, and interred. Secondly, they signify his victory over death and the grave (20:20).[445] Therefore, the primary objective behind displaying his wounds was to share his triumph with the community of witnesses and reveal the crux of their message.[446] Additionally, it sets the commission—the disciples' participation in God's

---

440. Brodie, *Gospel According to John*, 547.

441. Keener, *John*, 1200.

442. Harris, *John*, 330; cf. Keener, *John*, 1200. The closed doors coupled with his mode of entrance underscores the miraculous nature of the act. Ridderbos, *John*, 641; Carson, *John*, 646; cf. Köstenberger, *John*, 572.

443. John 20:20; cf. John 16:20-24; 17:13; Köstenberger, *John*, 572; Ridderbos, *John*, 642; Harris, *John*, 330; Carson, *John*, 647; Talbert, *Reading John*, 263; Keener, *John*, 1201.

444. See Keener, *John*, 1201.

445. Ridderbos, *John*, 641; cf. Köstenberger, *John*, 572.

446. See Ridderbos, *John*, 641; Carson, *John*, 647.

mission—in a proper context, given that it involves testifying about Jesus (cf. John 20:21).

Speaking to the disciples, he bequeaths peace to them twice (John 20:19, 21; cf. 14:27; 16:33). The first statement about peace accompanies his appearance (John 20:19). However, the narrative ties the latter to the commissioning of the disciples (20:21). Therefore, it seems appropriate to surmise that the first statement aims to dispel their fears, considering the frightened state of the community (cf. John 20:19).[447] However, the latter statement is a source of encouragement for a community bound for persecution because of their mission.[448]

The commissioning of the disciples is the narrative focus (John 20:21).[449] The authorization is critical because it allows the disciples to participate in the divine mission as a community of witnesses.[450] Jesus summarizes the relationship between the two roles in the commissioning statement: As the Father has sent me, so I send you (cf. John 20:21). It is pertinent to caution against promulgating two types of sending because of the different expressions employed in the statement for Jesus and the disciples; John uses them interchangeably.[451] He expresses the same thought, thereby drawing the disciples into the unity and mission of the eternal community.[452] The indication is that the believing community continues Jesus' mission.[453] The collocation aims to strengthen the community, knowing that it guarantees his participation in their mission. Ridderbos aptly notes: Similar to how Jesus accomplished his mission through functional unity with the Father, he also continues to have a significant impact on the mission of his disciples.[454]

To demonstrate the participation of the eternal community in what he has commissioned them for, he breathed the Spirit into the community (John 20:22). The generally accepted view on the narratological significance of the incident is that it envisions the empowerment of the

---

447. Köstenberger, *John*, 572; Morris, *John*, 745.
448. Keener, *John*, 1202.
449. Köstenberger, *John*, 574.
450. Harris, *John*, 330; Keener, *John*, 1204; Köstenberger, *John*, 575.
451. See Harris, *John*, 330; Keener, *John*, 1203; Carson, *John*, 647; Ridderbos, *John*, 642.
452. Köstenberger, *John*, 573; Ridderbos, *John*, 642.
453. Keener, *John*, 1203; Harris, *John*, 330.
454. Ridderbos, *John*, 642.

disciples.[455] The scholarly acceptance of this interpretation is based on its alignment with the contextual elements of the story, specifically the depiction of the disciples in a condition of petrification and their subsequent commissioning (cf. John 20:19–23). However, it is pertinent to note that two forms of this view exist in Johannine scholarship: partial and complete empowerment. Primarily, the proponents of the first view arrive at this conclusion by trying to reconcile what transpired here with Pentecost by juxtaposing the disciples' behavior after Jesus breathed on them with the account in Acts 2.[456] Köstenberger, for instance, asserts that their behavior after the present incident would also be puzzling had they already received the Spirit.[457] Arguing along that trajectory, Carson writes that the event is a kind of acted parable pointing forward to the full enduement still to come.[458] Alternatively, most scholars affirm that what transpires here is the transmission of the working of the Spirit.[459] Unlike the above scholars, who interpret the event through the prism of Lukan pneumatology in Acts, they focus on Johannine theology. Therefore, they interpret the event predominantly as the time when Jesus empowers the believing community for the mission preceding the act.[460] Consequently, though both views interpret the narrative distinctly, the common denominator is the agreement that the event empowers the community. The consensus emanates from the shared understanding that divine empowerment is a prerequisite for the fulfillment of what they were commissioned to do.

Concluding Remarks

The narrative development of the concept of community allows us to see the Johannine strategy employed to demonstrate the foundation of community in John, the conception and mission of the believing community, the problem of community, and how the believing community can imitate God. In John, God is the foundation of community; the narrative grounds this on the principle that God is the first community. From the

455. Ridderbos, *John*, 643; Keener, *John*, 1204; Talbert, *Reading John*, 264; Harris, *John*, 331.

456. Carson, *John*, 653–54; Köstenberger, *John*, 574–75.

457. Köstenberger, *John*, 574–75.

458. Carson, *John*, 653–54.

459. Ridderbos, *John*, 643.

460. Ridderbos, *John*, 643; Keener, *John*, 1204–5; Talbert, *Reading John*, 264.

prologue, the characterization of God as the first community stems from God's nature and the relational dimension of community demonstrated by the eternal distinctions in their union and the collectivistic attributes that culminated in the creation of the world (cf. John 1:1–5).

Since creation is a product of this relationship, it must participate in the community of God.[461] Nevertheless, its participation is dependent on divine assistance and invitation. Thus, God sends John the Baptist, one who fits into the Johannine qualification for witnesses, to extend an invitation to his community through his testimony concerning the Light.[462] As the precursor and witness, John fulfilled his role. He ushered in the messianic era by identifying the Messiah for the community (John 1:29–34). Additionally, his ministry inaugurated the assemblage of the members of the community of God: two of his disciples became the first members of the community of God through his testimony (John 1:35–39).

Furthermore, to demonstrate the role of the new community, John ties its narrative development to its religious and sociocultural mandate. Through narratives that evoke Jewish religious and cultural symbolism, John uncovers the religious-cultural maladies, presenting the new community as God's response to these challenges. For instance, John employs the sign of turning water into wine to demonstrate the community's role, characterizing it as a group whose social presence must address sociocultural challenges (cf. John 2:1–11). Additionally, the narrative casts Jesus' response to the abuse of the Gentile court in the Jewish symbol of community identity as the redefinition of community identity (John 2:13–22). Therefore, John proceeds to address the universalization of the community of God, buttressing the earlier notion that in Christ, God's purpose for community identity manifests (cf. John 4).

It is also pertinent to note that the abuse of the Gentile court, coupled with the tension between the Jews and the Samaritans, exposes the leaders' inability to incarnate their religious values. They have a temple court that allows Gentiles to participate in their communal worship, indicating that the divine purpose for the community of God is an interracial community serving one God.[463] Therefore, their disruption of Gentile worship reveals their struggle with becoming the conduit for incarnating the

---

461. Grenz, *Community of God*, 112; cf. Kanagaraj, *John*, 2; Bauckham, *Gospel of Glory*, 48.

462. See Brant, *John*, 31; Keener, *John*, 392.

463. See Köstenberger, *John*, 102.

community identity prescribed by God. Again, the same community that allowed a Gentile court in their temple had relationship challenges with their neighbors on religious grounds, defeating its theological essence.

Moreover, the problems of the community reflect the internal challenges of Jewish society. It is evident in the societal maladies that plagued the microcosmic community of Bethesda and the religious leaders' response to the remedy Jesus provides (John 5). The apparent colossal cultural failure creates lacunae, necessitating a paradigm for emulation.

Consequently, the farewell discourse addresses how the human community can represent the community of God. The farewell address reveals that the incarnation of the community of God is a divine-human partnership where both partners play their participatory roles. Thus, Jesus teaches the community how it can play its role and demonstrate in his final moments on the cross the application of the truths proclaimed earlier. Finally, he commissions and empowers the community to fulfill its mission. As discussed earlier, the community's mission is binary in nature: *going* and *living*. It is, therefore, reasonable to surmise that the purpose of the commissioning and empowerment is to fulfill these.

In the fourth chapter, the study exegetes the Akan concept of community. We consider this a critical step because the study recognizes that the contextualization of the biblical text completes the hermeneutical cycle. Thus, exploring how the interpreter's context perceives the theme is a prerequisite. The focus of this chapter (the narrative development of the community theme) helped identify the call to action for the interpreter's context. Consequently, studying the Akan reality will also impel an informed understanding of its sociocultural context and the call to action, an integral substratum for intercultural exegesis.

4

The Akan Concept of Community

Introduction

THIS CHAPTER CONCENTRATES ON the second step of the methodology: the exegesis of the Akan reality. The study indicates that reading the text interculturally requires a biblical culture and a contemporary cultural context.[1] Chapters 2 and 3 examine the biblical culture, namely, the Johannine concept of community. This chapter evaluates the second partner of an intercultural exegesis: the interpreter's culture. Thus, the study performs an academic autopsy on the Akan community concept to understand their community ideations and interrogate the veracity of the views in the academic literature enunciating this subject. It is also a prerequisite for determining the call to action (communicative force). Finally, the study explores the Akan sociocultural milieu because of the commonalities between the Johannine and Akan contexts, namely the emphasis on the community theme. The correlation, we believe, will allow the *modus vivendi* prescribed for the community of God in John to serve as a critique of the culture of the Akan Christian or see how the Akan culture enriches the understanding of the text.[2]

For an informed understanding of the Akan concept of community, it is critical to analyze their proverbs. Thus, the subsequent section examines the place of Akan proverbs to appreciate their impact on their

---

1. See Loba-Mkole, "Intercultural Biblical Exegesis," 1347–59.
2. See Ukpong, "Reading the Bible," 6; West, "African Biblical Scholarship," 249.

philosophy of life. Further, understanding the value of Akan proverbial lore culminates in establishing their concept of a community.

Proverbs in Akan Epistemology and Philosophy

In deliberating on the African philosophy of life, we cannot neglect or downgrade their proverbs. The reason is that these aphorisms are mines or repositories from which we can excavate their cultures. Commenting on this subject, Mbiti perspicaciously notes that "in the realm of oral literature, we (Africans) find the immensely rich world of stories, fables, recitations, songs, poetry, and proverbs."[3]

Similarly, the Akan counterparts of the Kenyan clergyman agree with him on the significance of proverbial lore in unearthing the thoughts of a traditional African.[4] In the Akan conceptual scheme, proverbs are sources and enormous residues of knowledge garnered from the real-life experiences of the community.[5] This ubiquitously held view on the impact of proverbs is the substratum of some of the works of Akan philosophers and scholars, such as Appiah et al., Gyekye, Opoku, Danquah, Yankah, and Bannerman, who have examined Akan proverbs to bring an informed understanding of the Akan culture.[6] They consider Akan proverbs as summations of knowledge of the surrounding world.[7] Thus, a short proverb can be equivalent to pages of philosophical discussions.[8]

Apart from proverbs being a source of knowledge, they also epitomize the wisdom of the community.[9] For the Akan, proper application of proverbs adorns or enriches the speech.[10] However, the goal is to contextualize the wisdom of the elders in the prevailing circumstances at the

---

3. Mbiti, "Children Confer Glory," ix.

4. See Opoku, *Akan Proverbs*, xviii; Boakye, "Akan Oral Tradition," 35.

5. Boakye, "Akan Oral Tradition," 35.

6. Appiah et al., *Proverbs*; Gyekye, *Akan Cultural Values*; Opoku, *Akan Proverbs*; Danquah, *Akan Doctrine of God*; Yankah, *Proverb*; Bannerman, *Ghanaian Proverbs*. See also Rattray, *Ashanti Proverbs*.

7. Appiah et al., *Proverbs*, xii; Nkansah-Kyeremateng, *Akans of Ghana*, 28; Gyekye, *African Philosophical Thought*, 14–15.

8. Appiah et al., *Proverbs*, xii.

9. Dzobo, "African Symbols and Proverbs," 94; Nkansah-Kyeremateng, *Akans of Ghana*, 28; Boakye, "Akan Oral Tradition," 35; Mbiti, *African Religions*, 86.

10. Opoku, *Akan Proverbs*, xviii; Nkansah-Kyeremateng, *Akans of Ghana*, 28; Boakye, "Akan Oral Tradition," 35.

time, not to display the richness of the speech.[11] It explains the Akan notion that the proper application of aphorisms is a mark of wisdom.[12] For Akans, wisdom is a prerequisite for accurate application and interpretation or understanding of proverbs.[13] They express this in two adages: "ɔba nyansafoɔ yɛbu ne bɛ, na yɛnka n'asɛm [we speak to the wise in proverbs, not in plain language]" and "ɔbkwasea na yɛbu ne bɛ a yɛkyerɛ no ase [communicating to a fool in proverbs requires explanations]."[14] Thus, Dzobo aptly observes that proverbs are a remarkably effective mode of communication, and society classifies their correct and persuasive use in speech as a sign of sound education, maturity, cultural sophistication, and wisdom.[15] Mbiti affirms that "it is in proverbs that we find the remains of the oldest forms of African religious and philosophical wisdom."[16] The ramification is that they provoke further reflection and deeper thinking about the meanings of the proverb and the aspect of life that the speaker seeks to promulgate or elucidate.[17]

Furthermore, in the awareness that adages are repertoires of knowledge and wisdom, every aspect of their lives is captured in their proverbial sayings.[18] Akan proverbs are sources and summations of knowledge, the philosophical reflections of the community, and concepts about every aspect of their lives. Their contents commend refined, tested, and proven community values.[19] Dzobo rightly affirms that proverbs display the main value orientations of the traditional African community, from the ethical, spiritual, humanistic, economic, and intellectual to the material.[20] Thus, scholars perspicaciously note that it is impossible to appreciate the philosophy and beliefs of Akans without studying their proverbs.[21] In

---

11. See Nkansah-Kyeremateng, *Akans of Ghana*, 28.

12. Opoku, *Akan Proverbs*, 42; cf. Dzobo, "African Symbols and Proverbs," 94–95; Boakye, "Akan Oral Tradition," 35.

13. Opoku, *Akan Proverbs*, 42; Gyekye, *Akan Cultural Values*, 141–42; Yankah, *Proverb*, 55.

14. See Opoku, *Akan Proverbs*, 42; Gyekye, *Akan Cultural Values*, 141–42.

15. Dzobo, "African Symbols and Proverbs," 94.

16. Mbiti, *African Religions*, 86.

17. Mbiti, "Children Confer Glory," ix.

18. Mbiti, "Children Confer Glory," ix; Christaller, *Ghanaian Proverbs*, 5; Boakye, "Akan Oral Tradition," 35.

19. Boakye, "Akan Oral Tradition," 35.

20. Dzobo, "African Symbols and Proverbs," 96.

21. Appiah et al., *Proverbs*, xii; Opoku, *Akan Proverbs*, xviii.

cognisance of these benefits, it is pertinent for works of this nature to incorporate or even concentrate on Akan proverbial lore. Consequently, the subsequent section explores the Akan community concept, focusing preponderantly on their aphorisms.

Community in Akan Thought

The Foundation of the Akan Community Concept

Akan philosophers emphasize the relational dimension as the determinant of community, not the territory (though it is an aspect) inhabited by a group of people.[22] To these thinkers, an aggregate of people devoid of quality relationships does not constitute a community. In their epistemology, a community is a group of individuals connected by interpersonal bonds who share common interests, values, and goals.[23]

Extrapolating the Akan philosophical ideations of humanity and community from their proverbs will culminate in describing their community concept as originating from God and thus natural to the human being. The Akan view of humans as theomorphic beings created for communal life is the ground for this postulation.[24] In this regard, two proverbs are worth noting: "*nnipa nyinaa ye Onyame mma* [all humans are children of God]" and "when a person descends from heaven, he lands into human society."[25] Gyekye maintains that the belief that *Onyame* (the Supreme Being) created human beings emanates from the idea that they descend from heaven into the human community.[26] For Akans, the relationship between God and humankind exceeds a Creator-creature relationship. Their aphorisms postulate that humans have an aspect of their Creator in their nature and, in consequence, are theomorphic beings.[27] Therefore, all humans are children of God; none are children of the earth.[28] This adage implies that all human beings are children of

---

22. Gyekye, *African Cultural Values*, 35–36; cf. Klink, *Sheep of the Fold*, 52.

23. Gyekye, *African Cultural Values*, 35–36.

24. Gyekye, *African Philosophical Thought*, 19–20; cf. Opoku, *Akan Proverbs*, 11; Appiah et al., *Proverbs*, 201.

25. See Appiah et al., *Proverbs*, 201; Gyekye, *African Philosophical Thought*, 155; Opoku, Akan *Proverbs*, 11.

26. Gyekye, *African Philosophical Thought*, 155.

27. Gyekye, *Akan Cultural Values*, 24.

28. Gyekye, *African Philosophical Thought*, 20; Appiah et al., *Proverbs*, 205.

God by creation, not procreation. It denotes that the Akans perceive all human beings as a community or family of children of God.[29] The Akan understanding of the brotherhood of humanity rests on this assumption. Their characterization of the human community shows that the Akan concept of brotherhood extends beyond blood ties.[30] To them, humanity has no boundary. They express this idea in the adage "*nnipa nua ne nipa* [man's brother is a man]."[31] Thus, Akan anthropology is the basis for their concept of communitarian egalitarianism and the indispensability of the community to a human being.

Alternatively, we can examine the foundation of the Akan ideations of the community through their view of the constitution of the human being. Akan thinkers perceive the constitution of human beings as an explanation for their sociality. The Akans hold a dualistic conception of the person, constituted by the immaterial and material constituent elements.[32] The spiritual elements consist of the ɔkra (soul) and *sunsum* (spirit). The two constitute a spiritual unity.[33] Akan cosmology intimates that the ɔkra (soul)—the innermost self and essence of a person—is a divine essence or spark of God in humans.[34] The soul is also the life, transmitter, and embodiment of a person's destiny. The spirit (*sunsum*), according to Danquah, determines the character dispositions and personality of a person.[35]

Whereas the ɔkra is from God and constitutes a spiritual unity with the *sunsum*, the *honam* (body) is material.[36] In their view of the nature of the human being, Akans also distinguish the *mogya* (blood) and the *ntorɔ* (father's spirit), both endowed by human beings.[37] They hold that whereas the *ntorɔ* comes from the father, the mother transmits the *mogya*

---

29. See Gyekye, *African Cultural Values*, 24; Danquah, *Akan Doctrine of God*, 101.

30. Gyekye, *African Cultural Values*, 26.

31. Gyekye, *African Cultural Values*, 28.

32. Gyekye elucidates that failure to see the spiritual unity of the ɔkra (soul) and *sunsum* (spirit) is the reason some think of a tripartite conception, constituted by the soul, spirit, and body (*honam*). See Gyekye, *African Philosophical Thought*, 99.

33. Gyekye, *African Cultural Values*, 99.

34. Gyekye, *African Philosophical Thought*, 85.

35. Danquah, *Akan Doctrine of God*, 66. Gyekye defines personality as a set of characteristics as evidenced in the behaviour of an individual. Gyekye, *African Philosophical Thought*, 90.

36. Gyekye, *African Philosophical Thought*, 94.

37. Gyekye, *African Philosophical Thought*, 94.

to the child.[38] In Akan anthropology, the two are responsible for the traits of parents that their children inherit.[39] The ramification of this philosophical construct is that the individual is not an "independent being" because his existence is the product of the collaborative work of God and the human community (parents). Against this background, human life revolves around society. Thus, for the Akan, to be human is to relate to others—community.[40]

Consequently, the Akans express this notion in the adage that when a person descends from heaven, he lands in human society. It suggests that human beings are naturally communal or social.[41] Akan thinkers ground the interpretation of this maxim on the principle that everyone is born into an existing community or lives as a community member.[42] Hence, in Akan philosophy, society is not merely a necessary condition for human existence but something natural to humanity. Living in a community is congruent with the nature of a human being.[43] Thus, human beings are naturally communitarian. It explains why banishment used to be one of the punishments for heinous crimes: it stripped a person of the privilege of belonging to his natural habitat. And since the naturalness of community originates from the fact that God created humanity as theomorphic beings and placed them in various communities, we can safely conjecture that Akan communitarianism is not a human invention but divine.

Furthermore, the origin of human beings in Akan epistemology is the root of Akan humanism. It defines the worth of a human being and how the community must value human life. If all human beings are perceived to be theomorphic, a universal community of children of *Onyame*, it follows that we must treat everyone with dignity. Gyekye succinctly notes:

> The insistent claim made in this maxim is based on the belief that there must be something intrinsically valuable in God: the human being, considered a child of God, presumably by reason of having been created by God and having in his or her nature

---

38. Gyekye, *African Philosophical Thought*, 94.
39. Gyekye, *African Philosophical Thought*, 94.
40. Opoku, *Akan Proverbs*, xviii.
41. Gyekye, *African Cultural Values*, 36; cf. Appiah et al., *Proverbs*, 201.
42. Gyekye, *African Cultural Values*, 36; Appiah et al., *Proverbs*, 201.
43. Gyekye, *African Philosophical Thought*, 155.

some aspect of God, ought also to be held as of intrinsic value, worthy of dignity and respect.[44]

Consequently, Akans have aphorisms indicating their appreciation for the dignity of the human being. To accentuate the worth of a person, some of the proverbs affirm the need to value people above wealth or material possessions.[45] The following are a few examples: "It is a human being that counts"; "I call upon gold, it answers not; I call upon cloth, it answers not";[46] "A human being is more beautiful than gold or money"; and "Man [a person] is more important than money."[47]

Analyzing these proverbial sayings through the prism of the Akan view of poverty and wealth is critical because it helps to appreciate their communicative intentions. Poverty is one of the necessitating factors in the degradation of the human spirit.[48] Akans avow that poverty is madness (that is, the poor person acts like a lunatic). The proverb that in the extremes of need, a human being will live in the forest also adds that poverty makes people live like animals.[49] Akans also perceive poverty as a disgrace because it necessitates disgraceful actions.[50] Their awareness of the impact of poverty makes their appreciation of money or wealth meaningful. Akan proverbs link wealth to an elevation of social status through the opportunities it creates and the encumbrances in life it helps to overcome. One of these is the adage "*sika yɛ nam sene sikan* [money is sharper than the sword]."[51] It is not surprising that wealth is the ultimate possession in Akan thought (when wealth comes and passes by, nothing comes after).[52] Therefore, the comparisons promulgated in these proverbs reflect the appreciation for the worth of the human being in the Akan concept of community.

---

44. Gyekye, *African Cultural Values*, 24.

45. See Opoku, *Akan Proverbs*, 12; Appiah et al., *Proverbs*, 201; Gyekye, *African Cultural Values*, 190–91.

46. Opoku, *Akan Proverbs*, 10; Gyekye, *African Cultural Values*, 190; Danquah, *Akan Doctrine of God*, 193.

47. Opoku, *Akan Proverbs*, 12; Gyekye, *African Cultural Values*, 25; Appiah et al., *Proverbs*, 201.

48. Gyekye, *African Cultural Values*, 104.

49. Gyekye, *African Cultural Values*, 104.

50. Opoku, *Akan Proverbs*, 54.

51. Gyekye, *African Cultural Values*, 98–99; Opoku, *Akan Proverbs*, 105.

52. Gyekye, *African Cultural Values*, 98–99.

And now, what are the implications of these proverbs? The proverb "It is a human being that counts" accentuates the worth of human beings above all material things.[53] Humans are to be considered above material things because the human being is of real value, especially in perilous or precarious times.[54] In such moments, material possessions do not respond. Since the human being responds in debilitating times—something material possessions cannot accomplish—"it is a human being that is needed" and "man [a person] is more important than money."[55] The appreciation of human worth is also a motivation for the Akan proverb, "a human being is more beautiful than gold or money."[56]

Understanding the worth of the human being in Akan epistemology and anthropology is pertinent because it defines how to treat human beings and builds a foundation for human fellowship.[57] First, these proverbs oblige us to accord humans the dignity and respect they deserve, proscribing inhumane acts against them. Hence the Akan proverbial saying "*Onipa nnyɛ nwura*," meaning that human beings are not weeds to be cut away or trampled upon.[58]

Additionally, proverbs that accentuate the worth of the human being aim to justify human fellowship by emphasizing its overriding importance for the well-being of the individual. Gyekye lists the following: "A human being is more beautiful than gold or money; it is a human being that counts or matters; it is a human being that is needed."[59] The first proverb deserves special mention because of its significance. Portraying the human being as beautiful denotes ascribing to humankind the property of beauty.[60] Gyekye elucidates that assigning this property (beauty) to humans means enjoying them for their own sake.[61] The Akan thinker clarifies that enjoyment in this context denotes appreciating the worth of a human being by showing compassion, generosity, and hospitality. Having this disposition towards the human being allows openness to the

---

53. Opoku, *Akan Proverbs*, 10; Gyekye, *African Cultural Values*, 25.
54. Gyekye, *African Cultural Values*, 25.
55. Gyekye, *African Cultural Values*, 25; Appiah et al., *Proverbs*, 201.
56. Opoku, *Akan Proverbs*, 12; Gyekye, *African Cultural Values*, 25.
57. See Opoku, *Akan Proverbs*, 11; Gyekye, *African Cultural Values*, 25–26.
58. Opoku, *Akan Proverbs*, 11; cf. Gyekye, *African Cultural Values*, 25–26.
59. Gyekye, *African Cultural Values*, 25; cf. Opoku, *Akan Proverbs*, 12; Appiah et al., *Proverbs*, 201.
60. Gyekye, *African Cultural Values*, 25.
61. Gyekye, *African Cultural Values*, 25.

interests of others, making it a moral responsibility to offer help when necessary.[62] The Akan concept of communitarianism rests on this understanding of human fellowship. Consequently, what follows discusses the Akan view of communalism.

Akan View of Communitarianism

The preceding discourse establishes that the Akan community concept is divine because of its inextricable link to the Children of God motif. This motif defines the intrinsic value of a human being, the brotherhood of humanity, and fellowship as the outflow and natural concomitant of appreciation for human value, explaining the substratum of the communalistic traits in the Akan social order.

Against this backdrop, Akans have multifarious proverbs that serve to explicate their perspective on communitarianism. Among these, the motivation for Akan communitarianism is a predominant motif. In this regard, certain proverbial sayings demonstrate that communitarianism in Akan philosophy hinges on the naturalness of society for the human being. One of these is, for instance, that when a person descends from *osoro* (heaven), he drops into human society.[63] The adage stresses that community is natural to a human being because it agrees with human nature as theomorphic beings and the habitat of their birth.[64]

Furthermore, the naturalness of community to the human being denotes the necessity of human fellowship for the well-being of an individual. Hence, Akans have proverbs expressing the preponderating significance of relationships, such as "it is a human being that is needed" and "a human being is sweet."[65] The second proverb deserves special mention because of its meaning: a human being is good to have. Explaining from the Akan perspective the intensity of the necessity of having a human being, Opoku asserts that a human being is so valuable that the Akan prize the presence of miscreants above empty homes.[66] It is pertinent to note that the maxim does not denote condoning social deviance by making

---

62. Gyekye, *African Cultural Values*, 25.

63. Gyekye, *African Philosophical Thought*, 155; cf. Appiah et al., *Proverbs*, 201; Opoku, *Akan Proverbs*, 11.

64. Gyekye, *African Cultural Values*, 36; cf. Appiah et al., *Proverbs*, 201.

65. Opoku, *Akan Proverbs*, 10; Gyekye, *African Cultural Values*, 25.

66. Opoku, *Akan Proverbs*, 10.

the house a haven for them. Akan proverbial lore forbids the concealment of such characters.[67] Therefore, though a house could symbolize security or safety, interpreting the maxim through this prism is at variance with the abhorrence of concealment of the wicked in the Akan view of communitarianism.[68] The focus is on brotherhood, which is also one of the meanings of a house.[69] For Akans, being human requires being in a relationship with others.[70] Why is human fellowship central to the Akan view of what community entails?

Studying the proverbs enumerated thus far meticulously shows a correlation between proverbs that prize human worth above material possessions and those that emphasize the necessity of human relationships; they all accentuate the need for human fellowship because of its concomitant prospects (for instance, a human being is sweet, and it is a human being who counts or matters).[71] One of these benefits (as we have already established) is that human beings count because of their ability to help or respond to the needs of fellow humans when the situation demands it.[72] The Akan view of human help makes the centrality of human fellowship even more perspicuous. An example of an adage helpful for probing the Akan thought on the interconnectedness of human relationships and assistance is the proverb "the human being needs help."[73] Gyekye explains that the Akan word *hia* (needs) has a normative connotation, making it a moral obligation to assist a human being because he or she deserves and ought to receive assistance.[74] However, receiving assistance can only transpire in the context of human fellowship, making it a prerequisite for such demonstrations. Therefore, the culture discourages a life of seclusion because it impedes the reception of help. Thus, human fellowship is central because it provides legitimacy as the conduit for help.[75]

---

67. See Appiah et al., *Proverbs*, 201.
68. Arthur, *Cloth as Metaphor*, 164.
69. See Opoku, *Akan Proverbs*, 10; Arthur, *Cloth as Metaphor*, 164.
70. Opoku, *Akan Proverbs*, 10.
71. See Opoku, *Akan Proverbs*, 12; Gyekye, *African Cultural Values*, 25.
72. Gyekye, *African Cultural Values*, 25.
73. Opoku, *Akan Proverbs*, 11; Gyekye, *African Cultural Values*, 24.
74. Gyekye, *African Cultural Values*, 24–25.
75. Gyekye, *African Cultural Values*, 24–25.

The necessity for help is rooted in the Akan view that a human being is not self-sufficient. In cognisance of this human reality, Akans employ multifarious proverbs to expound their view of human insufficiency. One of them states: "A person is not a palm tree that he should be self-complete or self-sufficient."[76] The explanation of Opoku is worth mentioning because it follows a literal translation of the proverb. His literal interpretation of the maxim, which reflects the Twi construction, suggests that the palm tree is self-complete or self-sufficient because its branches surround it.[77] Since human hands, by nature, do not surround the body like the branches of a palm tree, a human being needs helping hands to accomplish many things. Perhaps the interpretation of the proverb promulgated by Appiah et al.—a human being cannot be self-sufficient—stems from the Akan's awareness that a human being is naturally insufficient and incapable of attaining a state of self-sufficiency.[78]

Furthermore, acknowledging human insufficiency necessitates a community where members complement each other, thereby creating the chain of interdependence necessary for accomplishing individual goals. Thus, *obi dan bi*, to wit: one person depends on another for his or her well-being.[79] Other aphorisms deserve consideration to understand the purpose of interdependence. One of them is the proverb, *onipa na oma onipa ye yiye*. It reveals that interdependence is necessary because the well-being of man depends on another.[80] The others include: the left arm washes the right arm and vice versa; the reason two deer walk together is that one must remove the mote from the other's eye.[81] Opoku and Gyekye explain that the first proverb, for instance, affirms that each hand is not self-sufficient because one hand cannot cleanse itself without the assistance of the other hand. However, it can wash the other hand. Therefore, the left hand must depend on the right, and vice versa, for cleansing.[82] Akans express a similar thought in other proverbs (two deer

---

76. Appiah et al., *Proverbs*, 203; Opoku, *Akan Proverbs*, 12; Gyekye, *African Cultural Values*, 37.

77. See Opoku, *Akan Proverbs*, 12.

78. Appiah et al., *Proverbs*, 203.

79. Opoku, *Akan Proverbs*, 11; Gyekye, *African Cultural Values*, 45.

80. See Danquah, *Akan Doctrine of God*, 193; Gyekye, *African Philosophical Thought*, 155.

81. Opoku, *Akan Proverbs*, 17; Gyekye, *African Cultural Values*, 188; Ackah, *Akan Ethics*, 52–53.

82. Opoku, *Akan Proverbs*, 17; Gyekye, *African Cultural Values*, 37.

walk together so that one would remove the mote from the other's eye).[83] These aphorisms imply that "human interdependence contributes to the development, security, and survival needs of the individual."[84] Consequently, Akan proverbial sayings that espouse the community concept express appreciation of the worth and pertinence of the community.

Since Akans recognize that human inadequacies warrant interdependence, they emphasize the significance of collectivism. Some adages that espouse the importance of collective efforts are: "*nsa baako nkukuru adesoa* [one finger cannot lift a thing or a heavy load]"; "*nnipa baanu so dua a, emmia* [when two people carry a log, it does not feel heavy]"; "*nsa-dodow kyere babin koro* [many hands catch a valiant man]"; and "*ɔbaakofo nkyekyere kurow* [one person alone cannot build a town]."[85] The first two proverbs teach, for instance, that cooperation minimizes the burden of work due to shared responsibility, thereby making it light.[86]

Another benefit of the interdependence espoused in these proverbs is that it produces a community of action that makes even challenging tasks achievable. Lifting a heavy object requires all fingers, not just one. A gallant man can also be powerless when confronted by many people. In both instances, strength, a natural concomitant of numbers, complements their inadequacies, thereby overcoming the insurmountable to accomplish tasks through the accumulative effects of collective endeavors. The interpretation is akin to the meaning of the second proverb: it underscores the centrality of cooperation in undertaking something worthwhile and extraordinary.[87]

Apart from the prospects of collective efforts enumerated above, Akans believe that there is safety in numbers. Hence the proverb, One person alone does not arrest a lunatic.[88] If a group of people apprehend a lunatic, it saves the individuals from potential harm because, collectively, they have an overpowering presence that prevents the lunatic from targeting anyone. Even if the lunatic attempts, the target can depend on the strength of the others for his safety.

---

83. See Opoku, *Akan Proverbs*, 17; Gyekye, *African Cultural Values*, 188.
84. Opoku, *Akan Proverbs*, 11.
85. Opoku, *Akan Proverbs*, 13–17, 83; Gyekye, *African Cultural Values*, 37.
86. Opoku, *Akan Proverbs*, 17.
87. Opoku, *Akan Proverbs*, 13.
88. Appiah et al., *Proverbs*, 19.

Finally, interdependence enhances decision-making. The Akans assert that "ɔbaakofoɔ tirim nni adwen," meaning that "the head of a single person has no thoughts."[89] The proverb underscores the difficulty of making wise decisions solely based on a person's cognitive strength. It does not suggest the impossibility of making personal decisions, but rather the difficulty of making some decisions without taking counsel from others. Consequently, the Akan indicates the necessity of making decisions with the assistance of others in the proverb, "Wisdom is not in the head of one person."[90] According to Gyekye, the maxim means some equally wise individuals may offer better ideas. Thus, the individual should not consider his opinions superior to others but expect them to evaluate his positions, thereby enriching them.[91]

The portrait of communalism espoused in these proverbs and Akan epistemology gives the impression that the individual has no place. But this is misleading. Thus, we shall now consider how the individual fits into Akan communitarianism.

The Place of the Individual in the Community

Most definitions of the Akan (or African) community concept suggest that the group subsumes individuality. Such interpretations are inaccurate. The Akan expression of communitarianism is not radical because it does not "reduce a person to intellectual inactivity, servility, and docility."[92] It recognizes that the individual, though a social being, exercises personal will and identity.[93] This characterization denotes the distinct nature of a person in Akan thought.

Akan proverbial sayings project the individuality of each person. These aphorisms mostly contain a word about the human head. Akan philosophers use it because of its communicative force; it is synonymous with the word person or individual.[94] Consequently, it is not surprising that they employ it to depict the distinctness of a human being. The following are some examples of proverbs that stress the individuality of a

---

89. Appiah et al., *Proverbs*, 19.
90. Gyekye, *African Philosophical Thought*, 50, 144.
91. Gyekye, *African Philosophical Thought*, 50, 144.
92. Gyekye, *African Cultural Values*, 56.
93. Gyekye, *African Cultural Values*, 47.
94. See Gyekye, *African Philosophical Thought*, 159; Appiah et al., *Proverbs*, 275.

human being: "All men have one head, but heads differ" and "All heads are alike, but the thoughts in them are not the same."[95] Akan scholars suggest that these proverbs mean that resemblance in looks is not tantamount to the sameness of character.[96] The point is that all human beings have different temperaments and attitudes; therefore, they are not the same.

Additionally, the idiosyncratic nature of the individual human being is evident in his capabilities. Thus, the Akan proverb: "If your head is oversized, it is not everything that you can carry."[97] The meaning of this adage is that everyone has a limit, irrespective of one's capacity.[98] It is pertinent to note that the adage does not denote the absence of potential but rather its limitedness. It means a human being has peculiar capacities that require the company of others or an environment that breeds shared obligations to flourish.[99] Opoku, for his part, opines that this is the import of the proverb. He argues that we must recognize that being human means to belong, and to do so, is to have an obligation to other community members.[100] He intimates that the community maintains its balance when we exercise this obligation. Society is based more on responsibilities than individual rights; it is a place where people assume their rights in exercising their duties, making society a chain of interrelationships.[101] Therefore, the individual has a responsibility not to break the chain but to ensure that his abilities, though limited, contribute to the general good of society.

Moreover, the individual has personal responsibility for fulfilling his dreams. Adapting the definition of Gyekye, responsibility is the caring attitude an individual must have concerning her well-being.[102] Individual responsibility towards society must not forbid individuals from seeking personal advancement in life. Conversely, appreciating the worth of the community does not imply that, in the Akan social order, the group performs the obligations of the individuals. Akans recognize that the

---

95. Opoku, *Akan Proverbs*, 19; Appiah et al., *Proverbs*, 275; Danquah, *Akan Doctrine of God*, 193.
96. Opoku, *Akan Proverbs*, 19; Appiah et al., *Proverbs*, 275.
97. Appiah et al., *Proverbs*, 275; Opoku, *Akan Proverbs*, 19.
98. Appiah et al., *Proverbs*, 275.
99. See Opoku, *Akan Proverbs*, 19.
100. Opoku, *Akan Proverbs*, 19.
101. Opoku, *Akan Proverbs*, 11; Gyekye, *African Philosophical Thought*, 156–62.
102. See Gyekye, *African Cultural Values*, 63.

individual, having a personal will and identity, must make them count.[103] The outcome of his life will depend on what he makes of it. Thus, the Akans say, life is as you make it.[104] It has the same import as the Swahili adage: A person becomes what he wants to become.[105]

The purpose of the adage is to conscientize the individual not to abuse the community's appreciation for interdependence by being overly dependent on others to the point of forgetting her responsibilities. Akans do not encourage excessive dependence. "The person who helps you carry your load," they say, "does not develop a hump." The implication is that the helper does not solely bear your burden.[106] Understanding this reality of life discourages the proclivity to blame others instead of ourselves for the results of our lives. When a person has a deep sense of personal responsibility that enjoins him from excessive dependence, it will be difficult for him to blame others for his failures. Consequently, this leads to another prospect of personal responsibility: the awareness that the individual has ultimate responsibility for the success or failure of his life. The proverb "It is by individual efforts that we can struggle for our heads," reminds the Akan of this personal responsibility.[107]

Finally, though the espousal of the significance of taking personal responsibility is beneficial for community life, a critical analysis of some proverbs culminates in a tension between communalistic and individualistic values in the Akan social order. This tension denotes that the traditional definition of the Akan social order rests on questionable assumptions. Thus, the subsequent section interrogates the interplay between individualistic and communalistic values in the Akan milieu.

Tension Between Communality and Individuality in Akan Proverbs

A careful study of some Akan proverbs reveals their "philosophical" constructs of community. These aphorisms unveil the communal life of the Akans and the place of the individual in this setting. However, when

---

103. Gyekye, *African Cultural Values*, 47.

104. Gyekye, *African Cultural Values*, 48; Appiah et al., *Proverbs*, 63. Though Appiah et al. decrypt the Akan proverb as a character is what you alone have formed, he places in parenthesis the word life as the literal translation of the word translated character. See Appiah et al., *Proverbs*, 63.

105. Gyekye, *African Cultural Values*, 65.

106. Gyekye, *African Cultural Values*, 49.

107. Gyekye, *African Cultural Values*, 48.

proverbs on communality and individuality are juxtaposed, it blurs the line between communalism and individualism, making it difficult to accept the traditional designation of the Akan social order as completely communalistic. To authenticate the candor of the communalistic label, what follows explores the implications of some Akan proverbs on their community concept.

Communalistic Features of Akan Social Order

Scholars generally describe the Akan social order as communalistic.[108] Two reasons inform this designation. First, the communalistic view of the Akan social order is an offshoot of the traditional understanding of the African concept of community. African scholars like Mbiti, Gyekye, Menkiti, Ikuenobe, and many others argue that indigenous Africans practice communitarian egalitarianism.[109] On the communalistic nature of the African community, Mbiti writes: "The philosophical awareness of the individual is I am because we are, and since we are, therefore, I am."[110] The existence of the individual is the existence of the group.

Secondly, the traditional Akan community manifests features of communitarianism. In the understanding of the Akan, to be human is to relate with others—the community.[111] The individual cannot exist alone, except corporately.[112] Communalism is the indigenous Akan's (African) authentication and validation of reality.[113] Consequently, some cultural practices and values of the Akans indicate that they value collectivism. These practices include marriage ceremonies, child-outdooring, and child-rearing.[114]

Among the Akans, marriage is not a union between the husband and wife but a group union; it is between two families.[115] Consequently, the

108. Gyekye, *African Philosophical Thought*, 154; Appiah et al., *Proverbs*, 201.

109. Mbiti, *African Religions*, 141; Gyekye, *African Philosophical Thought*, 154; Menkiti, "Person and Community," 171–81; Ikuenobe, *Philosophical Perspectives on Communalism*, 53; Dickson, *Religion and Life*, 4.

110. Mbiti, *African Religions*, 141.

111. Opoku, *Akan Proverbs*, xviii; cf. Mbiti *African Religions*, 101.

112. Gyekye, *African Philosophical Thought*, 155; Mbiti, *African Religions*, 106.

113. Dogbe, "Concept of Community," 790.

114. Dogbe, "Concept of Community," 792–95; Gyekye, *African Cultural Values*, 76–81.

115. Nkansah-Kyeremateng, *Akans of Ghana*, 67; Gyekye, *African Cultural Values*,

families of prospective couples play various roles. These responsibilities commence before the marriage ceremony. When a man of marriageable age identifies a woman he would like to marry, he informs his parents to investigate her background.[116] However, this is not the privilege of one family. Custom requires that contracting families make inquiries about each family to ascertain if there are no traces of despicable and nefarious factors—congenital diseases, suicide, or traits of anomalous behaviors—to prevent the recurrence of these traits if they accept to marry their relative.[117] The proverb "investigate before marrying" emanates from the awareness of these communal responsibilities.[118] But since the woman needs to be sure about the proposal before investigating his background, it is most likely that her family will be the last to do their background check before accepting their request. After this, courtship begins. Subsequently, there is a formal introduction through the father of the to-be husband, where parents jointly seek their daughter's consent.[119] Then the family invites the parents to perform the necessary rites to schedule a day for the formal presentation of their daughter to the groom on the wedding day.

In Akan tradition, weddings are not private events; they bring together families and friends from far and near to commemorate the ceremony. It transpires whether they hold the wedding in a rural or urban community. The presence of the immediate family, especially parents, is pertinent for two reasons. First, the community considers it a sign of approval. Second, the parents (or immediate family) are not mere witnesses; they are participants. For instance, traditionally, the bride's father (and, in his absence, his representative) gives the hand of his daughter willingly in marriage. Consequently, you cannot conduct the ceremony with only individuals. Even if it is done "privately" (in the presence of a few family members and friends), these people and other members of both families must be around to witness and welcome the person into the family.

Given that both families performed these responsibilities in the awareness that marriage is between two families, they expect the couple to perform some duties towards their families and the new family they

---

79; Asante, *Toward an African Christian Theology*, 138; cf. Nukunya, *Tradition and Change*, 52.

116. Nkansah-Kyeremateng, *Akans of Ghana*, 67–68.

117. Opoku, *Akan Proverbs*, 26; Nkansah-Kyeremateng, *Akans of Ghana*, 67–68.

118. Opoku, *Akan Proverbs*, 26.

119. Nkansah-Kyeremateng, *Akans of Ghana*, 68.

married into or from. Custom requires that they show concern for the welfare of these families to the best of their abilities or risk being branded selfish by the families.[120] Showing concern for the families entails participating in their moments of sorrow and joy. Thus, members expect their presence and gifts during events like marriages and child-outdoor ceremonies. The bereaved expect that they will be around to mourn with them. The Akan maxim, "the family loves a corpse," sums up these responsibilities.[121] It enjoins family members to participate in all activities that funeral rites and burials entail, including contributing money to offset debts after burials when necessary. These factors give credence to the saying that marriage is a group union and showcase marriage as one of the communalistic features of the Akan community.

Akans perceive marriage as a sacred institution that legitimizes the establishment and continuity of families through procreation.[122] Thus, in the Akan conceptual scheme, one of the functions of marriage is procreation.[123] Like the celebration of marriage, the birth of a child and its concomitant cultural practices portray it as one of the communal features of the Akan social order. In a traditional Akan setup, procreation is critical because it is the basis of life and ensures the continuity of the family.[124] So, children belong to the community, not just their parents. It explains the proverbial saying that children resemble their father but belong to a family.[125] However, to consider children as part of the family, physical birth is not enough unless accompanied by rites that incorporate them into the larger community.[126] Therefore, parents wait until eight days after birth before outdooring the child.[127] This cultural practice emanates from the belief that the newly born are ghosts whose ghost-mothers are searching for them and could culminate in their death.[128] Thus, they interpret their

---

120. Gyekye, *African Cultural Values*, 79.

121. Opoku, *Akan Proverbs*, 29.

122. Nkansah-Kyeremateng, *Akans of Ghana*, 68–69; Gyekye, *African Cultural Values*, 76–77.

123. See Nukunya, *Tradition and Change*, 63; Gyekye, *African Cultural Values*, 76.

124. Nkansah-Kyeremateng, *Akan*, 107; Nkansah-Kyeremateng, *Akans of Ghana*, 67.

125. Opoku, *Akan Proverbs*, 42.

126. See Mbiti, *African Religions*, 106.

127. Nkansah-Kyeremateng, *Akan*, 107; Tanye, *Church as a Family*, 270.

128. Nkansah-Kyeremateng, *Akans of Ghana*, 70.

survival as an abandonment of the search or an indication that the child has come to stay and, consequently, name the child on the eighth day.[129]

Given that children belong to the family, the parents alone do not decide on the name the child will bear or perform the rites. Before the outdooring, the father consults his father for the child's name.[130] On the day of the occasion, the family outdoors the child. The term derives its meaning from the purpose of the customary act: a day to introduce the child to the world.[131] It is also the day the parents incorporate the child into the family through rites performed during the naming ceremony.[132] Therefore, they are significant family rites that bring together family and community members and conclude with communal feasting and drinking.[133] In the awareness that the child belongs to the family and community, traditional Akans and Africans generally see the new-born child incorporated into the family as "our child," not "my child."[134]

Since the child belongs to the community, the responsibilities of society towards the child commence after his incorporation. Like any traditional African community, the community raises a child, not just his parents.[135] Hence the proverb, "It takes a village to raise a child."[136]

These cultural practices and many others affirm the communalistic features of the Akan community concept. It is pertinent to note that these cultural practices have a foundation. Communalism thrives in an enabling environment—a community where members appreciate and demonstrate collectivistic values. The root of the communalistic tendencies in the Akan social order is their communalistic values. They underpin and guide their social relationships. Gyekye writes:

> Communal values are those values that express appreciation of
> the worth and importance of the community, those values that

---

129. Nkansah-Kyeremateng, *Akans of Ghana*, 70.

130. Customarily, if the child is a male, he is named after his grandfather. Conversely, the child is named after the grandmother if she is a girl. However, the grandfather can still direct that the first baby bears his name. See Nkansah-Kyeremateng, *Akans of Ghana*, 70.

131. Dogbe, "Concept of Community," 792.

132. Tanye, *Church as a Family*, 270; Salm and Falola, *Culture and Customs*, 128.

133. Tanye, *Church as a Family*, 270–71; Nkansah-Kyeremateng, *Akans of Ghana*, 71.

134. See Mbiti, *African Religions*, 107.

135. See Dogbe, "Concept of Community," 793–94; Mbiti, *African Religions*, 107.

136. Mbiti, *Introduction*, 23.

underpin and guide the type of social relations, and behaviour that ought to exist between individuals who live together in a community, sharing a social life and having a sense of common good.[137]

Examples of communal values include unity, love, care, service, reciprocal obligation, and communality.[138] Akan epistemology is replete with aphorisms espousing appreciation for these values. We will give attention to a few examples and make a passing reference because the next chapter comprehensively examines these communalistic values.

Most Akan proverbs accentuate more than one cultural value. Proverbial expressions such as "the left arm washes the right arm, and the right arm washes the left arm," "the tortoise says, the hand goes, and a hand comes," and "the reason two deer walk together is that one must take the moth from the other's eyes," stress the need and significance of reciprocity.[139] They also denote mutual help, service, and cooperation.[140] Akans also express the importance of unity in proverbs. One of the proverbs employed predominantly for this purpose draws lessons from the functions of a broom to emphasize the strength of staying united. It states that when you remove one broomstick, it breaks. But when you put all the broomsticks together, they do not split.[141] Finally, love is one of the communalistic values in Akan epistemology that the community encourages and promulgates proverbially. If someone loves you, love him in return is one of them.[142]

However, it is pertinent to note that interpretations differ when scholars describe the Akan social order as one that emphasizes communitarianism. Some hold an overly simplistic view that suggests that the Akan community is purely communalistic. And in so doing, no attention is given to individuality. Opokua, for instance, notes: "Akan community living is communal, not individualistic."[143] In Gyekye's view, this position

---

137. Gyekye, *African Cultural Values*, 35. See also Opokuwaa, *Akan Protocol*, 26; Sogolo, *Foundations of African Philosophy*, 119.

138. Gyekye, *African Cultural Values*, 35.

139. Opoku, *Akan Proverbs*, 17; Gyekye, *African Cultural Values*, 188–89; cf. Ackah, *Akan Ethics*, 52–53.

140. Ackah, *Akan Ethics*, 52–53.

141. Boakye, "Akan Oral Tradition," 36.

142. Opoku, *Akan Proverbs*, 77–78.

143. Opokuwaa, *Akan Protocol*, 26.

prejudges the place given to individuality because it reduces a person to rational inactivity.[144]

In cognizance of this problem, some scholars opine that, in practice, it is inaccurate to describe the Akan community as purely communalistic. It would be more accurate to define it as amphibious because it expresses both communalistic and individualistic features.[145] Unless the individual is willing to cooperate or collaborate with others, there will be no communalistic community.[146] Thus, it is legitimate to recognize individuality as a significant feature in any discourse on Akan communalism.

The Individualistic Features: Character and Implications

As Gyekye rightly affirms, the "African communal system does not exclude individualistic values";[147] it recognizes that social beings also have individuality and personal will that must be permitted to express themselves.[148] Thus, in the Akan context, both concepts coexist because there is a meaningful cooperative relationship between them.[149] Indeed, the presence of cooperation, reciprocity, and other values that characterize communalism requires distinct individuals who are willing to express these tenets.

In consequence, just like communitarian egalitarianism, Akans have multitudinous proverbial expressions to that effect. The following are some examples of proverbs that intimate the place of individuality in the Akan community: "The clan is like a cluster of trees which, when seen from afar, appear huddled together, but which would be seen to stand *individually* when closely approached."[150] The proverb establishes

144. Gyekye, *African Philosophical Thought*, 56.

145. Wiredu, "*Moral Foundations*," 202–3; Gyekye, *African Philosophical Thought*, 154.

146. Opoku, *Akan Proverbs*, 11; Gyekye, *African Philosophical Thought*, 156–62. To demonstrate how individual roles enhance communalism, Danquah uses the traditional dance as a metaphor to describe this harmony. In such a dance, he notes, "there is a recurrence of accent—rhythimic, elegant, concordant, harmonious, orchestral, unified, in which each individual contributes in order for a communal experience to take place." See Danquah, *Akan Doctrine of God*, 136.

147. Gyekye, *African Philosophical Thought*, 154.

148. Gyekye, *African Cultural Values*, 47.

149. Neequaye, "Personhood," 100; Gyekye, *African Cultural Values*, 47–50.

150. Appiah et al., *Proverbs*, 67; Gyekye, *African Cultural Values*, 47. This maxim is translated differently by various authors. Blay, for instance, translates as: "The clan is

that the presence of the cluster (the Akan family, with its concomitant sense of communalism) does not imply the submergence or obliteration of *the individual* tree (the individual). Individuals express distinct personalities. The following aphorisms explain the import of the above: "All men's thoughts are not alike," "All people have heads, but their heads are not alike,"[151] or "All heads are alike, but the thoughts in them are not the same."[152]

It is pertinent to note that allowing space for individuality has both merits and demerits. And depending on where the pendulum swings, it could either enhance communalism or breed individualism. When proverbs on communalistic and individualistic values are juxtaposed, one discovers a precarious relationship that exposes the deep-rooted individualistic proclivities in the Akan social order. The following adages exemplify the problem: "A tree is not a forest" or one big tree does not constitute a forest[153] and "The clan is like a cluster of trees which, when seen from afar, appear huddled together, but which would appear to stand *individually* when closely approached."[154] The first one teaches that the human being is not self-sufficient and, therefore, needs a community to become a forest (reach their goals or be complete). The second proverb indicates that even if this "tree" finds itself in a cluster of trees constituting a forest, it only appears huddled together when seen from afar but stands *individually*. Hence, "The clan is (mere) a multitude," meaning that "there are no specific and reliable persons to turn to for the fulfillment of one's needs."[155] Thus, everyone must be responsible for what they want to become ("Life is as you make it").[156]

The portrayal of the family in these proverbs is noteworthy because of what it reveals about the Akan community concept. Accentuating the significance of the family unit is one of the distinct characteristics of African societies.[157] The emphasis emanates from the roles that traditional

---

like a forest. When you are outside, it is dense; when you are inside, you see that each tree has its place." However, they express the same thought. See Blay, "Akan," 24.

151. Appiah et al., *Proverbs*, 204.
152. Opoku, *Akan Proverbs*, 19.
153. Opoku, *Akan Proverbs*, 82; Apt, "Coping," 225.
154. See Appiah et al., *Proverbs*, 67; Gyekye, *African Philosophical Thought*, 158; Blay, "Akan," 24.
155. Gyekye, *African Cultural Values*, 47–48.
156. Gyekye, *African Cultural Values*, 48.
157. Gyekye, *African Cultural Values*, 75.

African communities, including the Akans, assign to the family. Opoku asserts that the Akans consider families a group of "people who are not isolated beings, but rather people who are welded together in a web of interrelationships and interpersonal bonds, resulting in the pursuit of shared values, interests, and goals."[158] Gyekye reveals that the Akans perceive the family as blood relatives whose genealogy is traceable to a common progenitor and held together by obligations to each member.[159] Opoku adds that the family structure is supported by reciprocal obligations that exist among its members, forming the fundamental basis for familial existence.[160] This mutual obligation requires that communalistic values—interdependence, solidarity, care, reciprocity, and mutual helpfulness—find their most heightened and extemporaneous expression in this institution.[161] Arguing along those lines, Nukunya identifies three functions of the traditional family: procreation, socialization, and economic cooperation. He asserts that there is economic cooperation in the family, allowing members to contribute to making a living.[162] Therefore, to suggest that "there are no specific and reliable persons to turn to for the fulfillment of one's needs (the clan is a multitude)" is paradoxical and antithetical to Akan ideations of a family. It exposes a colossal cultural failure. Even though Gyekye suggests that the adage points to the value of self-reliance, this explanation alone is not satisfactory.[163] Indeed, he admits that the maxim denotes that Akans exaggerate the relevance of the clan.[164] Hence, though the multitude is not amorphous or fictitious, there are no specific and reliable people to turn to to address your needs because it appears huddled together, but members stand *individually*.

Akan proverbial expressions reveal what could account for this: the concept of personal responsibility. Most of the adages enumerated as expressing a sense of responsibility seem to point to a sense of individualism. For instance, consider the proverbs, "Each of us protects his head" and "It is by individual effort that we can struggle."[165] The meaning

---

158. Opoku, *Akan Proverbs*, 29.
159. Gyekye, *African Cultural Values*, 75.
160. Opoku, *Akan Proverbs*, 28.
161. Gyekye, *African Cultural Values*, 75.
162. Nukunya, *Tradition and Change*, 63.
163. Gyekye, *African Cultural Values*, 49.
164. Gyekye, *African Cultural Values*, 161.
165. Gyekye, *African Cultural Values*, 48; Appiah et al., *Proverbs*, 275.

of the first one is that each person cares for himself or herself first.[166] The implication is that the individual's interests take precedence over group interests. The second maxim reveals how prioritizing individual interests affects the group. Gyekye explains that the word "head" denotes fortunes, interests, and goals.[167] According to him, the adage underscores the role of individual effort in reaching our goals or fulfilling our needs. He indicates further that the phrase (we can struggle) refers to competition (or the effort required to fulfill individual goals) and that African social thought recognizes it.

Even though encouraging the need for individual efforts is noteworthy, recognizing competition in African (or Akan) social thought is problematic; it is at variance with the tenets of collectivism. A community that allows competition or contests to fulfill individual goals produces competitors instead of partners. Cooperation flourishes more in an environment where community members partner with one another. But competition disrupts social harmony.[168] As a result, there could be attempts to outsmart one another. Hence, "If fish eats fish, then it grows fat," meaning, we climb by pushing down others.[169] Thus, in the end, what should trigger a sense of personal responsibility breeds selfishness and exacerbates the tension between communalism and individualism. When people cannot find reliable persons to benefit from the chain of interrelationships in a community that prides itself on being communalistic and resorts to competing with one another, the balance between communality and individuality tilts more in favor of individualism.[170]

Finally, many things militate against the tenets of collectivism. These factors reveal the substratum of individualistic proclivities in the Akan social order. One of these is the Akan's thoughts on the value and acquisition of wealth. As already highlighted, some proverbs indicate that the Akan emphasizes the worth of human beings above all material things. For instance, "I call upon gold, it answers not; I call upon cloth, it answers not";[171] "A human being is more beautiful than gold or

---

166. Appiah et al., *Proverbs*, 275.
167. Gyekye, *African Cultural Values*, 48.
168. Malina, "Collectivism," 22.
169. Appiah et al., *Proverbs*, 104.
170. Opoku, *Akan Proverbs*, 11.
171. Opoku, *Akan Proverbs*, 10; Gyekye, *African Cultural Values*, 190; Danquah, *Akan Doctrine of God*, 193.

money;[172] and "Man [a person] is more important than money."[173] Yet, in some instances, they suggest otherwise. Whereas some make wealth the most pertinent thing in life, others seem to put human value and wealth on a pedestal—a disposition that blurs the line concerning what the community considers valuable. For instance, the paradox of affirming the worth of human beings above material possessions and yet classifying money as the ultimate possession in life creates ambiguity.[174] Some maxims also indicate that money can make up for the absence of family and friends if you are rich. For example, "The brother of a single person is money."[175] The proverb equates money with family—human beings—and the only milieu where communalistic values find their highest expression. The characterization of money and the comparison between money and family in these aphorisms stem from the materialistic or acquisitive elements in the Akan character, something many scholars overlook.[176] The characteristics of materialism, coupled with the concept of personal responsibility, blur the line between appreciation of the worth of collectivism and individualism.

Other possible factors contributing to individualistic propensities are urbanization and economic challenges.[177] These two are inseparable; urbanization can occasion cultural changes, causing the subservience of traditional communal values to individualistic tendencies because of the pristine socio-economic conditions in the cities.[178] Commenting on the impact of urbanisation on communalism, Abraham correctly notes:

> Again, all African countries have experienced urbanization and technological expansion. These are processes which have brought with them influxes of populations from the country into the cities. These movements have disrupted the protective connections and the certitudes which generate the bonds and fellowship of rural life. The material facet of rural life, including property systems, and relations to land and labour; the institutional facet of rural life, including customs, ritual, political and

---

172. Opoku, *Akan Proverbs*, 12; Gyekye, *African Cultural Values*, 25.
173. Appiah et al., *Proverbs*, 201.
174. See Gyekye, *African Cultural Values*, 98–99.
175. Appiah et al., *Proverbs*, 19.
176. See Gyekye, *African Cultural Values*, 99.
177. Abraham, "Crisis," 14; Gyekye, *African Cultural Values*, 51; Howard-Hassmann, *Human Right*, 28.
178. Gyekye, *African Cultural Values*, 51; Abraham, "Crisis," 14.

social relations; the value facet of rural life, including ethics, religion, art, and the aspirations and wisdom which they enshrine: everything falls, in different degrees, into abeyance in the face of such mass population movements.[179]

He argues further:

> Urban Africans and Africans, trained for urban living, think, learn, work, conceive their hopes and aspirations within a new belief system which comes with its own axioms and postulates, its own norms, and its own ethic. In consequence, problems of the individual psyche, problems of the relations between individuals, problems relating to the responsibilities of individuals to the group, and the individual's attitude to nature, indeed the very idioms of interpersonal discourse, are deprived of the context of traditional cultures, and arise like outcroppings of rock in a bed of sand.[180]

Given the materialistic character of the Akan social order, evident in their concept of wealth and wealth acquisition, urbanization with its concomitant economic situation, is more likely to provoke individualism. Because of these circumstances, maintaining a balance between being communalistic and individualistic is not easy.[181] Thus, the community tilts more in favor of individualism. These elements expose the tension between communalism and individualism and the conditions militating against the foundation of communitarianism in the Akan social order.

Other Issues

Many other issues reveal why the Akan Christian needs something beyond his culture to revitalize the sense of communitarianism plagued by materialistic elements and individualistic proclivities due to factors such as urbanization and economic conditions. As previously described, the Akan community concept hinges on the value and worth of humans as theomorphic beings because it defines the brotherhood of humanity, the naturality of community, and how a human being must be treated.[182] Thus, the Akan conceptual scheme stresses the intrinsic worth of a human

---

179. Abraham, "Crisis," 14.
180. Abraham, "Crisis," 16.
181. Gyekye, *African Cultural Values*, 51; cf. Abraham, "Crisis," 16.
182. See Gyekye, *African Philosophical Thought*, 19–20; Opoku, *Akan Proverbs*, 11; Appiah et al., *Proverbs*, 201.

being and the universalization of the family of God. The proverb "humanity has no boundary" espouses this idea.[183] Yet, in practice, some Akan Christians set boundaries in some spheres of their lives. One well-known example is marriage. They prohibit their children from intermarriages in the Ghanaian context on tribal grounds. The irony is that some of them allow their children to marry citizens of foreign nations—Europeans and Americans especially—for economic reasons and the joy of having mixed-race descendants. It affirms what we have discussed previously: the acquisitive elements in the Akan character. We can also attribute it to individualistic tendencies because individual interests cause these things.

Moreover, Gyekye notes another paradox in the Akan character: the coexistence of the appreciation of human worth and the twin evils of domestic slavery and human sacrifice prevalent in some communities decades ago.[184] These evils are at variance with the Akan's appreciation of the intrinsic worth of a human being. Given that the appreciation of the value of a human being is the substratum of Akan communalism, domestic slavery and human sacrifices raise issues about whether collectivism exists purely in theory, praxis, or both.

Against this background, Akan believers need something outside their traditional epistemology about the community concept that will help to revaluate and revitalize their cultural values challenged by individualism, materialism, and urbanization. Given that Akan Christians believe in the transformative power of the word of God and that communalism is also a theological and missiological value, they can rely on the Johannine community concept because it allows them to critique, challenge, and transform the situation. Consequently, the subsequent chapter engages some of the cultural values in the text and Akan reality through an intercultural reading.

---

183. Gyekye, *African Cultural Values*, 22.
184. Gyekye, *African Cultural Values*, 29.

5

Intercultural Reading

Introduction

THE PRESENT CHAPTER FOCUSES on the ultimate phase of the methodology, namely, an intercultural reading. Numerous exegetes who analyze the Bible in the African context use the term "intercultural exegesis" to facilitate the process of enculturating the Bible. Ukpong posits that intercultural reading involves an interactive engagement between the biblical text and a contemporary sociocultural issue.[1] In this context, the gospel message serves as a critique of the culture, while the cultural perspective enriches the understanding of the text. The term is utilized by Gatti within the framework of dialogic hermeneutics, wherein the text and culture are regarded as interlocutors engaged in a dialogue that elicits a call to action directed towards the believing community.[2] The use of the term in the communicative approach by Ossom-Batsa is comparable.[3] Thus, with regard to the implementation of intercultural exegesis across various tiers, this investigation adheres to the description provided by Loba-Mkole.[4] The author employs the term "intercultural reading" to denote a constructive dialogue between the cultural context of the biblical text and a receptive audience. The present study utilizes intercultural

---

1. Ukpong, "Reading the Bible," 6.
2. Gatti, "Toward a Dialogic Hermeneutics."
3. Ossom-Batsa, "Biblical Exegesis."
4. Loba-Mkole, "Intercultural Biblical Exegesis."

reading as a means of facilitating constructive dialogue between the community concepts of the Johannine and Akan societies.

The study employs this intercultural exegesis because it recognizes that the interpretation of the Bible is incomplete until the text meets the reader. The theoretical foundation of this idea is the philosophical hermeneutics of Gadamer, which proposes a fusion of the horizons of the reader and that of the text.[5] In his view, understanding emanates from a fusion between the reader's preconceptions and the text. Similarly, when Akan Christians read the Johannine community concept, there is a fusion of horizons: Akan preconceptions about communalistic values and the cultural values, or *modus vivendi*, of the community of God in John. Since Akan Christians and John belong to different cultures, the fusion or dialogue between the two concepts is intercultural, allowing the gospel message to critique the culture or the cultural perspective to enlarge and enrich the understanding of the text.[6]

The Call to Action in the Text

From the narrative analyses in chapters 2 and 3, the understanding that emanates from the study is that John casts the believing community as a panacea to its religious and sociocultural problems. As the divine remedy to these maladies, the narrative characterizes the believing community as culturally collectivistic. There are three reasons why God requires the disciples to be communalistic: the composition, character, and calling of the believing community.

The formation of the believing community entails an engagement between two cultures: divine and human. The eternal community engages people in a collectivistic society through the incarnation. The interaction between the two communities culminates in incarnating, exegeting the ideal community, and inviting the human community to participate in the "social" Trinity.[7] The Logos, who was with God the Father from eternity, becomes flesh to incarnate and explicate the concept of a community of God as the only authoritative expositor (John 1:1–18). The objective (as explained in chapter 1) is to invite the human community to participate and mirror its divine purpose. Thus, those who accept the

---

5. Gadamer, *Truth*, 415.
6. See Ukpong, "Reading the Bible," 6.
7. See Grenz, *Community of God*, 112.

invitation enter the kingdom of God through spiritual birth, becoming children of God.⁸ They become part of an inclusive community constituting Jews and Gentiles, united in Christ, the Vine.⁹ Thus, we can describe the group as a universalized and collectivistic community, given that it entails translating people from diverse communities into a unified body with one community identity.¹⁰

Moreover, the community's character is communalistic. As the paradigm, the community of God has its own peculiar culture, prescribing and proscribing certain attitudes to those who enjoy the grace of participating in it. The analyses of selected narratives and the narrative development of the theme indicate that John characterizes the relationship between the Father and the Son as communalistic. To cultivate that culture, the disciples' involvement in the community of God conditions a lifestyle that reflects their identity and opposes values at variance with the character of the community they represent.¹¹ The purpose of such values is to enable the believing community to fulfill its calling.

The disciples have a calling to incarnate the divine community (cf. John 13:34; 15:12, 17). The vine metaphor ties the character of the community to its calling. The metaphor teaches that abiding in the Vine makes individuals members of society—the community of God.¹² In this community, members have a calling to be fruitful. Being fruitful, in this context, includes the fruitfulness of Christian life or mission as *living*.¹³ It is a life that reflects the communal values experienced in the community of God.¹⁴ In the farewell discourse, Jesus highlights unity, love, service, care, reciprocity, and communality as examples of these values.

In the awareness that inculturation allows the gospel message to critique a particular contemporary sociocultural issue and the interpreter's preconceptions enlarge the understanding of the text, the subsequent discussions focus on how Akan Christians can appropriate these cultural

---

8. Vincent, *Word Studies*, 49; Morris, *John*, 87.

9. Köstenberger, *John*, 449; Ridderbos, *John*, 516; Keener, *John*, 993.

10. See Ngewa, *John*, 17.

11. See Ridderbos, *John*, 523; Köstenberger, *John*, 464; Carson, *John*, 525; Brodie, *Gospel According to John*, 485.

12. Köstenberger, *John*, 449; Ridderbos, *John*, 516; Keener, *John*, 993.

13. Ridderbos, *John*, 522.

14. See Brodie, *Gospel According to John*, 483; Keener, *John*, 1004; Ridderbos, *John*, 520; Moloney, *Glory Not Dishonor*, 64.

values to revitalize and redefine their communalistic values through the prism of the concept of community in John in an intercultural reading.

Intercultural Reading

From the exegesis of the Johannine and Akan community concepts, the reader discovers that they share some commonalities: they affirm that the community label is a derivative of the quality relationship a group of people demonstrate in their interactions with group members. They are also collectivistic cultures. Consequently, they reveal that a communalistic culture must manifest features such as unity, love, service, care, reciprocity, and communality. However, the difference is that whereas Akan communalistic values focus on personal gains, the other derives its impetus from the eternal community and its paradigm from what Jesus demonstrated. The acquisitive character of Akan cultural values stems from their purpose: to fill the lacuna created by the insufficiency of the human being. Thus, they derive their impetus from the benefits gained through the reciprocity of collectivism. However, the community of God exists to fulfill a divine mandate. Therefore, even though its cultural or communalistic values bring mutual benefits to the community members, the aim is to reflect God, incarnate its values, testify about the community, and continue the salvific work of Jesus and the Spirit. It, thus, raises the standard and redefines community life. Given that the study focuses on Akan Christians, the intercultural reading, which considers the interplay between both cultures, allows them to critique and transform their values to reflect the community of God.

Generally speaking, values are qualities and directions of life that human beings are required to epitomize in their behavior.[15] Thus, communalistic values are those qualities underpinning and guiding the behavior that ought to exist between individuals who live together in a community.[16] In the Akan culture and believing community of John, unity, love, service, care, reciprocity, and communality are examples of these communal values. Hence, the subsequent section engages these values interculturally.

---

15. Pilch and Malina, "Introduction," xiii; cf. Gyekye, *African Cultural Values*, 35.
16. Gyekye, *African Cultural Values*, 35; cf. Pilch and Malina, "Introduction," xiii.

A United Community

Akan Ideation of Unity

In the Akan conceptual scheme, unity is one of the communalistic values that stress their appreciation for the worth of the community. In the discussions on the place of the person in the Akan community concept, we did indicate that the community does not subsume individuality because Akans hold that though humans are social beings, they exercise personal will and identity.[17] Thus, Akans understand unity as distinct individuals operating in harmony.

Furthermore, the Akan concept of unity receives its impetus from the benefits it produces. Thus, it raises the question of the possibility of upholding these tenets in the absence of personal interests. Proverbial expressions that espouse the Akan ideation of unity legitimize these concerns. The adage that focuses on lessons drawn from the functions of a broom (a symbol of unity) is an example of how personal benefits sustain unity in Akan thought. The proverb states: When you remove one broomstick, it breaks easily. But when combined, they are unbreakable.[18] The proverb contrasts the strength of a collection of broomsticks with that of a single rib. It reveals that in a group, broomsticks are unbreakable, especially with the hand. But they are fragile when isolated. The lesson is that there is strength in numbers; thus, being united benefits the individual members of the community, not just the community.[19] The communicative force of the proverb becomes even more perspicuous when situated in its cultural context. Traditional Akan communities manufacture brooms from the ribs of the leaflets of palm trees. For the broom to sweep rubbish effectively, irrespective of its weight and size, they tie together a sizeable number of ribs to accomplish the task through their collective strength. But when one attempts to perform the same chore with a rib of the leaflet of a palm tree, it will either break or cannot sweep that quantity of refuse from that compound within that time limit. The implication is that working in unison benefits the individual and the group.

Other proverbs that stress the significance of unity affirm that the benefits of a community of action that unity occasions are the motivation for unity and define the Akan view of unity. The reason is that Akans

---

17. Gyekye, *African Cultural Values*, 47.
18. Boakye, "Akan Oral Tradition," 36.
19. Boakye, "Akan Oral Tradition," 36.

appreciate this communal value because of the insufficiency of the human being.[20] The inadequacy of a human being requires that he cooperate with others to achieve his purpose.[21] Thus, adages like one finger cannot lift a thing (like the broom), and if a person scraps the bark of a tree for use as medicine, the pieces fall to the ground, emphasize the notion that unity of action is a prerequisite for mutual benefits and the accomplishment of anything worthwhile and extraordinary.[22]

This characterization of unity can enrich and enlarge the understanding of oneness in John; it enhances appreciation for the role of oneness in the eternal community's incarnation of the ideal community concept and the significance of unity to the believing community's role in that mission. John ties oneness in the divine community to the collaborative works of its members (John 10:38; 14:10; cf. 5:17–20). Additionally, he situates the prayer for unity in the original and future believing communities in a missiological context—their mission to the world (John 17:20–22). The Akan concept deepens the meaning of the Johannine unity concept because it espouses the importance of unison for accomplishing tasks and, therefore, helps to understand it. For instance, the proverbs above, concerning the impact of the collective efforts of fingers and the leaflets of the palm trees united as brooms, give the reader an informed understanding of the narrative context of the oneness prayer; they help to appreciate the Johannine significance of making unity a prerequisite for witnessing, demonstrating how the bond of unity allows Christians to accomplish this worthwhile mission.[23] They also illustrate how Christians can remain unbreakable and fulfill their mission amidst hostilities or persecutions (just like how the united leaflets of a broom overcome obstacles to perform their role as a natural concomitant of unison).

However, the Akan concept of unity poses several challenges for the Akan community concept. It makes personal and reciprocal benefits the motivation for building a united community. Thus, rather than unite for human fellowship, community members might naturally become attached to people based on personal interests when we make accomplishments the purpose of unity. Therefore, many may connect with people whose contributions can help them accomplish their goals, not with

20. See Appiah et al., *Proverbs*, 203; Opoku, *Akan Proverbs*, 12; Gyekye, *African Cultural Values*, 37; Danquah, *Akan Doctrine of God*, 193.

21. See Opoku, *Akan Proverbs*, 11; Gyekye, *African Cultural Values*, 45.

22. Opoku, *Akan Proverbs*, 13, 17, 83; Gyekye, *African Cultural Values*, 37.

23. See Opoku, *Akan Proverbs*, 13, 17, 83; Gyekye, *African Cultural Values*, 37.

individuals incapable of rendering any significant assistance in their area of interest. The implication is that human relationships become a means to an end, not the cultivation of a sense of communalism. The ripple effect is that it might be uncommon to expect unity if it does not culminate in fulfilling personal interests.

Most importantly, placing benefits above enjoying communalism for the sake of humanity defeats the purpose of belonging to the Akan community because it contravenes Akan tenets of communalism. For instance, maxims that explain the Akan belief that the human being is worth more than material gains emphasize that depicting human beings as beautiful implies that community members should enjoy human beings just for being humans and nothing else.[24] However, from the above, the contrary is the case: what counts in praxis is not always the human being but what that individual contributes to advance the life of the one he partners with or a community member.

Against this background, the Akan Christian seeking an informed understanding of a united community can read John for the character of unity worthy of believers because it contains Jesus' redefinition and illustration of what this entails and provides a paradigm for contextualization. Finally, its applicability to the Akan believing community emanates from the fact that Jesus makes the implications of the paradigm he delivers to the messianic community a prerequisite for future believers (cf. John 17:20–22).

The Revelation and Transformation that John Provides

The Johannine concept of unity offers insights that can transform the Akan Christian community into a society that reflects God's purpose for creation. Thus, it is expedient for the Akan reader to note the theological foundation established by Jesus as the substratum of unity to appreciate the theological import of the concept in John. Explaining the theological foundation for unity among members of the community of God, Jesus employs the term "one," given its theological potency, to promulgate the unity between him and the Father and its implications for the community (cf. John 10:30; 17:11, 21–22). Since unity is a theological value that

---

24. It is a human being that counts; a human being is more important than money, and a human being is more beautiful than gold or money. See Opoku, *Akan Proverbs*, 10–12; Gyekye, *African Cultural Values*, 25, 190; Appiah et al., *Proverbs*, 201; Danquah, *Akan Doctrine of God*, 193.

the believing community must imbibe from the eternal community, we can only appreciate its theological import when we situate it within its narrative context, considering the oneness statements.[25]

In John, the oneness statements emerge from interactions between Jesus and the Jewish leaders and his farewell prayer for the disciples (cf. John 10:30; 17:11, 21–23). Explicating his relationship with the Father to the Jews, Jesus posits that he is one with the Father (John 10:30; cf. 17:11, 21–23). Having been accused of blasphemy because of this assertion, he restates his claim, indicating to the Jewish interlocutors that he is in the Father and vice versa (John 10:38). Analyzing these statements allows the reader to appreciate the Johannine elucidations on unity in the Godhead and its reverberations on the culture of the believing community. Thus, the subsequent discussion situates the statements within John's narrative context for their theological import.

In the prologue, John establishes how the concept of ontological equivalence and some communal attributes function inextricably to portray the relationship between the Logos and God as a community (cf. John 1:1–2). Employing the phrase ἐν ἀρχῇ (*en archē*), he promulgates that the Logos and God (the Father) enjoy eternity and coeternity and are, therefore, ontologically equal (cf. John 1:1). The Greek preposition πρὸς (*pros*), which describes the character of the relationship, also distinguishes between the Logos (the Son) and the Father, indicating that the Father is not the Son and vice versa.[26] However, John ties the personal distinctions in the Godhead, coupled with coeternity and ontological equivalence, to an intimate relationship to justify its communalistic character (cf. John 1:1–2).[27]

Consequently, the interpretation of the oneness statement can only be complementary (not contradictory) to the idea of eternal distinctions already underscored, given the impact of the prologue on the themes in John.[28] Thus, their oneness and the perichoretic relationship they enjoy do not denote the sameness of persons. The Jewish ecclesiastical authorities did not interpret the communicative force of the statement as the

25. Gharbin and Van Eck, "United Community," 3.

26. Harris, *John*, 18–19; Ridderbos, *John*, 24; Vincent, *Word Studies*, 34–35; Mounce, *Biblical Greek Grammar*, 27; Borchert, *John 12—21*, 106; Kanagaraj, *John*, 1–2; Voorwinde, "John's Prologue," 32.

27. Vincent, *Word Studies*, 34; Harris, *John*, 18; Kanagaraj, *John*, 1; Keener, *John*, 369; Morris, *John*, 70; Tenney, *John*, 64.

28. See Carson, *John*, 394.

sameness of persons; they understood his oneness with the Father as ontological equality with God (John 10:33).[29] It is in line with the concept of mutual penetration (being in one another) that the perichoretic union denotes unity of being,[30] a relationship that allows the individuality of the eternal distinctions to be maintained while sharing in the life of each other.[31] As a term, "one" denotes two things: singularity (or individuality) and unity.[32] However, in the community of God, both meanings converge; unity requires the unification of two or more distinct individuals.

The implication is that unity is one of the intrinsic values of the community, born out of ontological unity, not a tool to fill the lacuna created by inadequacies. The Father and the Son demonstrate unity because they are united in being; it is one of the two compatible sides of the eternal God.[33] Their union establishes ontological equality as the reason for participating in the lives of each other and unity as a natural concomitant of being one in essence. It further suggests that unity should be the *modus vivendi* of beings who enjoy ontological equivalence, not a means to an end. They were ontological coequals eternally before collaborating to create the world (cf. John 1:1–3). Thus, their functional unity is only an outflow of what existed ontologically or a manifestation of what is compatible with the divine nature. The oneness of will and task, a unity of purpose producing a community of actions, proceeds from this.[34] Jesus attributes the functional unity he enjoys with the Father—his works and words—to his ontological unity and mutual interpenetration with the Father, considering them as products of divine partnership (John 10:38; John 14:10; cf. 5:17–20).

Similarly, the imitators of the community of God must bear these marks in their expression of unity as a theological and communal value.[35] Thus, Jesus reveals that unity in the believing community is analogous to the community of God (John 17:11, 21–22).[36] In the farewell prayer, Jesus prays to the Father for the disciples that they will be one just as he

29. See Harris, *John*, 202–3.
30. Köstenberger, *John*, 431.
31. See McGrath, *Christian Theology*, 325; Carson, *John*, 494; Bauckham, *Beloved Disciple*, 251.
32. Bauckham, *Gospel of Glory*, 19.
33. Borchert, *John 12—21*, 106; cf. Grenz, *Community of God*, 112.
34. See Carson, *John*, 394–95.
35. See Carson, *John*, 394.
36. See Carson, *John*, 568.

and the Father are (John 17:11, 21–22). The Greek word καθώς (*kathōs*) is both causative and comparative, affirming that divine unity is the cause of Christian unity and that the believing community is analogous to the community of God.[37] What relationship exists between the divine and human communities to warrant the comparison?

Akin to the meaning of oneness in the eternal community, John does not imply the sameness of persons in his application of the term to the relationships that must characterize the believing community. Such a description would be antithetical to the oneness theology in John, given its application to the community of God and the fact that the believer's goal is to participate in the mission of Jesus: incarnating the eternal community (cf. John 10:33).[38] The kind of unity required of them is akin to the community whose interests it represents.[39] Bauckham affirms that, in line with the Johannine theology of the community of God, the term concentrates on the unity of persons, not the singularity of persons.[40] In the farewell discourse where Jesus promulgates unity as a theological value, for instance, he often addresses the disciples employing the second person plural, indicating the plurality of persons (for example, John 13:12; 15:3–12). Further, he likens the disciples to the community of God (John 17:11, 21–22). Thus, what Jesus requires from the disciples are cultural values redolent of the eternal community—that they imitate the unity existing between the Father and the Son (cf. John 17:11, 21–22).

Therefore, in Johannine theology, oneness is the unification of distinct ontological coequals into one body with a unity of purpose. Their ontological unity stems from how God incorporates believers into the community. John indicates that membership is not by blood nor by the will of the flesh nor by the will of a human being, an indication that natural birth does not give the individual the authority to become a member of this community (cf. John 1:13). It is critical because natural birth defines national identity or nationality. In a status-conscious social system such as the first-century Mediterranean world, status is a concomitant feature of natural procreation.[41] Permitting human reproduction as a means of entry is tantamount to allowing the factors that produce social

---

37. Harris, *John*, 293; cf. Carson, *John*, 568.
38. Harris, *John*, 202–3; Bauckham, *Gospel of Glory*, 26.
39. Carson, *John*, 568.
40. Bauckham, *Gospel of Glory*, 26.
41. See Malina, *New Testament*, 107; Keener, *John*, 468.

classifications to continue. Spiritual procreation proscribes unity based on social standing because it ushers all believers into a new status despite their social status or identity.[42] It redefines community as a group of people joined together primarily on the grounds of ontological equivalence, enjoying an intimate familial relationship with God, and sharing in the community life of God.[43] It is a relationship centered on the "community of nature," allowing believers to participate in the divine nature,[44] that is, the life of the "social Trinity."[45] Consequently, their interpersonal relationships mirror the oneness of the Trinity and not the dictates of their societies, plagued by social classifications.

Just like the community of the Trinity, ontological equality must define functional unity—the oneness of will and task. Rather than considering functional unity merely as an instrument for accomplishing personal goals, community members must see their ontological equivalence as the common denominator and need for cooperation. In God's community, ontological unity translates into the oneness of purpose (John 10:38; 14:10; 5:17–20).[46] John traces Jesus' words and works to his ontological equality with the Father and the relationship of mutual penetration or unity, providing a paradigm for the believing community (John 10:38; 14:10; 5:17–20).[47] Given that the members of the believing community are part of the community of God and exist to incarnate it, their concept of unity is akin to its paradigm: translating ontological equality into the unity of purpose.

What is the significance of the unity of purpose for the historical and Akan disciples? In the narrative context of the prayer, Jesus ties the oneness of the believing community to their participation in the divine activity of *sending* or mission as *going* (John 17:18, 20–26). In John, the sent are witnesses who testify about the community: John the Baptist (John 1:7–8, 15; 3:26; 5:33), Jesus (3:11; 8:18), the disciples (15:27; 17:20), and the Spirit (15:26). As elucidated in the participatory role of the believing community, believers have a responsibility to witness to expand

---

42. Morris, *John*, 87; Watt, *Family of the King*, 182.

43. Watt, *Family of the King*, 182; cf. Keener, *John*, 403.

44. Vincent, *Word Studies*, 49; Morris, *John*, 87.

45. Grenz, *Community of God*, 112; Grenz, *Created for Community*, 49; cf. Kanagaraj, *John*, 2; Bauckham, *Gospel of Glory*, 48.

46. See Carson, *John*, 394–95.

47. See Carson, *John*, 394–95.

the community.⁴⁸ The foundational principle of genuine Christian expansion is witnessing.⁴⁹ Therefore, John calls the disciples and Akan Christians to unity, given that it is a necessary provision for a productive and God-pleasing mission.⁵⁰ Moreover, since the creation of the believing community was by divine unity, its sustenance requires the oneness of the human community called to participate in the mission. Thus, Akan Christians must see unity as a prerequisite for witnessing and employ it in this divine mandate.

Mission as *living* is the other aspect of the binary character of mission in John, where God requires unity from the believing community in their relationship with one another. It is a paradigm set by God. John portrays the Father and the Son as distinct ontological coequals preexisting in unity and demonstrating functional unity as a natural concomitant of ontological unity (cf. John 1:1–5). Similarly, being disciples requires the believing community to imitate God. Whereas witnessing is their responsibility to the world, being united is their duty to each other. Thus, the oneness of the disciples also entails living in unity with each other (cf. John 17:11, 20–22). Jesus makes it a prerequisite for the believing community of all generations by praying this prayer for the successive communities of believers (cf. John 17:20–22). The implication for every believing community is that unity is a mark of obedience to the Lord, fulfillment of their communal obligation, and testimony of reflecting the community of God. When this becomes the motivation, personal benefits and interests do not determine and contaminate the kind of unity undergirding interpersonal relationships.

Loving as a Community of God

Love in Akan Epistemology

Love is one of the communalistic values in the Akan culture that John challenges Akan Christians to revisit. Akans consider love the greatest virtue.⁵¹ This is the import of the Akan proverb, "When charity comes and passes by, nothing comes after."⁵²

---

48. Carson, *John*, 159; cf. Talbert, *Reading John*, 86; Köstenberger, *John*, 453.
49. Carson, *John*, 159; cf. Talbert, *Reading John*, 86.
50. Borchert, *John 1—11*, 197.
51. Gyekye, *African Cultural Values*, 70; Opoku, *Akan Proverbs*, 77.
52. Gyekye, *African Cultural Values*, 70; Opoku, *Akan Proverbs*, 77.

Gleaning the Akan concept of love from their proverbial lore, three distinctions of love are apparent: sexual love, parental love, and brotherly love. However, we can classify all of them as familial love, as they are demonstrated in the context of familial relationships. For instance, sexual love is the love expected to exist between spouses, that is, a husband (a man) and wife (a woman). The term "sexual love," as described by Opoku and Ackah, extends beyond the physical act of sexual intercourse and encompasses the entirety of the commitment and dedication expected from both partners in a relationship.[53] Opoku posits that this is the explanation of the proverb "love is death."[54]

Parental love, on the other hand, is the natural love between parents and children.[55] To expound on the Akan understanding of parental love, the mother metaphor is usually employed in proverbial sayings to depict the extent to which parents go or should go to demonstrate love to their children. Some of them are "It is the mother who knows what her children will eat," "The tortoise does not have breast milk, but it knows how to take care of its child when it gives birth," and "If *Tintimme* (mother locust) says she will eat a stone, she shares it with her little one (*Sekyere Amprofiri*)." The import of these adages is that motherly or parental love is a prerequisite for parental sacrifices.[56]

Moreover, fraternal affection represents the most significant manifestation of kinship love. In contrast to the preceding two, the aforementioned approach expands its purview to encompass all members of the community as well as those beyond it. According to Gyekye, the Akan people perceive brotherhood as a notion that surpasses biological relationships.[57] According to their perspective, the concept of humanity is limitless. The concept of fraternity is conveyed through the proverbial expression "man's (human being) brother is man (another human being)."[58] Consequently, brotherly love refers to the innate fondness towards individuals within human society.[59]

---

53. Opoku, *Akan Proverbs*, 77; Ackah, *Akan Ethics*, 57.
54. Opoku, *Akan Proverbs*, 77.
55. Opoku, *Akan Proverbs*, 77–78.
56. Opoku, *Akan Proverbs*, 78, 109.
57. Gyekye, *African Cultural Values*, 26–28.
58. Gyekye, *African Cultural Values*, 28.
59. Ackah, *Akan Ethics*, 29, 56–57.

From the discussions on the varied forms of love, it has become increasingly clear that, according to the Akan conceptual scheme, there are characteristics of love. Therefore, some Akan proverbial sayings reveal what they identify as a mark of love or differentiate genuine from spurious love. Money-induced love is, for instance, considered spurious. Proverbs such as "true love is not motivated by wealth" and "love that money buys can also be destroyed by money" expose the dangers and inauthenticity of love prompted by wealth.[60]

Conversely, the preponderant character of genuine love espoused in Akan epistemology or proverbs is that it impels sacrificial giving.[61] One of these adages is, for instance, "It is out of love that Esiamma bit a raw fish into two."[62] The proverb portrays someone dividing raw fish with her teeth (instead of a knife), disregarding the risk of getting injured by bones because of her willingness to give. Understanding the etymology of the name further clarifies the import of the proverb. Esiamma means a parsimonious or tight-fisted person called Esi.[63] Thus, the act reveals how love motivates stingy people to give sacrificially, something uncharacteristic of their nature.

An exemplification of sacrifice driven by love within Akan philosophy is the act of visitation. According to Opoku, the Akans express their recognition of the efforts individuals put into visiting their family members, friends, and loved ones through the proverbial statement, "It is the river that loves you that enters your drinking pot."[64] This activity is regarded as sacrificial, particularly when the individual being visited resides at a considerable distance, as the visitor willingly relinquishes their time, energy, and occasionally resources in its pursuit. Hence, both visitors and inhabitants colloquially designate these locations as "*dɔ me a bra*" (a phrase denoting an invitation to come or visit as an expression of affection), acknowledging the aforementioned reasons.

Furthermore, Akan proverbs emphasize reciprocal love. Thus, Akans say, "If someone loves you, love him in return."[65] The maxim implies that, for the Akan, love is reciprocal. Thus, the one who loves

---

60. See Opoku, *Akan Proverbs*, 77.
61. Ackah, *Akan Ethics*, 29, 56–57; cf. Opoku, *Akan Proverbs*, 78.
62. Ackah, *Akan Ethics*, 29, 56–57; cf. Opoku, *Akan Proverbs*, 78.
63. Ackah, *Akan Ethics*, 29, 56–57; Opoku, *Akan Proverbs*, 78.
64. Opoku, *Akan Proverbs*, 77.
65. Opoku, *Akan Proverbs*, 77.

expects reciprocation. And the individual who receives love understands the responsibility that accompanies it.

Despite the inherent difficulties associated with this particular portrayal of love, as we shall presently observe, one notable advantage is its capacity to augment the comprehension of love among adherents of the Akan tradition in the context of the Gospel of John. Akan Christians possess a unique advantage in comprehending key elements of love in the gospel of John, specifically sacrifices motivated by love and the reciprocation of love. This advantage stems from the fact that these attributes align with the concept of the Johannine community, allowing Akan Christians to approach the Gospel with a mindset that already incorporates notions of sacrificial acts and the mutual exchange of love. The reader can utilise the individual's preconceived notions about love as a starting point and a lens through which to examine the Johannine concept of love.

However, the portrayal of love in Akan philosophy is not without its challenges. The aforementioned proverb implies that individuals who are typically reluctant to be generous may be inspired to make selfless contributions through the power of love. Nevertheless, it is difficult to reconcile the concept of parsimoniousness with acts of giving that are driven by love or sacrifice. The rationale behind this assertion is that individuals who exhibit a tight-fisted disposition tend to possess inherent qualities of self-centeredness and a lack of generosity. Hence, the concepts of stinginess and love, or sacrificial giving, are inherently contradictory as they involve the manifestation of behaviors that are incongruous with one's typical disposition. As a result, when an individual who is reluctant to spend money makes a sacrifice, it is possible that they have an underlying motive or an expectation of receiving something in return.

Moreover, the Akan conceptualization of love propagates a form of love that is contingent upon certain conditions. For instance, the adage on reciprocal love (if someone loves you) makes love "conditional" in the Akan setting because it obliges an individual to reciprocate love only upon reception. This is noteworthy because many consider Akans to have a communalistic society and love as their greatest virtue.[66] Therefore, it is legitimate to expect that demonstrating love will not be predicated on conditionalities. Enjoining community members to reciprocate love on the condition that they receive it has further consequences. Members will only show love to those who love them. Additionally, they would not be

---

66. Gyekye, *African Cultural Values*, 70; Opoku, *Akan Proverbs*, 77.

obliged to initiate love. Given that love in this context is predicated upon reception, the absence of initiation creates the possibility of a society where encountering love is not a certainty, as the individual may or may not experience it.

Moreover, between wealth and love, Akan proverbs blur the line concerning what is more important. Proverbial sayings that espouse the value of wealth and love express a similar thought about the two. Akans say, "When charity comes and passes by, nothing comes after."[67] Similarly, one of their proverbs on money suggests that "When wealth comes and passes by, nothing comes after."[68] The ramification is that whereas wealth is the ultimate possession, love is the greatest virtue in Akan thought.[69] The materialistic elements in the Akan culture and the recognition of wealth-impelled love make it legitimate to think of the difficulty of striking a balance when wealth is involved.

In light of the aforementioned difficulties, what strategies can be employed by Akans who have adopted Christianity in order to cultivate a cultural environment that aligns with their collective purpose as a community of God? One of the potential approaches suggested by the New Testament writings involves embracing the concept of community as elucidated and propagated by Jesus in the gospel of John. Consequently, the following section delves into the Johannine concept of love through an analysis of the imperative to love.

The Call to Love

John invites the Akan Christian reader to learn how to demonstrate love as members of the community of God.[70] The Johannine narrative, therefore, offers a paradigm to epitomize. It begins with understanding the love relationship between the Father and the Son. There are multiple justifications for the critical examination of the nature of love within the divine community as the foundational basis for any scholarly investigation into this communal virtue. The community concept and its concomitant values in John are divine. The believing community also exists to imitate the community of God. Moreover, love flows from the divine to the believing

---

67. Gyekye, *African Cultural Values*, 70; Opoku, *Akan Proverbs*, 77.
68. Gyekye, *African Cultural Values*, 98–99.
69. Gyekye, *African Cultural Values*, 70; Opoku, *Akan Proverbs*, 77.
70. Gharbin and Van Eck, "Redefining Love," 5.

community.⁷¹ Hence, it is expedient to trace its thematic development back to the eternal community, the originator of the community concept in the Johannine gospel.

The discussions on the love relationship in the ideal community concentrate on how Jesus and the Father relate, describing their union primarily as a loving relationship (John 3:35; 5:20; 10:17; 14:31; 15:9–10; 17:23, 24, 26).⁷² In this relationship, Ridderbos correctly notes that the Father is the source and energy of love.⁷³ Thus, John defines the Father's love as the substratum of his actions connected to the contextualization of the community, employing two verbs: "to give" and "to show" (cf. John 3:16, 35; 17). The narrative traces the incarnation of the Logos to the Father's act of giving (John 3:16). Love is also the reason for putting all things into the hands of the Son (John 3:35; 13:3). Beyond these, in the farewell prayer, Jesus enumerates many things the Father gave him: authority (John 17:2), believers (17:2, 6, 9, 24), words (17:8), the divine name (17:11–12), and glory (17:22, 24). The application and interconnectedness of love and giving characterize giving as a natural constituent element of love. It marks the loving community as a society where giving is a lifestyle.

Furthermore, John relates love to the verb "show," another love-motivated act of the Father (John 5:20). The verb is critical because of its connection to the functional unity of the Father and Son. Jesus proclaims that his works are products of paternal love—that is, he only accomplishes or replicates what the Father does and shows him out of love (5:19–20). In the narrative context, "works" refers to judgment and life-giving prerogatives (5:20–30).⁷⁴ However, in John, Jesus employs the word "works" to refer to his vocation and everything he does (4:34; 5:36; 17:4).⁷⁵ By extension, what the Father unveils to the Son includes all the above, and as the obedient Son, Jesus does what he sees the Father doing (5:19). The adverb "likewise" indicates the identity of *action* (functional unity), culminating in perfect parallelism between the Father and the Son (5:19).⁷⁶ In essence, it amalgamates the functions in such a manner that

71. See Bauckham, *Gospel of Glory*, 31–32.
72. Malina, "Love," 112.
73. Ridderbos, *John*, 519.
74. Morris, *John*, 278; Moloney, *John*, 178, 182; Köstenberger, *John*, 183; Harris, *John*, 113; Beutler, *Judaism and the Jews*, 154.
75. Painter, "Signs of the Messiah," 242.
76. See Vincent, *Word Studies*, 135; Carson, *John*, 252.

the resultant product is a collaborative effort between the Father and the Son, constituting a singular work.[77] Thus, it would be accurate to surmise that the connection established between love and the verbs demonstrates that in the community of God, love initiates, undergirds, underpins, and contributes to the functional unity of its members, given that the entire process originates from it (cf. John 5:19–20).

Moreover, it is noteworthy that while the Father is the source and impetus of love, the Son reciprocates the Father's love, creating an environment of mutual love. John discusses the reciprocity of love between the Father and Jesus in the prologue and the narrative (cf. John 1:1–2, 18; 14:31). The prologue commences on the note that the Logos enjoys communion and intimacy with God[78] and ends with the indication that the Son is in the bosom of the Father, an expression that depicts mutual love.[79] The narrative reiterates this idea, revealing Jesus' love for the Father and demonstrating his commitment to the love relationship through perfect obedience to his commands out of love (John 14:31; 15:9–10).[80] By doing so, he affirms the concept of reciprocal love that was previously discussed in the prologue.

Moreover, John conceptualizes love as a perpetual communal principle within the divine community. The implicit perpetuity of the reciprocal nature of love can be observed within the grammatical and theological aspects of the Johannine prologue and narrative. The prologue sets the discussions on the community of God in the context of eternity, evoking Genesis 1 and employing the imperfect tense (which shows the continuing existence of a state) to establish that the relationship between the Son and the Father predates the creation (John 1:1–2).[81] The prologue situates the loving relationship that the community members enjoy in this milieu through the preposition "with" and asseverates that the Son is in the bosom of the Father (John 1:1–2, 18). It means that the Son enjoys unparalleled and timeless intimacy with the Father (1:1–2, 18).[82]

---

77. Kysar, *John*, 43; Thompson, *Gospel of John*, 77–78; Barrett, *Gospel According to St. John*, 260; Ngewa, *John*, 88.

78. Vincent, *Word Studies*, 34; Harris, *John*, 18; Kanagaraj, *John*, 1; Morris, *John*, 70; Borchert, *John 12—21*, 103; Tenney, *John*, 64; Wuest, *New Testament*, 209.

79. Carson, *John*, 134.

80. Köstenberger, *John*, 456; cf. Harris, *John*, 269.

81. Köstenberger, *John*, 25, 115; Ngewa, *John*, 11; Vincent, *Word Studies*, 24.

82. Köstenberger, *John*, 49; Voorwinde, "John's Prologue," 32; Vincent, *Word Studies*, 60.

In the farewell prayer, Jesus affirms the eternality of the Father's love by declaring that it precedes the foundation of the world (John 17:24). The clues from the prologue and narrative suggest that John ties the community's existence to eternal and reciprocal love, thereby rendering them coeternal and inextricable.

Before proceeding further, it is pertinent to recap some conclusions drawn from love in the quintessential community. The study has established the nature of love that characterizes the community of God, revealing that it provokes giving and fosters functional unity through the virtue of transparency. It also contends that though the love between the Father and the Son is mutual, the Father's love is the substratum and origin. Finally, it affirms the eternality of love. These points are salient because love flows from the ideal community to the disciples, and the paradigm is Jesus' love, a reflection of the Father.[83] Therefore, it is of utmost importance to acknowledge the manifestation of love within the divine community, as it holds profound implications for Jesus' paradigm of love towards the believing community.

Jesus' love for the believing community replicates what he enjoys with the Father. He patterns his love for the disciples after the eternal love relationship; therefore, it shares similarities with the attributes of the quintessential community (John 15:9–10).[84] Akin to the divine model, the relationship between Jesus and the believing community portrays an inextricable connection between love, giving, and showing (15:13–15). However, it is vital to note that whereas the two expressions are not employed explicitly, the narrative maintains their import: showing and giving because of love.

The farewell discourse in the gospel of John highlights two actions undertaken by Jesus out of love: the sacrifice of his life for the disciples and the bestowal of an elevated status upon them (John 15:13–15; cf. 17:26). The narrative makes love the motivation for surrendering his life for his friends—what he labels greater love (15:13).[85] Laying down one's life for a friend is the ultimate sacrifice friends can make for each other.[86] Therefore, through the act of making this the prevailing model and

---

83. Carson, *John*, 520; Köstenberger, *John*, 456.

84. Carson, *John*, 520; Köstenberger, *John*, 456; Barrett, *Gospel According to St. John*, 475.

85. See Harris, *John*, 269; Barrett, *Gospel According to St. John*, 476; Carson, *John*, 521–22; Beasley-Murray, *John*, 274.

86. Ridderbos, *John*, 520.

exemplifying it through his demise, Jesus establishes the essential nature of love that is expected from his companions.

Moreover, John ties love to the elevated status of the believers. From the gathering and inception of the community of faith, John describes the members as disciples of Jesus. However, in the farewell address, the people who were hitherto classified as disciples become friends of Jesus (15:13–16).[87] The change of identity to friends is a more elevated status.[88] He gives them this new status as an act of love.[89]

In the context of this elevated status or friendship, there is transparency (or *showing*). The reader discovers that the new relationship occasions the transmission of heavenly information to the believing community, just as the narrative makes the intimate relationship in the ideal community a prerequisite for the transparent disposition of the Father towards the Son.[90] Similar to the Father, Jesus does not withhold any information from his companions but rather imparts to them all that he has heard from the Father. This culminates in his interpretation of the Father, as indicated in John 15:15 and 17:26.

Most importantly, the narrative flow of the theme indicates that the goal of Jesus' exegesis and demonstration of love to the believing community is to prepare them to imbibe the culture of his community (cf. John 1:18). It is evident in the love commandment issued to the disciples (cf. John 13:34; 15:9, 12, 17). Jesus commands the community of faith to remain or abide in his love (John 15:9). Within the framework of the gospel of John, the concept being discussed pertains to the affectionate devotion of the Father, wherein love emanates from Him (cf. John 15:9).[91] Moreover, Jesus corroborates this assertion, making the love of his Father the model of what he demonstrates: he loves just as the Father (John 15:9). Thus, the imperative implies continuing the chain of love initiated by the Father and replicated by the Son (cf. John 15:9). Hence, it furnishes us with a hermeneutical framework for comprehending the significance of the love command—that we must interpret it through the

---

87. Köstenberger, *John*, 459; Beasley-Murray, *John*, 274; Barrett, *Gospel According to St. John*, 477; Brodie, *Gospel According to John*, 483.

88. Köstenberger, *John*, 459; Schnackenburg, *Gospel*, 110; cf. Esler and Piper, *Lazarus, Mary, and Martha*, 91.

89. Beasley-Murray, *John*, 274; Barrett, *Gospel According to St. John*, 477; Brodie, *Gospel According to John*, 483; Keener, *John*, 911.

90. Harris, *John*, 270; Carson, *John*, 522–23.

91. Ridderbos, *John*, 519.

prism of the eternal relationship since Jesus makes his imperative to the believers analogous to his obedience to the commandments of the Father (cf. John 15:10). In the familial relationship, Jesus keeps the commands of the Father out of love.[92] Therefore, the implication for the followers is to abide in the love of Jesus through adherence to his instructions as a manifestation of love rather than through coercion, since obedience based on force is not an expression of love.[93] Conversely, love devoid of adherence to commands is uncharacteristic of the community of God because the two are mutually dependent.[94]

Moreover, the directive elucidates the nature of love that is anticipated from the community of believers. To abide in the love of Jesus entails the act of loving one another in the same manner that he has demonstrated his love towards them (John 13:34; 15:9, 12, 17). The Greek word καθώς (*kathōs*) has a comparative and causative force.[95] However, in the context of love, Jesus employs it preponderantly to compare the quintessential and believing communities, making love (and other communal values) in the former the paradigm for the latter (cf. John 13:34; 15:9–12; 17:11). Thus, loving one another as he has loved them denotes demonstrating what is comparable or analogous to the ideal model Jesus promulgates to the believing community. The comparison with its concomitant responsibilities allows believers to see a new portrait of love.

The aforementioned observations indicate the presence of certain attributes within the community of God that Jesus expects Akan Christians to emulate as they strive to incarnate and propagate the cultural principles upheld by the community of God. For example, the directive to exhibit love towards one another suggests that individuals within the community should display reciprocal affection.[96] It evokes the reciprocity of love in the community of God (cf. John 1:1–2, 18; 14:31). In the divine portrait, community members love and receive love in return. Thus, the command to mirror the eternal paradigm mandates all members to love and be loved. It is also pertinent to note that the paradigm of reciprocity in love does not promulgate conditional love. Jesus neither enjoins believers to demonstrate love as a response to the reception of love nor gives

92. Köstenberger, *John*, 456; cf. Harris, *John*, 269; Keener, *John*, 1003.
93. Ridderbos, *John*, 519; Carson, *John*, 520.
94. Barrett, *Gospel According to St. John*, 476.
95. Harris, *John*, 293.
96. See Köstenberger, *John*, 457; Carson, *John*, 521; Ridderbos, *John*, 520; Beasley-Murray, *John*, 274; Barrett, *Gospel According to St. John*, 476.

specific conditions to warrant it. He only commands everyone to love just as he loves (John 13:34; 15:12, 17). Therefore, the community members must exhibit love out of obedience to the divine imperative, whether they enjoy reciprocation of love or not. The implication is that John invites Akan believers to incarnate the love of Christ in their cultural expression or become an extension of his humanity.

In addition, John calls on Akan readers to reconsider the principles that undergird functional unity. The text challenges Akans to make love the undergirding and necessitating factor of functional unity, like the quintessential community, not cooperation instigated by human inadequacy and benefits. Whereas the former encourages fellowship, the latter employs human relationships for self-aggrandizement.

Love is the undergirding and necessitating factor of unity in the quintessential community. It promotes the level of transparency necessary for a community of actions exhibited in incarnating the community of God (John 5:19–20). Since the community anthropomorphized its concept through functional unity, its continuation rests on the collaborative work of the witnesses. Indeed, the advancement of incarnating God's idea of community necessitates the participation of a community of witnesses that obeys the foundational principle of Christian expansion through a repeated process of testifying about Jesus to others (cf. John 15:27).[97] It is a role that gives them the privilege of participating in a mission initiated and sustained through the functional unity of the community of God, and so they need this quality to perpetuate it. Therefore, akin to the quintessential community, imbibing the love culture of the Father and Son stimulates the functional unity necessary for the mission.

Beyond this, the narrative reveals what must characterize the interpersonal relationships of the members of the Akan Christian community: the character of relationships demonstrated by community members should reflect Jesus' example since their mission demands replicating him. In this regard, John states that Jesus loves his own (John 13:1). The phrase evokes what Jesus reveals in the Good Shepherd metaphor about his relationship with his disciples (10:1–21). Here, Jesus identifies them as his own sheep (10:3). Evoking this concept, John employs the expression (his own) as a designation for the disciples of Jesus as the object of his love.[98] Loving his own makes it the shared responsibility of Akan

---

97. Carson, *John*, 159; Talbert, *Reading John*, 86.

98. Kruse, *Gospel According to John*, 279; Harris, *John*, 242; Köstenberger, *John*, 395; Carson, *John*, 460–61.

readers to love their own, something that the love command reiterates (John 10:1–21; cf. 13:34–35; 15:12, 17).

Another issue revealed in this example is the extent of his love and its reverberations in the community of God (cf. John 13:1). The theological import of this love for the believers lies in the interpretation of the Greek phrase εἰς τέλος (*eis telos*). It could be adverbial or temporal.[99] If considered adverbially, the focus is on the intensity or quality of love: uttermost love.[100] When taken temporally, the communicative force is that Jesus loved them to the end of his life.[101] In his relationship with the disciples, he demonstrated both: he loved to the uttermost and to the end of his life.[102] Not only did Jesus love to the end of his life, but love also ended his life. He sacrificed his life for love. Uttermost love is sacrificial love. He epitomized this as the Good Shepherd laying down his life for his sheep or a human being for his friends (cf. John 10:11; 15:13–15).

Hence, the text implores Akan Christians to reassess and redefine their comprehension of sacrificial love. The substitution of conditional love with a deeper manifestation of love, as expounded by Jesus as greater love, is of utmost importance. The concept involves demonstrating unwavering affection towards individuals within the community, exemplifying a love that is all-encompassing and characterized by reciprocal sacrifices.[103] By demonstrating mutual sacrificial love, they incarnate the culture of the ultimate community, with giving as a paradigmatic feature. A community in which members reciprocate sacrificial love will not struggle with demonstrating all other forms of giving that are not at variance with the culture of the community of God, given that this is the ultimate, greater love. Further, their obedience to the command identifies them (not makes them) as his friends (cf. John 15:14)[104] and evokes the image of the self-sacrificial love of Jesus for sinful humanity (cf. John 13:35).[105]

---

99. Kruse, *Gospel According to John*, 279; Harris, *John*, 242; Carson, *John*, 460–61.

100. Harris, *John*, 242; Kruse, *Gospel According to John*, 279; Carson, *John*, 460–61; Ridderbos, *John*, 452; Keener, *John*, 899.

101. Kruse, *Gospel According to John*, 279; Harris, *John*, 242; Carson, *John*, 460–61; Keener, *John*, 899.

102. Kruse, *Gospel According to John*, 279; Ridderbos, *John*, 452; Köstenberger, *John*, 402.

103. Barrett, *Gospel According to St. John*, 476; Carson, *John*, 521–22.

104. Harris, *John*, 269; Carson, *John*, 522.

105. Ridderbos, *John*, 477.

A Call to Godly Service and Care

Serving and Caring in Akan thought

In light of Akan epistemology's acknowledgment of the insufficiency of the human being, the culture promotes mutual care and service as essential tools for realizing individual and collective goals. Opoku, Ackah, and Gyekye outline the following proverbs to that effect: "The left arm washes the right arm, and the right arm washes the left arm," "The tortoise says, the hand goes, and a hand comes," and "The reason two deer walk together is that one must take the moth from the other's eyes."[106] In the scenarios above, a pair of deer are witnessed partaking in acts of service or caregiving towards one another. Similarly, the left arm undertakes the duty of attending to the left hand, and vice versa. As a result, the aphorisms portray a manifestation of care or service.

From the aforementioned proverbs, it is evident that two distinct conclusions can be drawn. One of them is that the adages reveal that the Akan conceptual framework espouses the notion of reciprocal service and care. The aforementioned examples exemplify the inherent reciprocity in the concepts of service and care, wherein an individual is both the bestower and recipient of these benevolent actions.

The proverbial expressions also reveal that the importance attributed to service and care in Akan philosophy is dependent on two key elements: the Akan viewpoint regarding ontological parity and the inherent constraints of human nature. In Akan philosophy, the use of elements such as the term "hands" as a synecdoche for human beings and the metaphorical representation of humankind as "two deer" serves to highlight the ontological equality of individuals. Moreover, the illustration of the hand's incapacity to cleanse itself or a deer's inability to eliminate a mote from its own eyes without the aid of another deer functions as a persistent reminder of human deficiencies within Akan philosophy.[107]

As a result, the culture advocates for the adoption of reciprocal care or service as the solution to these challenges. This is the significance of the two aforementioned proverbs.[108] The establishment of a communal framework is necessary due to the inherent limitations of the human

---

106. Opoku, *Akan Proverbs*, 17; Ackah, *Akan Ethics*, 52–53; Gyekye, *African Cultural Values*, 188–89.

107. See Opoku, *Akan Proverbs*, 17; Gyekye, *African Cultural Values*, 37.

108. Opoku, *Akan Proverbs*, 17; Gyekye, *African Cultural Values*, 37.

condition, which require individuals to engage in reciprocal care and service towards one another. Opoku and Gyekye expound upon the meaning of the second proverb, suggesting that it signifies the inherent interdependence of individual hands, which are incapable of cleansing themselves without the assistance of the other hand.[109] However, reciprocity holds a prominent position within this particular context. As a result, the process of cleansing requires reciprocal interdependence between the right hand and the left hand. In a similar manner, one can posit that a deer is dependent on the aid or consideration of another entity (the deer) to eliminate any extraneous items impeding its visual perception, as elucidated by Opoku and Gyekye.[110] Therefore, the aphorisms put forth indicate that the fulfillment of an individual's developmental, security, and survival needs is contingent upon the presence of human interdependence.[111] Furthermore, they place great importance on communal values, such as reciprocal care and service, as crucial elements for promoting individual well-being.[112]

The aphorisms presented herein exemplify the potential of Akan concepts to enrich the Johannine notions of care and service. They elucidate the indispensability and advantages of reciprocal acts of service and care within the context of communal existence. John's discussion lacks an elaboration or explicit mention of the societal advantages associated with these communalistic principles. Instead, he merely asserts that they are divine mandates that the faithful community must adhere to and embody. The Akan concepts emphasize and illustrate the indispensability of mutual service and care for both the individual and the community, as human beings are inherently interdependent and incapable of complete self-sufficiency. Therefore, the preconceived notions of communal values held by the Akan community can enhance our comprehension of the Johannine concept.

Even though the purpose of these values is to complement one another, individual interests drive the Akan concepts of care and service. For instance, the concept that rewards or personal benefits play a role in the Akan concept of service (and care) is corroborated by the proverb, "A slave who possesses the ability to serve inherits the possessions of their

---

109. Opoku, *Akan Proverbs*, 17; Gyekye, *African Cultural Values*, 37.
110. Opoku, *Akan Proverbs*, 17; Gyekye, *African Cultural Values*, 188.
111. Opoku, *Akan Proverbs*, 11.
112. See Opoku, *Akan Proverbs*, 17; Ackah, *Akan Ethics*, 52–53.

master." According to Appiah and Appiah, this proverb conveys the notion that participating in acts of good service results in obtaining the corresponding benefits.[113] It presupposes that the people performing these *communalistic* acts have their interests in mind. However, this does not mean that we cannot find genuine care and service among the Akans, but that the community members generally tie reciprocal care and service to personal benefits. We can extrapolate from the character of the above proverbs the premise for this conclusion.

The first two proverbs have some commonalities. Employing how human hands function during bathing, the adages demonstrate how reciprocal service and care culminate in mutual helpfulness in the Akan culture. It is pertinent to note that the relationship is between members of a pair of hands, not the hands and another body part. The latter presents a scenario where reciprocity is most unlikely. For instance, the head cannot reciprocate the services of the hands after washing it. However, the first scenario, the intent of the adage, warrants reciprocity: the two hands bathe each other because complete cleansing requires mutual care and service. Thus, they are conditional services grounded on personal benefits and not genuine concern for others.

The third adage exhibits a similar analogy to the preceding two. It establishes a connection between two entities of equal ontological status (two deer) who possess a common area of focus. The depiction presented illustrates a representation of service that is intrinsically linked to individual inclinations and the anticipation of mutual exchange: a deer engages in acts of service and nurturing towards another deer with the expectation of receiving comparable advantages in return. The implication is that observing individuals engaging in acts of service towards those who are less privileged or unable to reciprocate without expecting significant personal benefits is not a frequent occurrence.

Service Redefined

Analyzing these cultural values through the prism of John, the reader recognizes that Jesus reveals how Akan Christians can transform their concept and practice to reflect their mandate as a community of God through his exemplary lifestyle (cf. John 13:3–17). For example, in the foot-washing narrative, he epitomizes, redefines, and calls on the

---

113. Appiah and Appiah, "Akan Proverbs," 123.

believing community (Akans included) to emulate what he reveals and exemplifies (cf. John 13:3–17). Ridderbos affirms that in the symbolic act of the foot-washing, Jesus lays down the foundation on which alone the future fellowship of the believing community as the church in the world could rest.[114] Thus, the activity and the perlocutionary force of the illocutionary act it occasioned are the substratum of reciprocal service in the community of God.[115]

However, to appreciate the implications of the symbolic act, paying attention to the narrative context is critical. John makes Jesus' awareness of his departure to the Father the motivation for his action (cf. John 13:4–5). Knowing the limitedness of his time on earth, he prepares to establish how the community must live when he is physically absent.[116] Therefore, he arose from the table, took off his outer robe, tied a towel around himself, and poured water into a basin to wash and wipe the feet of the disciples (cf. John 13:4–5). Peter, the first person Jesus decided to wash his feet with, initially contested the act by questioning the motive behind it (cf. John 13:6). Given the cultural connotation of foot-washing—that it was the responsibility of servants, a status that both Jews and Gentiles despised—the question was legitimate.[117] It is pertinent to note that though Gentile servants performed the task of foot-washing, wives and children did it sometimes.[118] However, what is happening is different because Jesus and the disciples do not fit into the scenarios above. There is no literary attestation in Jewish or Greco-Roman sources suggesting that superiors washed the feet of inferiors.[119] Thus, Harris asserts that only the expression of the deepest love, the love that makes one willing to be a servant to the beloved, would warrant the performance of the most humiliating acts of service.[120]

The love that prompted Jesus' willingness to take the form of a servant and serve the disciples is evident in the process that culminated in the foot-washing, not just the act of washing their feet (cf. John 13:4–5).

---

114. Ridderbos, *John*, 458; cf. Carson, *John*, 462; Keener, *John*, 907.

115. Gharbin, "Service and Care," 498.

116. See Ridderbos, *John*, 458; Carson, *John*, 462; Keener, *John*, 907.

117. Köstenberger, *John*, 402; Carson, *John*, 463; Ridderbos, *John*, 460; Keener, *John*, 904; Bauckham, *Gospel of Glory*, 62–63; Harris, *John*, 243.

118. Harris, *John*, 243; Talbert, *Reading John*, 199; cf. Keene, *John*, 903; Carson, *John*, 461–63.

119. Köstenberger, *John*, 405; Harris, *John*, 243.

120. Harris, *John*, 243; cf. Carson, *John*, 462.

By his actions—laying aside his outer garment and girding around his waist a towel for this menial task—he demonstrates humility to serve.[121] Beyond this ubiquitously held view, most scholars opine that the phrases (lay aside and take up) echo the words (I lay down my life and take it) of Jesus in the narrative of the Good Shepherd (John 10:17–18).[122] If so, John ties the footwashing to the crucifixion and resurrection of Jesus, painting a portrait of sacrificial service.[123]

Further, performing the servile act of foot-washing affirms the point above. By doing so, Jesus accomplishes what had no historical antecedent for the disciples, thereby reversing the role.[124] For the disciple, executing any act of service to a master is an obligation.[125] However, it excluded dealing with the feet since that was too degrading for a free person.[126] It explains why Peter resisted initially (John 13:6). The Greek construction accentuates and clarifies the force of the implication of the decision to wash Peter's feet and its concomitant astonishment. By juxtaposing the Greek emphatic pronoun σύ (*su* or you) to μου (*mou* or me) and commencing the sentence with Κύριε (*Kyrie* or Lord) and ending with πόδας (*podas* or feet), the narrative indicates indignant emphasis: Jesus, their Lord and Master, is performing what the society classified as ignominious for even disciples to do for their masters.[127] The narrative later affirms the humility demonstrated by Jesus in his appropriation of the servile act for the disciples through the inversion of the order of Κύριος (*Kyrios* or Lord) and Διδάσκαλος (*Didaskalos* or Teacher) (cf. John 13:13–14). As Harris correctly notes, it highlights the humbleness of the Κύριος in acting as a servant in the foot-washing.[128]

Finally, the primary purpose of inverting the order is to indicate the perlocutionary effect of the servile act on the communal life of the disciples—to make it a model that will define the future interpersonal relationships of the disciples and subsequent believing community members

---

121. See Carson, *John*, 463; Harris, *John*, 243; Köstenberger, *John*, 404; Keener, *John*, 908.

122. Ridderbos, *John*, 458; Talbert, *Reading John*, 199.

123. See Köstenberger, *John*, 405.

124. Köstenberger, *John*, 405; Harris, *John*, 243.

125. Köstenberger, *John*, 405.

126. Keener, *John*, 911.

127. See Keener, *John*, 908–9; Carson, *John*, 463; Harris, *John*, 243; Ridderbos, *John*, 459; Köstenberger, *John*, 405.

128. Harris, *John*, 245.

(John 13:14–15). The culture considered it honorable for leaders to motivate followers by the virtues they epitomized.[129] Similarly, the imports of ὑπόδειγμα (*hypodeigma*) and καθὼς (*kathōs*) in the narrative suggest that Jesus does that and even more. The Greek term ὑπόδειγμα denotes a pattern or an example.[130] Furthermore, several Second Temple texts and Greco-Roman writings associate the word with virtues.[131] Consequently, Jesus motivates the disciples to demonstrate virtues worthy of their calling by his example through the foot-washing act. The Greek conjunction καθὼς affirms that there is a connection between the pattern and its motivating effect on the disciples; it indicates not only similarity and devotion to a standard but also the substratum on which this discipleship rests and the source from which it gains its strength.[132]

In this narrative, what Jesus models and motivates the community to imitate through the performance of the menial task is humility for service.[133] Hence, the command to imitate his example is not to wash the feet of one another as a required act of devotion but to emulate the servanthood of Jesus through humility, mutual service, and renouncing every form of power game in the community.[134] Jesus does not only want the community to know, but he also wants them to practice. He demands that orthodoxy beget orthopraxy or that orthopraxy accompany orthodoxy concomitantly. It means that their practise must match the teachings they received and not be at variance with the divine will.[135]

Similarly, Jesus calls on the Akan Christians to reassess their perspective on service, taking into consideration the paradigm that has been established by the portrayal of Jesus in the Johannine tradition. The successful application of this model requires the emulation of Jesus' servanthood. John draws a correlation between Jesus' demonstration of servanthood and qualities such as love, selflessness, and a readiness to serve. Additionally, the Gospel establishes Jesus' love as the fundamental foundation for his inclination towards acts of service that are characterized by selflessness. Therefore, this paradigm advocates for the prioritization of

129. Keener, *John*, 904.

130. Köstenberger, *John*, 405; Carson, *John*, 467; Harris, *John*, 245.

131. Köstenberger, *John*, 405.

132. Ridderbos, *John*, 463.

133. Ridderbos, *John*, 462; Harris, *John*, 245; Keener, *John*, 902; Carson, *John*, 467–69.

134. Harris, *John*, 245; cf. Ridderbos, *John*, 462; Carson, *John*, 467–69.

135. See Harris, *John*, 245.

Christ's love as the foundational principle for communal and reciprocal acts of service. In accordance with the theological viewpoint of John, the notion of love empowers members of the faith community to partake in voluntary, sacrificial, and humble acts of service towards each other. Through this process, the individual's conceptual framework experiences a profound shift, wherein the self-interested mindset of engaging in reciprocal service is replaced by a mindset focused on sacrificial service, devoid of any expectation of personal benefits resulting from the reciprocation of such acts.

Furthermore, the adoption of an innovative approach to service by Jesus, devoid of any historical precedent, aimed at inspiring his disciples and future communities of believers, can serve as a source of motivation for Akan believers, especially leaders, to inspire fellow community members to demonstrate virtues that align with their divine calling. This can be achieved by emulating the selfless service exemplified by Christ. The concept of role reversal holds significance among Akan Christians, amplifying the urgency of the call to action. This is exemplified by the proverb "A slave who possesses the ability to serve inherits the possessions of their master," which establishes the duty of service for a servant.[136] Hence, by emulating the actions of Jesus, the notion of service is redefined, giving rise to a novel understanding wherein social status no longer exerts influence over acts of service.

Pastoral Care

John identifies pastoral and reciprocal care as two ways of caring for community members that can transform the Akan Christian's cultural concept of care. Whereas pastoral care defines how leaders of the believing community must cater for the people under their leadership, the latter concentrates on the responsibility of the members towards each other. Nonetheless, both are inextricable, given that reciprocity is their point of confluence or convergence. To restate, leaders are also community members and, thus, beneficiaries of reciprocal care.

In the epilogue of John, the encounter between the resurrected Jesus and his friends offers a teachable moment for an informed understanding of the Johannine concept of pastoral care (cf. John 21:1–17).[137] After

---

136. Appiah and Appiah, "Akan Proverbs," 123.
137. Carson, *John*, 678; Ridderbos, *John*, 666; Talbert, *Reading John*, 272.

directing the disciples to harvest a multitudinous number of fish after a fruitless night, Jesus invites them for breakfast (John 21:3-12) and initiates a conversation, asking Peter slightly divergent questions on three occasions (John 21:15-17). The Greek construction of the first question has generated two main views (ἀγαπᾷς με πλέον τούτων;).[138] Since other gospel narratives declare that Peter boasted of a greater loyal love for Jesus than his friends before the crucifixion, scholars generally agree that the phrase (more than these) refers to the disciples (John 21:15).[139] For these scholars, Jesus is asking if Peter still stands by his confession, considering the present action—fishing. Furthermore, some scholars assert the possibility that Jesus had Peter's profession also in mind when asking the question, given the narrative context.[140] However, we cannot also overlook the possibility that the question is redolent of the need to prioritize Christ over earthly food, as in the Bread of Life image, since the breakfast precedes it.[141]

Why does Jesus question Peter's love for him repeatedly? There are two possible reasons: the betrayal of Peter and the role of love in the assignment given to him after his reinstatement. The betrayal of Peter is one of the reasons for repeating the question.[142] He betrayed Jesus three times; therefore, his restoration must reflect the number of times he demonstrated that perfidious character.[143] Most importantly, however, his reinstatement, with its associated charge, makes it more reasonable to surmise that the question was necessary because of the responsibility given to Peter concerning the community (John 21:15-17).[144]

To give the charge its proper context, Jesus employs the metaphor that is one of the most recurring portraits of the care of the church—the shepherd imagery. Both the Old and New Testaments are awash with the shepherd metaphor. It is rooted in the portrayal of God as the shepherd of his people.[145] Given that it originates from God, the Old Testament es-

---

138. *Agapas me pleon toutōn* [Do you love me more than these?].

139. Morris, *John*, 768; Köstenberger, *John*, 597; Carson, *John*, 675-76; Harris, *John*, 343.

140. Talbert, *Reading John*, 271; Keener, *John*, 1236; Harris, *John*, 343.

141. Keener, *John*, 1236.

142. See Carson, *John*, 678; Ridderbos, *John*, 665; Köstenberger, *John*, 595.

143. See Carson, *John*, 678; Ridderbos, *John*, 665; Köstenberger, *John*, 595; Harris, *John*, 343.

144. Keener, *John*, 1237; Carson, *John*, 678; Köstenberger, *John*, 596.

145. Ridderbos, *John*, 666.

tablishes a relationship between devotion to God, the source, and caring for his flock (Ezra 34; Jer 3:15).[146] It explains why the New Testament and John portray only Jesus, the incarnate Word, as the Good and Chief Shepherd (cf. John 10:11–18). Therefore, employing the imagery implies evoking John 10 to draw attention to something patterned after the concern or care of the Good Shepherd for the believing community (cf. John 10:11–18).[147] It explains Jesus' questions to Peter before entrusting him with such responsibilities, given that their execution flows from his love for the Lord.[148]

As a natural consequence of his love for Jesus, Peter must demonstrate pastoral care for the community. To clarify what this entails, Jesus employs the verbs βόσκε and ποιμαίνω because, together, they are redolent of the fullness of the task.[149] By employing verbs and not nouns to define the ministry, the focus is on working, not holding an office.[150] Consequently, the idea of Peter's elevation to pastoral primacy promulgated by some scholars because of this narrative rests on questionable assumptions.[151] Like the other disciples, Peter is also an undershepherd of Jesus.[152] As an undershepherd, the verb βόσκω denotes that he is obligated to feed the flock.[153] Furthermore, his role entails performing the entire responsibilities of a shepherd, such as guiding and protecting the sheep, as the verb ποιμαίνω denotes.[154] Thus, the two verbs are purposefully combined to stress the measure of attention required from Peter and pastoral care: the total or all-inclusive care of a shepherd.[155] Performing the functions of a shepherd, just like Jesus epitomized, is a call to utter self-sacrifice and potentially death, given that the work of the Chief

---

146. See Köstenberger, *John*, 597.

147. Ridderbos, *John*, 666.

148. See Carson, *John*, 678; Harris, *John*, 343; Köstenberge, *John*, 596.

149. Köstenberger, *John*, 2004. Whereas *boske* comes from the verb to feed, *poimaine* means to shepherd.

150. Carson, *John*, 678.

151. See Ridderbos, *John*, 666; Carson, *John*, 678–79; Harris, *John*, 343; Keener, *John*, 1237.

152. See Ridderbos, *John*, 666; Carson, *John*, 678–79; Harris, *John*, 343; Keener, *John*, 1237.

153. Keener, *John*, 1237; Harris, *John*, 343; Köstenberger, *John*, 597.

154. Harris, *John*, 343; Keener, *John*, 1237.

155. Harris, *John*, 343; Ridderbos, *John*, 666; Keener, *John*, 1237.

Shepherd, the model for Johannine pastoral care, culminated in sacrificing his life for the flock (John 10:11, 15; 21:18-19).[156]

Thus, the above portrait reveals that John invites the Akan Christian to view pastoral care through the prism of the revelations that proceed from the interaction between Jesus and Peter. In this, John projects pastoral care as a call to love and utter sacrifice. Leaders must recognize that pastoral care is a natural consequence of their love for Jesus (cf. John 21:15-17). John ties love for Jesus to the observance of his commandment (John 14:15). Consequently, loving Jesus is a prerequisite for the pastoral role, given that it entails fulfilling the command to feed and performing the total care of a shepherd. Finally, following the example of Jesus, Akan Christians must see pastoral care as a call to utter self-sacrifice.

Reciprocal Care

Apart from pastoral care, the narrative addresses how members of the community of God must care for one another. We can look at this in two ways: by examining the new relationship established at the foot of the cross and the interconnection between this and other communalistic values. John employs what transpires at the foot of the cross—a portrait of profound care—to define the new interpersonal relationships that must characterize the believing community.[157] In the crucifixion scene, Jesus establishes a mother-son relationship between Mary and the beloved disciple, entrusting Mary to the beloved disciple as a mother and vice versa (John 19:25-27). The beloved disciple responds to this by taking Mary to his own home. Many interpret Jesus' words and the corresponding response of the disciple as the responsibility of caring for her.[158] Additionally, most scholars agree that the import of the narrative—caring for one another—applies to the believing community.[159] Thus, as part of the universal community of God, John invites the Akan Christian to participate in the quality of interpersonal relationships Jesus establishes at the foot of the cross for the microcosmic messianic community: reciprocal care.

156. Keener, *John*, 1237; cf. Talbert, *Reading John*, 272.

157. See Brodie, *Gospel According to John*, 547; Moloney, *Glory Not Dishonor*, 146; Ridderbos, *John*, 613; Keener, *John*, 1145.

158. Harris, *John*, 316; Ridderbos, *John*, 613; cf. Brodie, *Gospel According to John*, 547.

159. See Brodie, *Gospel According to John*, 547; Moloney, *Glory Not Dishonor*, 146; Ridderbos, *John*, 613; Keener, *John*, 1145.

Another way of analyzing how community members must care for one another is by assessing how demonstrating the various communalistic values culminates in reciprocal care in the community of God. The established relationship between pastoral care, love, and service makes it increasingly conspicuous that demonstrating concern for community members is not an independent value. John connects it to other communal values, especially communalism, unity, love, and service. Thus, it is impossible to live in a united, loving community that demonstrates reciprocal service without witnessing the virtue of mutual care, since the divine pattern and the command to replicate these communalistic values make its expectation natural.

In the first place, the entire concept of the community of God hinges on reciprocal care. Borchert concisely and correctly notes that community and unity are two compatible sides of God.[160] This affirmation implies that God exists as a community.[161] The prologue clarifies what legitimizes this union as a community by indicating that the distinct ontological coequals do not live independently but demonstrate community and unity (ontological and functional) through coeternity and the intimate union or communion they enjoy.[162] The narrative also reiterates that these attributes characterize the community of God. The portrait of the community presented is redolent of reciprocal care between ontological coequals because of God's character and the values upheld by the community members. These factors make it impossible to assume that mutual concern is not inherent in the community members or implied in their coeternity, unity, and intimate relationships.

The reverberation of this conclusion on the Akan believing community is that the invitation to be part of the community of God is a call to participate in this communalistic life.[163] It explains the motivation for making the concept of community, unity, and love in the believing community analogous to the community of God.[164] Therefore, to exist as a community of God requires replicating this social life by imbibing its values, including caring for one another.

160. Borchert, *John 12—21*, 106.

161. Borchert, *John 12—21*, 106.

162. See Vincent, *Word Studies*, 34; Morris, *John*, 70; Tenney, *John*, 64; Harris, *John*, 18; Kanagaraj, *John*, 1; Voorwinde, "John's Prologue," 32; Newman and Nida, *Gospel of John*, 8.

163. Grenz, *Community of God*, 112; *Created for Community*, 49.

164. See Carson, *John*, 568.

Moreover, a critical analysis of the communalistic values indicates that mutual love and care are intertwined. The study affirms the reciprocity of love in the eternal relationship of the Father and the Son, indicating that the Son enjoys communion and intimacy with God.[165] Further, the narrative establishes that the Father is the source of love and that Jesus patterns what he demonstrates to the believing community after that fatherly love.[166] In the first relationship, love motivates the giving and disclosure of the works of the Father to the Son (John 3:35; 5:19–20; 13:3; 17). Contextualizing this in the believing community, Jesus demonstrates love by giving the disciples an elevated status to warrant the disclosure of what he receives from the Father and the ultimate sacrifice—laying down his life for his friends (John 15:13–15; 17:26).[167] He presents this love as the model for imitation and commands a mutual demonstration in the believing community (cf. John 13:34; 15:9, 12, 17). Given its character, we can infer that the idea of reciprocal care is inherent in the love command; anyone who can sacrifice his life for a person is showing that he cares. Moreover, Jesus, the model of love, applies a title to himself suggestive of care: the Good Shepherd (cf. John 10:11–18).[168] He also interprets his sacrificial love through the prism of the holistic care of the Good Shepherd, making it impossible to detach care from the greater love he requires the community to emulate (cf. John 10:11–18).[169]

Furthermore, the narrative establishes a correlation between reciprocal service and mutual care through love. There exist two compelling rationales to support the notion that love serves as the cohesive force that unites these communalistic principles. Firstly, this assertion is grounded in the depiction of the exemplar, and secondly, it is reinforced by the injunction to emulate the conduct epitomized by Jesus. Many scholars affirm that by indicating that Jesus laid down his garment to wash the feet of the disciples, John evokes the Good Shepherd narrative, a metaphor for care,[170] and ties the event to the crucifixion to make it an act of

---

165. Vincent, *Word Studies*, 34; Harris, *John*, 18; Kanagaraj, *John*, 1; Morris, *John*, 70; Carson, *John*, 134.

166. See Ridderbos, *John*, 519.

167. See Harris, *John*, 269; Carson, *John*, 521–22; Brodie, *Gospel According to John*, 483; Keener, *John*, 911.

168. Ridderbos, *John*, 666.

169. Ridderbos, *John*, 666; Harris, *John*, 343; Keener, *John*, 1237.

170. Ridderbos, *John*, 458; Talbert, *Reading John*, 199.

sacrificial service.¹⁷¹ Furthermore, the foot-washing is an expression of the most profound love, given that only love can make an individual, most especially the Lord, perform the most humiliating acts of service for his disciples.¹⁷² Secondly, John indicates that this sacrificial service, which originates from love, is an example for the community to replicate reciprocally (John 13:15). The interconnection among the depictions of care, love, and service necessitates the Akan community to reexamine and construe its notion of reciprocal love, service, and care through the lens of the principles espoused by Jesus in the book of John.

Reciprocity

Reciprocity in the Akan Culture

The principle of reciprocity holds a significant place within the Akan community framework, as it embodies the cherished communalistic values that are appreciated. The inherent significance of reciprocation becomes apparent through its inseparable correlation with other communal virtues, namely love, unity, service, and care. By examining the intricate interplay between reciprocity and communalistic principles within Akan epistemology and culture, one can discern that the Akan community ethos inherently demands reciprocation within the context of love. In this particular context, it is worth noting the presence of certain adages. One notable example pertains to the reciprocity of affection, wherein it is suggested that if someone loves you, reciprocate it.¹⁷³ Likewise, it is worth noting that various other maxims serve to reinforce the Akan cultural perspective that the essence of communal existence necessitates the reciprocal exchange of communal values such as service and care. For instance, consider the notion that the left arm dutifully cleanses the right arm, while conversely, the right arm reciprocates this act of cleanliness upon the left arm. Similarly, the rationale behind two deer walking in tandem lies in the imperative for one deer to alleviate the other of an ocular affliction caused by a moth.

Hence, the advantageous aspect of this notion for John lies in the Akan Christian preconceptions regarding the role of reciprocity in enhancing the well-being of community members. By supplementing their

---

171. See Köstenberger, *John*, 405.
172. Harris, *John*, 243; cf. Carson, *John*, 462.
173. See Opoku, *Akan Proverbs*, 77.

individual deficiencies to accomplish what one party alone cannot, this concept expands John's comprehension of the interconnectedness and interdependence inherent in mutual relationships.

Moreover, it is worth noting that though there exists a profound appreciation for the concept of reciprocation within the Akan culture, it is primarily focused on fostering positive mutuality, wherein individuals are encouraged to reciprocate acts of kindness rather than engaging in negative reciprocity. Negative reciprocity, which involves repaying evil with evil or considering evil as a form of recompense for good, is not endorsed within the Akan cultural framework.[174] According to the Akans, it is imperative to abstain from the pursuit of malevolence.[175] It is imperative to acknowledge that they do not espouse the notion of substituting malevolence with benevolence either.

Nevertheless, because reciprocity is a point of convergence for the various communal values, the challenges associated with expressing these communalistic principles affect the Akan practice of reciprocity. For instance, the study has demonstrated that Akan proverbs, the repository of inestimable information pertaining to this cultural milieu, propagate conditional love, wherein the reciprocation of love is contingent upon its initial bestowal. As a result, members mostly show love to those who love them or do not feel obliged to initiate that process of demonstrating love. Thus, though the Akan concept of love encourages sacrificial and reciprocal love, not everyone is likely to enjoy it because of the above and other factors, such as the acquisitive elements in Akan culture, the recognition that wealth impels love, and the difficulty of maintaining the balance between love and money. Further, since Akans regard love as the greatest virtue, any cultural delinquency has ripple effects on the Akan expression of other communalistic values.[176]

Moreover, this cultural deficiency significantly impacts the Akan paradigm of care and service. Akan epistemology espouses the notion that the cultural milieu places great significance on the principles of reciprocal care and service. Nevertheless, upon conducting a meticulous examination of Akan maxims pertaining to this matter, it becomes apparent that these esteemed principles are predominantly exemplified within the framework of self-interest, as community members commonly

---

174. Ackah, *Akan Ethics*, 62, 75.
175. Ackah, *Akan Ethics*, 62, 75.
176. See Gyekye, *African Cultural Values*, 70; Opoku, *Akan Proverbs*, 77.

associate reciprocal care and service with personal advantages. The ultimate consequence is that the aspiration to satisfy individual interests supplants a sincere regard for others or members of the community, thereby transforming what should be manifestations of collectivist principles into contingent acts of service and care due to the anticipation of reciprocation.

Reciprocity in a Community of God

John makes reciprocity in the eternal community the substratum of the reciprocal relationship required of the human community. The portrait of the relationship between the Father and the Son presented in John shows the eternal distinctions demonstrating reciprocity in diverse ways. In the narrative, the intimate relationship between the Father and Son is reciprocal (John 1:1–2, 18). Thus, love is mutual, though it flows from the Father (John 1:1–2, 18; 14:31).[177] Reciprocity is evident even in the Johannine characterization of unity; it suggests that the distinct ontological coequals participate in the lives of one another.[178]

It is worth noting that John does not cast reciprocity as a panacea or remedy for the inadequacy of the members of the eternal society. The only portrait given is that it is an intrinsic and communalistic value characterizing and legitimizing the relationship between the eternal distinctions as a community. To state it differently, the undergirding principle of reciprocity demonstrated by the Father and the Son is love for communalism, not mutual benefits. Given that Jesus makes the tenets of reciprocity in the eternal community the standard for the believing community, this is necessary to note.

The call to participate in the life of the "social" Trinity entails replicating the character of reciprocity epitomized by the eternal community. Therefore, Jesus employs the language of reciprocity (doing something for one another) in promulgating the application or contextualization of communalistic values. Given that Jesus applies the values that characterize the eternal relationship as the ideal concept of reciprocity to the believing community, he redefines reciprocity. He requires from the believing community reciprocal love (John 13:34; 15:9, 12, 17), service

---

177. Ridderbos, *John*, 519.

178. See McGrath, *Christian Theology*, 325; Carson, *John*, 494; Bauckham, *Beloved Disciple*, 251.

(13:13–15), care (19:25–27), and unity (17:11, 21–22), values known to Akan Christians. However, since Jesus redefines these communalistic values, the rudiments of reciprocity, it has a ripple effect on the concept of reciprocity required of the Akan believing community. For instance, whereas mutual benefits inform the Akan expression of reciprocal love, service, care, and unity, Jesus invites Akan Christians to demonstrate reciprocity as an expression of their love for communalism, not because of mutual benefits. Thus, he does not make the demonstration of communalistic values a requirement for reciprocation. In other words, he does not command the disciples to love or serve in response to love or service. The command is to love and serve the community members, whether the one who is loved or served reciprocates it or not. It is nonetheless legitimate to expect reciprocation because Jesus commands the community to remain in his love by obeying his commands.[179] Love and obedience are mutually dependent.[180]

Furthermore, the first-century Mediterranean culture believed in the need to fulfill the expectations of other community members.[181] They reveal these communal obligations, and members respond accordingly.[182] One of these is to seek the good of one's neighbor.[183] Therefore, since the command on reciprocation possesses these attributes and entails seeking the welfare of each other, one expects the believing community to approach adherence to the communalistic values as a collective responsibility, thus creating a chain of interdependence.

Communality

Discussing communality as one of the values that must characterize the believing community is vital because communal values presuppose or warrant a community; they find expression in the community context. Additionally, the goal of expressing these communalistic values—unity, love, service, reciprocity, and care—is to build a communalistic community. Moreover, the focus of the previous discussions has been on how the theoretical and practical values guide the reader towards an informed

---

179. See Ridderbos, *John*, 519; Carson, *John*, 520.
180. Barrett, *Gospel According to St. John*, 476.
181. Malina, *New Testament*, 68.
182. Neyrey, "Group Orientation," 88.
183. Neyrey, "Group Orientation," 89.

understanding of the Johannine and Akan concepts of communalism. Hence, it is proper to conclude with a summary of how these values culminate in appreciating communalism in both cultures and the revelation and transformation John provides for the Akan believing community.

Given the impact of communal values on the character of communalism in a particular sociocultural context, we can conclude that the Akan Christian needs to redefine communalism because of the gap between the theoretical and practical values and the impact of the acquisitive elements on the Akan expression of unity, love, service, care, and reciprocity. Communal values grounded in the insufficiency of a human being and driven by personal interests and the material elements of the Akan culture defeat the purpose of communalism because these traits are antithetical to the tenets of collectivism and breed individualistic propensities.

Therefore, John invites the Akan believing community to emulate the true character of communalism. In John, the call to communal living is divine. The narrative, especially the farewell discourse, reveals that God expects believers to live as a collectivistic society and not be individualistic. As this study has reiterated, this is the purpose of God for the human community: to participate in the social life of God.[184] Thus, the various symbols employed for the believing community point in this direction. For instance, the prologue indicates that believing culminates in a familial relationship with God as one of the children of God (John 1:12).[185] It is a relationship that allows believers to share in the community life of God.[186]

Consequently, participating in the social life of God is an invitation to mirror the character of relationships in the eternal community. One of the attributes of the community of God is that it is communalistic. Therefore, any community replicating God must epitomize this trait. Jesus employs two metaphors to accentuate this: the Vine and the temple. In the temple cleansing narrative, Jesus refers to his body as a temple, signifying the universalized community of God or the new place where God's purpose for universal communal worship transpires.[187] He employs the vine metaphor for a similar purpose. The metaphor denotes the new

---

184. See Borchert, *John 12–21*, 106; Grenz, *Community of God*, 112.

185. Watt, *Family of the King*, 166, 182.

186. Watt, *Family of the King*, 166, 182; cf. Keener, *John*, 403.

187. See Köstenberger, *John*, 105; Brodie, *Gospel According to John*, 179.

community of God constituted by believing gentiles and Jews.[188] And the command to abide in the Vine implies remaining in the community of God (John 15:4).[189] It stands to reason that God wants the believing community to coexist (in him) communally. It also justifies the communalistic values prescribed as imperatives for the believing community to embody.

However, communal living is not foreign to the culture of the Johannine community. An analysis of the New Testament reveals that we can only learn about people by their relationship to someone or something—to place, school, family, clan, and nation.[190] Similarly, collectivism features prominently in the Akan concept of community. The difference, however, is that John interprets communitarianism through the prism of the eternal community and the model Jesus presented to the disciples. Hence, John characterizes the Christian community as a society with a collectivistic social structure patterned after the community of God, proscribes individualistic tendencies, and promotes communalism. He requires community members to be united in line with their divine mission and mandates the believing community to see collectivism as a *modus vivendi*, not a means to an end. Finally, the narrative requires love as the undergirding principle of communal values: reciprocity, mutual love, care, service, and communality.

Concluding Remarks

The reader concludes that Akan believers must fulfill their mission—incarnate the communalistic values of the divine community—like Jesus and live like the quintessential community. Incarnating God's concept of a community like Jesus entails loving, serving, and caring like Jesus. To love like Jesus, they must demonstrate love in practice, not theoretically. Such love requires transparency (cf. John 15:15; 17:26). It is inseparable from giving (15:13-15). In this context, it is a call to love to the uttermost and to the end.[191] Such love requires loving their own (John 10:1-21; cf.

---

188. See Köstenberger, *John*, 449; Ridderbos, *John*, 516; Keener, *John*, 993.

189. See Köstenberger, *John*, 449; Ridderbos, *John*, 516; Keener, *John*, 993.

190. Neyrey, "Dyadism," 49-51; "Group Orientation," 88-89; Malina, "Love," 100.

191. Kruse, *Gospel According to John*, 279; Ridderbos, *John*, 452; Köstenberger, *John*, 402; cf. Harris, *John*, 242.

13:34–35; 15:12, 17) and performing the ultimate reciprocal sacrifice of sacrificial giving.[192]

Furthermore, being in a believing community entails serving like Jesus. John makes the service of Jesus a pattern or an example for believers.[193] The pattern calls believers to sacrificial service.[194] As such, it requires humility for service, that is, getting down from the table, laying aside the outer garment, and girding around our waist a towel to perform menial tasks.[195] However, this is only possible when there is love; the willingness to serve sacrificially is a derivative of love.[196]

Beyond this, the Akan believing community must characterize the caring nature of Jesus through exemplary leadership and the interpersonal relationships of community members. John's concept of pastoral care portrays the leader as a worker, not an officeholder.[197] Like Peter, leaders are undershepherds who emulate the Chief and Good Shepherd.[198] By its very nature, the leader's work is a call to utter self-sacrifice; it entails performing the total or all-inclusive care of shepherds.[199]

Also, the portrait presented by the community at the foot of the cross indicates that caring for one another is a communal responsibility (John 19:25–27).[200] The commands of reciprocation for love and service reinforce this thought. The divine imperatives affirm that belonging to the community of God requires demonstrating characteristics that express the appreciation of the significance of community, culminating in the replication and reciprocation of values such as love and service. Obedience to the commands makes it a corporate responsibility for Akan Christians to care for each other.

Therefore, the criticality of love is undeniable in the concept of the community of God, considering its place in communalistic values; it is the cord that binds service and care together. As elucidated earlier, the

---

192. Ridderbos, *John*, 520; Carson, *John*, 521–22.

193. Köstenberger, *John*, 405; Carson, *John*, 467; Harris, *John*, 245.

194. See Köstenberger, *John*, 405.

195. See Carson, *John*, 463; Harris, *John*, 243; Köstenberger, *John*, 404; Keener, *John*, 908.

196. Harris, *John*, 243.

197. Carson, *John*, 678.

198. See Ridderbos, *John*, 666; Carson, *John*, 678–79; Keener, *John*, 1237.

199. See Harris, *John*, 343; Ridderbos, *John*, 666; Keener, *John*, 1237.

200. See Brodie, *Gospel According to John*, 547; Ridderbos, *John*, 613; Keener, *John*, 1145.

pattern of service and care epitomized by Jesus is love-motivated. Consequently, it is not surprising that Jesus emphasizes the necessity of remaining in his love and reciprocating it. A loving community will naturally serve and care for one another. Therefore, the Akan believing community must recognize that it must operate all communalistic values in love to be different from its culture.

Furthermore, these values affirm that being a community of God entails living like the quintessential community: being collectivistic. Borchert perspicaciously and aptly notes that community and unity are two compatible sides of the eternal God.[201] The implication is that God exists as a community of united, coeternal, and ontological coequals. Again, there is reciprocity in this relationship (cf. John 1:1–3, 18). Hence, a believing community demonstrates unity, mutuality, and communality as part of its calling. It is pertinent to note that in the theology of John, these are not independent but represent a community of interconnected communalistic values. Therefore, being a believing community requires exhibiting these attributes. We can legitimately label a group of individuals as a community only if they are communalistic.

---

201. Borchert, *John 12—21*, 106.

6

Summary, Conclusions, and Recommendations

THIS CHAPTER CONCLUDES THE study with a synopsis of the work and critical research findings, considering the research objectives and questions that shaped the study. It also recommends future research.

Summary

This work is an intercultural reading of the community ideations of John and the Akans. The study emanates from the commonalities between the biblical culture and the Akan reality: the emphasis on communalism and the inability to incarnate the communalistic values of their respective cultures. Thus, the research aimed to explore how John addresses this sociocultural crisis and examine its ramifications for the Akan believers plagued by this sociocultural malady.

Consequently, the study implemented Ossom-Batsa's communicative approach as the theoretical framework. He proposes a frame of interpretation—a tripartite level—constituted by adherence to the text, attention to the call to action, and the interpreter's context. The study employed the Narrative Criticism proposed by Marguerat and Bourquin for the first and second steps concomitantly—adherence to the biblical narrative—to establish the communicative force of the community theme in John. Further, it analyzed Akan proverbs for their preunderstanding of community. Finally, the study engaged the call to action in John in the sociocultural context of Akans in the intercultural exegesis to see how John helps the Akan believer transform their communalistic values and

SUMMARY, CONCLUSIONS, AND RECOMMENDATIONS

the questions the Akan culture poses to the text. Thus, the organization of chapters followed the progression of thought captured by the methodology of the study.

Chapters 2 and 3 focus preponderantly on the exegesis of the biblical culture, that is, the concept of community in John. Chapter 2 explores the community theme by analyzing four selected narratives (John 1:1–18; 5; 15—16:3; 17), laying the foundation to trace the narrative development of the concept of community in chapter 3. The study considers the prologue as the substratum of the community theme and thus commences with its analysis. The analysis allows the reader to discover the origin, meaning, and characterization of the Johannine community concept. Further, it guides the reader to ascertain the relationship between the incarnation of the Logos and his critical role in the explication and replication of the divine concept of community in the human community. It also reveals the invitation given to the human community and the appropriate response it must elicit. Finally, it prepares the reader for the exegesis of God—the divine community.

Furthermore, studying John 5 through the lens of the community theme culminates in appreciating the need for the explication and imitation of the divine community concept. John selects the marginalized (the paralytic) in the microcosmic community and the magnified (religious authorities) to demonstrate how the Johannine community failed to fulfill the divine intentions for its establishment. The Bethesda community fails to live by the religious-cultural values worthy of a religious community. The response of the custodians of the law—the Jews—to the healing and the exegesis on the eternal community it occasioned also discloses the exacerbated nature of the problem: the custodians of the law are neither willing to accept the incarnate Logos nor have the word of God abiding in them (John 4:38–40). The failure of the Jewish ecclesiastical authorities necessitates the introduction of a new community that imitates God.

Against this background, the chapter concludes with the analysis of John 15:1—16:33 and 17 to establish the proposed solutions to the problem. In this regard, John employs the vine metaphor to demonstrate how Jesus presents the community of God as the divine remedy. The metaphor evokes the vine (a symbol of the old believing community) to depict an inclusive community of believers called to participate in the mission of the Logos—expanding the community of God through witnessing and contextualizing its communal values in their culture, thereby becoming the cure for the religious, cultural, and social problems of the community.

Finally, the character of a community redolent of the community of God is revealed in Jesus' inventory of his ministry and prayer for the Johannine and future community of believers.

Building on this foundation, chapter 3 traces the narrative development of the community theme, focusing on narratives that develop the foundation and formation of the ideal (divine) community, expose the sociocultural maladies, and reveal the proposed remedy. Thus, the study analyzes the foundation of the Johannine community concept, establishing the significance of the eternal relationship in the prologue to the Johannine community concept. Further, it explores the conception and the mission of the community of God, revealing that John ties the narrative development of the believing community to its sociocultural malady, thereby exposing the root of the social, cultural, and religious problem. Given these challenges, the study explores the proposed remedy: the divine portrait of a community and the participatory roles of the eternal and believing communities in the incarnation of the ideal community paradigm.

Given that intercultural reading requires a biblical culture and a contemporary sociocultural context, chapter 4 exegetes the Akan community's concept as the second partner of the intercultural exegesis. The examination of the Akan community concept reveals that though the community is amphibious (manifests both collectivistic and individualistic traits), the acquisitive elements in the Akan culture militate against the genuine expression of collectivism; they tie communalism to personal interests. Communalism, grounded in personal gains, sounds more like individualism because it focuses on the individual.

Therefore, chapter 5 engages some cultural and communal values that emanate from the narrative analysis of John and the exegesis of Akan reality: unity, love, service, care, reciprocity, and communality. It explores the Akan Christian's pre-understanding of the subject and the challenges with the Akan concept. Finally, it challenges Akan believers to evaluate their communalistic values through the prism of what Jesus proscribes and prescribes for the members of the Johannine believing community as the divine response to the sociocultural problems in their milieu: the struggle with the incarnation of religious-cultural values.

Conclusions

The study aimed to explore the narrative development of the concept of community in John through narrative analyses of relevant narratives and examine its significance for the Akan community in an intercultural reading, using the communicative approach as the theoretical framework. It presents the summary of the findings below.

The Community of God

The study aimed to investigate the relational dimension of community in the eternal community—the quality of interpersonal relationships between the eternal distinctions—and its reverberations on the believing community.[1] The findings indicate that John provides the reader with a different perspective on the scholarly labeling of community. In John, the community concept originates from the eternal community because they coexist coeternally in an intimate relationship (John 1:1–3, 18). The Johannine portrayal of the eternal distinctions legitimizes their relationship as the first and only paradigm of community.

It also redefines a community as a group of people participating in the eternal community, not just demonstrating quality relationships. Consequently, John distinguishes creation (or the world) from the community of God, given that the definition restricts the community to a section of humanity (1:12–13). The participants are individuals who either accept the Son or experience a spiritual rebirth (1:12–13; 3:3). The condition of spiritual birth explains why not everyone who has gone through biological birth is part of this community. It also implies that anyone who fulfills the requirement, irrespective of race or gender, can be part of the community; it is the participation of children of God in the community of God (1:12–13). The implication is that John elevates the community concept above the anthropological view, making it a theological value.

The relationship between the anthropological and Johannine views is that they converge and diverge at some point. The convergent point is the relational dimension of community, supported by the two concepts. However, the difference is that, whereas the anthropological view makes the people or culture the determinant of quality interpersonal relationships, John makes God the paradigm. The implication is that it is possible

---

1. See Gusfield, *Community*, xv–xvi; Cohen, *Symbolic Construction*, 12; Klink, *Sheep of the Fold*, 52.

to express "quality" relationships without belonging to the community of God (the community concept presented by John); nevertheless, self-interests are often the motivation for such relationships (as the discussions on the Akan community concept have demonstrated). Furthermore, culture is dynamic; thus, with time, many factors affect cultures, drawing a line between the theoretical values and practices of a community. However, the culture required of the believing community is unchanging and time-tested; it is an eternal concept prescribed for all generations (cf. John 1:1–3; 17:20–22). Further, God requires that believers dwell on the collective and missiological significance of living communally (John 13:34–35).

John enumerates various reasons as justification for these differences. The narrative clearly defines the character of relationships within a community of God through what Jesus teaches and personifies. Thus, "quality relationships" is not an ambiguous term but simply participating in the culture of the eternal community. John affirms that abiding in the Vine prescribes the lifestyle that must be evident in the community: they must demonstrate communal values experienced in God.[2] It also establishes a relationship of mutual indwelling, giving them the impetus to meet this divine standard (cf. John 15:4–5).[3] It implies that the community of believers receives strength to demonstrate what God requires of them (mission as *going* and *living*) as members of the community of God, akin to the vine-branch relationship (John 15:4–5). Finally, demonstrating the values of the community of God is a divine imperative they obey in love.[4]

The Logos' Contribution to the Incarnation of the Divine Community

The study aimed to explore the contribution of the Logos to the exegesis and incarnation of the eternal community. What does this mean? John employs three designations for Jesus in the prologue in this order: the pre-incarnate Logos (John 1:1–3), the incarnate Word (1:14), and the Son (1:18). He does not employ the title Logos after identifying him as the one who incarnated and dwelt in a human community. However, he

---

2. See Brodie, *Gospel According to John*, 483; Keener, *John*, 1004.
3. Köstenberger, *John*, 451; Ridderbos, *John*, 517.
4. See Ridderbos, *John*, 519; Carson, *John*, 520; Köstenberger, *John*, 253.

sustains the characterization of the Logos as the Son in the narrative and identifies him as Jesus. Thus, the focus is to examine the contributions of Jesus, the pre-incarnate and incarnate Word, to the incarnation of the eternal community concept.

The study indicates that the Logos' relationship with God makes the concept of the eternal community meaningful. The pre-incarnate Word's (Logos) coeternal relationship with the Father is the origin of the Johannine community concept; it defines what it entails to be a community (cf. John 1:1–5). The values characterizing this eternal relationship—union, intimacy, fellowship, reciprocal love, and functional and ontological unity—legitimize the characterization of the relationship as a community, furnishing the reader with an idea of what constitutes a community in John.[5] It further presents the prologue as a hermeneutical key for an academic autopsy on the community theme, given the impact of the prologue on the themes in John: it *tells* what the narrative *shows*.[6]

As the incarnate Word, his identity and relationship with God also present him as the only authoritative exegete of the eternal community (cf. John 1:18; 3:13). Thus, John ties the exegesis of the community of God to the goals of the incarnation, revealing that ἐξηγήσατο (*exēgesato*) encompasses in a glimpse the whole life of Jesus on earth; therefore, the reader should read the narrative, a compendium of incalculable information about the community theme, as his exegesis on the subject.[7] John reveals that the declarations on the ideal community entail two things: his relationship with the Father and the relationship between the eternal and human societies (cf. John 5:20–23; 10:30; 14:7–11; 15). Whereas the former focuses preponderantly on his ontological and functional unity with the Father and the shared values, the latter entails human participation in the community of God and its concomitant fruits worthy of the new identity (cf. John 5:20–23; 10:30; 14:7–11; 15). Consequently, one of the contributions of the Logos to the incarnation of the community is that he exegetes the community as its sole authoritative expositor.

Additionally, through his earthly ministry, the divine purpose for the human community becomes clearer. For instance, he redefines the identity and sociocultural role of the community. Jesus reveals that God's purpose is an inclusive community constituted by both Jews and Gentiles,

---

5. Harris, *John*, 18; Kanagaraj, *John*, 1.
6. See Moloney, *Belief in the Word*, 24; Köstenberger, *Encountering John*, 44.
7. See Harris, *John*, 39.

or a universalized community of believers in Christ, with the mandate of becoming a remedy to the sociocultural maladies of their communities (cf. John 2:1–11, 13–21; 4; 5:6–9).

Moreover, John links the incarnation to the conception of the believing community, making it part of the contributions of Jesus to the contextualization of the community. The invitation to the human community that culminated in the conception of the believing community is the product of the incarnation (John 1:12–13, 35–42). The gathering of the first community affirms the entry requirements of the community of God stipulated in the prologue, allowing subsequent believers to understand how to become members of the community (cf. John 1:12).

Furthermore, through the incarnation, Jesus demonstrates the possibility of contextualizing the values of the eternal society in the world and how the disciples must live as participants in the community of God. For instance, in the foot-washing narrative, he demonstrates the nature of reciprocal service that must characterize the community by washing the feet of the disciples and making that value a paradigm for emulation (John 13:3–17). Additionally, he redefines love for the disciples through his death by demonstrating what it must impel—sacrificial giving—and commands them to imitate him through reciprocal love (cf. John 15:13, 17).

Most importantly, the death of Jesus is an essential component of the mission of universalizing the community of God. Though Jesus discussed the theme of the universalization of the believing community before his crucifixion and Gentiles became part of the community, his death reinforced this reality. Through his death, he destroyed the temple wall that divided worshippers into Jews and Gentiles and enforced the divine will for the new community of God.[8] Given that the crucifixion could only happen in the context of the incarnation (not in his pre-incarnate state), it serves as one of the contributions of the Son to the mission of contextualizing the eternal community.

Thus, the above indicators reveal that the Logos (Jesus) plays a critical role in establishing the origin and character of the concept of an eternal community in John and the incarnation of its values on earth. It further indicates that building a genuine communalistic community starts with a relationship with Jesus as the Way and expositor (John 1:18; 14:6). Union with Jesus, the Way, gives the individual access to the

---

8. Barrett, *Gospel According to St. John*, 195; Brodie, *Gospel According to John*, 179; Köstenberger, *John*, 105.

community of God. Furthermore, as the expositor of the ideal community, embracing Jesus culminates in receiving the revelation about the *modus vivendi*, or character, of the community of God and the impetus necessary for transforming the believing community into a society that participates in the mission of God for the world by incarnating its values.

The Relationship Between John's Culture and that of the Akans

The study aimed to analyze the relationship between John's culture and that of the Akans because it helps establish how the biblical culture can guide Akan Christians to revitalize their tradition of communalism, which is challenged by urbanization, globalization, and the materialistic elements in the Akan culture. The study indicates that both cultures share similarities that legitimize the application of solutions proposed by John to Akan sociocultural maladies. Some of these are, for instance, the emphasis on communalism and the struggle to incarnate cultural values.

The study reveals that both cultures appreciate collectivism. Communalism in the Akan culture emanates from Akan anthropology: the creation of human beings and their placement on earth. It commences with the theomorphic view of a human being, an Akan anthropological position on the origin of the human being that teaches that all human beings have a part of God, the Creator, in them and, therefore, are children of God.[9] The Akan anthropological concept further promulgates that when God brings these children onto the earth, they descend into a human community, making a society natural to humanity.[10] And while on earth, they must live communally because none of them is self-sufficient.[11]

Similarly, the culture of John—the first-century Mediterranean culture—is communalistic: it promotes seeking the neighbor's good and, therefore, does not countenance competition because it culminates in social disharmony.[12] Furthermore, a critical analysis of John reveals that the narrative ties the appreciation for the worth of the community in the culture to their relationship with God, making it a theological value. For instance, the temple symbolizes their national, communal, and religious

---

9. Gyekye, *African Cultural Values*, 24; Appiah et al., *Proverbs*, 205.
10. Gyekye, *African Cultural* Values, 36.
11. Gyekye, *African Cultural Values*, 37; Appiah et al., *Proverbs*, 203.
12. Malina, "Collectivism," 22; Neyrey, "Group Orientation," 89.

identities.¹³ Therefore, their connection to God through temple worship creates a community of worshippers united by one God and temple. Moreover, Jewish feasts feature prominently in John because of their significance in the communal life and piety of the believing community.¹⁴ An example of a feast connected to community life is the Sabbath. One of the goals of the Shabbath celebration is to destroy social classifications and re-enact in the community the original status of humanity.¹⁵ Therefore, breaking it is practically tantamount to touching their communal identity.¹⁶

Nevertheless, the Akan and Johannine cultures grapple with incarnating their cultural values. In his submissions on communalism in the Akan culture, Gyekye admits that even though society fulfills its duty of imparting various forms of moral knowledge from generation to generation, not everyone practices the values communicated to them.¹⁷ Furthermore, the analysis of Akan maxims in chapters 4 and 5 uncovers the tension between Akan ideations on communalistic values and practices and the impact of the acquisitive element on their concept of collectivism.

Similarly, the biblical culture has its challenges. In John, the marginalized microcosmic religious community (Bethesda) that lived in expectation of divine mercies does not demonstrate values worthy of its identity (cf. John 5:1–8). Moreover, the abuse of the court of Gentiles exposes the Jews' lack of understanding of the theological significance of the temple for God's agenda for the human community and their inability to incarnate their religious values.¹⁸ The cultural challenges in marginalized and religious communities (religious leaders) reveal the magnitude of the problem—that it transcends gender and social standing.

Consequently, John can guide Akan Christians to reevaluate their concept of communalism. The reasons are that the Akan reader identifies with John because of his emphasis on collectivism and the struggle with incarnating cultural values. These elements in John indicate an appreciation of the problems confronting Akan communalism. Additionally, John addresses some sociocultural challenges, such as the problem of

---

13. See Köstenberger, *John*, 105.
14. Yee, *Jewish Feasts*, 27.
15. Nelson, *Deuteronomy*, 83; Hasel, "Sabbath," 32.
16. O'Day and Hylen, *John*, 64.
17. Gyekye, *Philosophy*, 212.
18. See Köstenberger, *John*, 102.

incarnating communalistic values. Furthermore, it explains the divine paradigm and how the believing community can become a remedy for its sociocultural challenges. Finally, Jesus demonstrates through his exemplary earthly life that it is possible to incarnate values worthy of the community of God. Since Akan Christians are part of the universalized community of God and have a call to imitate God, they can depend on the proposed solutions in John because of their revelatory and transformative character: participating in the eternal and ideal community by dwelling in the Vine for the strength to contextualize its communal values (cf. John 15:1–17).

Recommendations

The study reveals that though the Akan community appreciates collectivism, the gap between theory and practice, coupled with the tension between communalism and individualism, makes it imperative for Akan Christians to reevaluate their cultural values through the lens of the idea of community in John. Therefore, the research makes the following academic and pastoral-oriented recommendations: For academia, the researcher recommends further research on the Akan culture, focusing on the aspect of the Akan community concept that many scholars overlook—the materialistic elements in the culture—for a better appraisal of Akan communalism. It also recommends further studies on the Johannine community concept to complement this study.

For pastoral ministry, the study recommends that Akan Christians consider the concept of the church as a "community of God" in John. Though Akan proverbial sayings postulate the idea of the children or community of God, the believing community exists to imitate God. Further, given the transformative power of the Word of God and the inadequacies of the Akan concept, paying attention to what Jesus proposes in John helps the believers fulfill their mission of imitating the eternal community.

Moreover, it urges the Akan believing community to redefine Christian leadership through the lens of the Johannine characterization of Jesus. Emulating the servant-leadership style of Jesus helps to renounce every form of power game and ignite a sense of humility, service, and sacrifice in the community of faith.

Finally, it advocates that love should be the undergirding principle of communalism, not mutual benefits.

Bibliography

Abbott, Edwin A. *Johannine Vocabulary: A Comparison of the Words of the Fourth Gospel with Those of the Three*. Eugene, OR: Wipf & Stock, 1905.

Abraham, W. Emmanuel. "Crisis in African Cultures." In *Person and Community: Ghanaian Philosophical Studies I*, edited by Kwasi Wiredu and Kwame Gyekye, 13–38. Washington DC: Council for Research in Values and Philosophy, 2010.

Ackah, Christian A. *Akan Ethics: A Study of the Moral Ideas and the Moral Behaviour of the Akan Tribes of Ghana*. Accra: Ghana Universities Press, 1988.

Adamo, David T. *Reading and Interpreting the Bible in African Indigenous Churches*. Eugene, OR: Wipf & Stock, 2001.

Anderson, Paul N. "Anti-Semitism and Religious Violence as Flawed Interpretations of the Gospel of John." In *John and Judaism: A Contested Relationship in Context*, edited by R. Alan Culpepper and Paul N. Anderson, 265–312. Atlanta: SBL, 2017. https://digitalcommons.georgefox.edu/ccs/289.

———. *The Riddles of the Fourth Gospel: An Introduction to John*. Minneapolis: Fortress, 2011.

Appiah, Peggy, and Kwame Anthony Appiah. "Some Akan Proverbs." *NER* 21 (2000) 119–27. https://www.jstor.org/stable/40244520.

Appiah, Peggy, et al. *Bu Me Bɛ: Proverbs of the Akans*. Oxfordshire: Ayebia Clarke, 2007.

Apt, Nana. "Coping with Old Age in Africa." In *Longevity and Quality of Life: Opportunities and Challenges*, edited by Robert N. Butler and Claude Jasmin, 225–34. New York: Kluwer, 2000.

Arthur, K. G. F. *Cloth as Metaphor: (Re)Reading the Adinkra Cloth Symbols of the Akan of Ghana*. Accra: Afoaks, 2001.

Asante, Emmanuel. *Toward an African Christian Theology of the Kingdom of God: The Kingship of Onyame*. New York: Mellen University Press, 1995.

Asiedu-Peprah, Martin. *Johannine Sabbath Conflicts as Juridical Controversy: An Exegetical Study of John 5 and 9:1—10:21*. New England Review 2.132. Tübingen: Mohr/Siebeck, 2001.

Aune, David E. *The Cultic Setting of Realized Eschatology in Early Christianity*. Leiden: Brill, 1972.

Aye-Addo, Charles S. *Akan Christology: An Analysis of the Christologies of John Samuel Pobee and Kwame Bediako in Conversation with the Theology of Karl Barth*. Eugene, OR: Pickwick, 2013.

Bannerman, Joseph Y. *Mfantse-Akan Mbebusem Nkyerekyeremu: Ghanaian Proverbs Explained and Translated into English*. Accra: Private Printing, 1927.

Barnes, Albert. "John 5." In *Notes on the Bible*. London: Blackie and Son, 1834. Internet Sacred Texts Archive. https://sacred-texts.com/bib/cmt/barnes/joh005.htm.

Barrett, Charles K. *The Gospel According to St. John: An Introduction with Commentary and Notes on the Greek Text*. 2nd ed. Philadelphia: Westminster John Knox, 1978.

Bauckham, Richard. *Gospel of Glory: Major Themes in Johannine Theology*. Grand Rapids: Baker Academic, 2015.

———. *The Testimony of the Beloved Disciple: Narrative, History, and Theology in the Gospel of John*. Grand Rapids: Baker Academic, 2007.

Beasley-Murray, George R. *John*. WBC 36. Waco, TX: Word, 1987.

Bediako, Kwame. *Christianity in Africa: The Renewal of a Non-Western Religion*. New York: Orbis, 1995.

———. *Theology and Identity: The Impact of Culture upon Christian Thought in the Second Century and Modern Africa*. Oxford: Regnum, 1999.

Beutler, Johannes. *A Commentary on the Gospel of John*. Translated by Michael Tait. Grand Rapids: Eerdmans, 2013.

———. *Judaism and the Jews in the Gospel of John*. subBi 30. Rome: Pontficio Instituto Biblico, 2006.

Blay, Yaba A. "Akan." In vol. 1 of *Encyclopedia of African Religion*, edited by Molefi K. Asante and Ama Mazama, 23–26. Los Angeles: Sage, 2009.

Boakye, Lawrence. "Akan Oral Tradition as Functional Epistemology in Scholarship, Social Change, and Development in Ghana." In *Religion and Sustainable Development: Ghanaian Perspectives*, edited by George Ossom-Batsa et al., 27–44. Rome: Urbaniana University Press, 2018.

Boer, Martinus C. de. "The Depiction of 'the Jews' in John's Gospel: Matters of Behaviour and Identity." In *Anti-Judaism and the Fourth Gospel*, edited by Reimund Bieringer et al., 141–57. Louisville: Westminster John Knox, 2001.

———. *Johannine Perspectives on the Death of Jesus*. Contributions to Biblical Exegesis and Theology 17. Kampen: Pharos, 1996.

Boismard, Mane-Émile. "Bethzatha ou Siloé." *RB* 106 (1999) 206–18.

———. *St. John's Prologue*. London: Blackfriars, 1957.

Borchert, Gerald L. *John 1—11: An Exegetical and Theological Exposition of Holy Scripture*. New American Commentary 25A. Nashville: B&H, 2002.

———. *John 12—21: An Exegetical and Theological Exposition of Holy Scripture*. New American Commentary 25B. Nashville: B&H, 1996.

Borgen, Peder. *The Gospel of John: More Light from Philo, Paul, and Archaeology*. Supplement to Novum Testamentum 154. Leiden: Brill, 2014.

———. "Logos Was the True Light: Contributions to the Interpretation of the Prologue of John." *NovT* 14 (1972) 115–30.

———. "Observations on the Targumic Character of the Prologue of John." *NTS* 16 (1970) 288–95.

Brant, Jo-Ann A. *John*. Paideia: Commentaries on the New Testament. Grand Rapids: Baker Academic, 2011.

Brodie, Thomas L. *The Gospel According to John: A Literary and Theological Commentary*. New York: Oxford University Press, 1993.

———. *The Quest for the Origin of John's Gospel: A Source-Oriented Approach*. New York: Oxford University Press, 1993.

Brown, Jeannine K. *The Disciples in Narrative Perspective: The Portrayal and Unction of the Matthean Disciples.* SBL Academia Biblica 9. Atlanta: Society of Biblical Literature, 2002.

———. *Scripture as Communication: Introducing Biblical Hermeneutics.* Grand Rapids: Baker Academic, 2007.

Brown, Raymond E. *The Community of the Beloved Disciple: The Life, Loves and Hate of an Individual Church in New Testament Times*: New York: Paulist, 1979.

———. *The Gospel According to John I-XII: Introduction, Translation, and Notes.* Anchor Bible. New York: Doubleday, 1996.

———. *The Gospel and Epistles of John: A Concise Commentary.* Collegeville, MN: Liturgical, 1988.

———. *An Introduction to the New Testament.* Anchor Yale Bible Reference Library. New Haven: Yale University Press, 2016.

Bruce, Frederick F. *The Gospel of John: Introduction, Exposition, and Notes.* Grand Rapids: Eerdmans, 1993.

Bruner, Frederick D. *The Gospel of John: A Commentary.* Grand Rapids: Eerdmans, 2012.

Bultmann, Rudolf. *The Gospel of John: A Commentary.* Translated by George R. Beasley-Murray. Philadelphia: Westminster John Knox, 1971.

Burge, Gary M. *The Anointed Community: The Holy Spirit in the Johannine Tradition.* Grand Rapids: Eerdmans, 1987.

———. *Jesus and the Land: How the New Testament Transformed "Holy Land" Theology.* Grand Rapids: Baker Academic, 2010.

Bystrom, Raymond. *God Among Us: Studies in the Gospel of John.* Luminaire Studies. Winnipeg, MB: Kindred, 2003.

Campbell, Joan C. *Kinship Relations in the Gospel of John.* Catholic Biblical Quarterly Monograph Series 42. Eugene, OR: Wipf & Stock, 2023.

Carson, Donald A. *The Gospel According to John.* Pillar New Testament Commentary. Grand Rapids: Eerdmans, 1991.

Chennattu, Rekha M. "Scripture." In *How John Works: Storytelling in the Fourth Gospel*, edited by Douglas Estes and Ruth Sheridan, 171–86. Atlanta: SBL, 2016.

Christaller, Johann G. *Three Thousand Six Hundred Ghanaian Proverbs: From the Asante and Fante Languages.* Translated by Kofi R. Lange. Studies in African Literature 2. Lewiston, NY: Edwin Mellen, 2000.

Cohen, Anthony P. *Symbolic Construction of Community.* London: Routledge, 1985.

Coloe, Mary L. "The Structure of the Johannine Prologue and Genesis 1." *ABR* 45 (1997) 40–55.

Coxon, Paul S. *Exploring the New Exodus in John: A Biblical Theological Investigation of John Chapters 5—10.* Eugene, OR: Wipf & Stock, 2014.

Culpepper, R. Alan. "Anti-Judaism in the Fourth Gospel as a Theological Problem for Christian Interpreters." In *Anti-Judaism and the Fourth Gospel*, edited by Reimund Bieringer et al., 61–82. Louisville: Westminster John Knox, 2001.

———. *The Gospel and Letters of John.* London: Abingdon, 1998.

———. "John 5:1–18: A Sample of Narrative-Critical Commentary." In *The Gospel of John as Literature: An Anthology of Twentieth-Century Perspectives*, edited by Mark W. G. Stibbe, 193–208. Leiden: Brill, 1993.

———. "The Pivot of John's Gospel." *NTS* 27 (1980) 1–31.

Daise, Michael A. *Feasts in John: Jewish Festivals and Jesus' Hour in the Fourth Gospel.* WUNT 2.229. Tübingen: Mohr/Siebeck, 2007.

Dalcour, Edward L. *A Definitive Look at Oneness Theology: Defending the Tri-Unity of God.* Lanham: University Press of America, 2005.

Danquah, Joseph B. *The Akan Doctrine of God: A Fragment of Gold Coast Ethics and Religion.* London: Frank Cass, 1968.

Dennison, James T. "The Prologue of John's Gospel." *Kerux* 8 (1993) 3–9.

Dickson, Kwesi A. *Aspects of Religion and Life in Africa.* Accra: Ghana Academy of Arts and Sciences, 1977.

Dodd, Charles H. "Behind a Johannine Dialogue." In *More New Testament Studies*, edited by Charles H. Dodd, 41–57. Manchester: Manchester University Press, 1968.

———. *Historical Tradition in the Fourth Gospel.* Cambridge: Cambridge University Press, 1963.

Dogbe, Korsi. "Concept of Community and Community Support Systems in Africa." *Anthropos* 75 (1980) 781–98.

Downs, David J. "Economics, Taxes, and Tithes." In *The World of the New Testament: Cultural, Social and Historical Contexts*, edited by Joel B. Green and Lee M. McDonald, 156–68. Grand Rapids: Baker Academic, 2013.

Dudovskiy, John. "Purposive Sampling." Business Research Methodology, n.d. https://research-methodology.net/sampling-in-primary-data-collection/purposive-sampling.

Dunn, James D. G. "The Embarrassment of History: Reflections on the Problem of 'Anti-Judaism' in the Fourth Gospel." In *Anti-Judaism and the Fourth Gospel*, edited by Reimund Bieringer et al., 41–60. Louisville: Westminster John Knox, 2001.

———. *The Evidence for Jesus.* Louisville: Westminster John Knox, 1985.

———. "Let John be John: A Gospel for Its Time." In *The Gospel and the Gospels*, edited by Peter Stuhlmacher, 293–322. Grand Rapids: Eerdmans, 1991.

Dzobo, Noah K. "African Symbols and Proverbs as Source of Knowledge and Truth." In *Person and Community: Ghanaian Philosophical Studies I*, edited by Kwasi Wiredu and Kwame Gyekye, 83–100. Washington DC: Council for Research in Values and Philosophy, 2010.

Esler, Philip F., and Ronald A. Piper. *Lazarus, Mary, and Martha: Social-Scientific Approaches to the Gospel of John.* Minneapolis: Fortress, 2006.

Estes, Douglas C. *The Questions of Jesus in John: Logic, Rhetoric and Persuasive Discourse.* Biblical Interpretation Series 115. Leiden: Brill, 2013.

Estrada, Rodolfo G., III. *A Pneumatology of Race in the Gospel of John: An Ethnocritical Study.* Eugene, OR: Wipf & Stock, 2019.

Evans, Craig A. *Word and Glory: On the Exegetical and Theological Background of John's Prologue.* Journal for the Study of the New Testament Supplement Series 89. Sheffield: Sheffield Academic, 1993.

Frey, Jörge. *The Glory of the Crucified One: Christology and Theology in the Gospel of John.* Translated by Wayne Coppins and Christoph Heilig. Waco, TX: Baylor University Press, 2018.

Fuhr, Richard A., Jr., and Andreas J. Köstenberger. *Inductive Bible Study: Observation, Interpretation, and Application through the Lenses of History, Literature, and Theology.* Nashville: B&H, 2016.

Gadamer, Hans-Georg, *Truth and Method.* Translated and revised by Joel Weinsheimer and Donald G. Marshall. London: Bloomsbury, 2013.

Gatti, Nicoletta. "Toward a Dialogic Hermeneutics: Reading Genesis 4:1–16 with Akan Eyes." *HBTH* 39 (2017) 46–67.

Getui, Mary N., et al., eds. *Interpreting the New Testament in Africa.* Nairobi: Acton, 2001.

Gharbin, Godibert K. "Service and Care in the Johannine and Akan Conceptual Schemas: Inculturation Hermeneutics." *ERATS* 9 (2023) 491–99.

Gharbin, Godibert K., and Ernest van Eck. "Building a United Community: Reading the Johannine Concept of Unity through the Eyes of an Akan Christian." *HvTSt* 79 (2023) 1–7.

———. "The Johannine Prologue: A Hermeneutical Key to the Community Theme." *VE* 43 (2022) 1–8.

———. "Redefining Love: Engaging the Johannine and Akan Concepts of Love through Dialogic Hermeneutics." *HvTSt* 79 (2023) 1–6.

———. "Solitude in the Multitude: A Christological Response to Loneliness in the Akan Community of God." *VE* 44 (2023) 1–8.

———. "The True Vine and the Branches: Exploring the Community Ideation in John 15:1—16:3." *VE* 44 (2023) 1–9.

Grenz, Stanley J. *Created for Community: Connecting Christian Belief with Christian Living.* Grand Rapids: Baker Academic, 1998.

———. *Theology for the Community of God.* Grand Rapids: Eerdmans, 2000.

Gusfield, Joseph R. *Community: A Critical Response.* Oxford: Basil Blackwell, 1975.

Gyekye, Kwame. *African Cultural Values: An Introduction.* Accra: Sankofa, 1996.

———. *An Essay on African Philosophical Thought: The Akan Conceptual Scheme.* Rev. ed. Philadelphia: Temple University Press, 1995.

———. *Philosophy, Culture, and Vision: African Perspectives.* Accra: Sub-Saharan, 2013.

Hamilton, Victor P. *The Book of Genesis: Chapters 1—17.* Grand Rapids: Eerdmans, 1990.

Harrington, Daniel J. "Biblical Perspectives." In *Jesus and Virtue Ethics: Building Bridges between New Testament Studies and Moral Theology,* edited by Daniel J. Harrington and James F. Keenan, 126–29. Chicago: Sheed and Ward, 2002.

Harris, Elizabeth. *Prologue and Gospel: The Theology of the Fourth Evangelist.* Journal for the Study of the New Testament Supplement Series 107. Sheffield: Sheffield Academic, 1994.

Harris, Murray J. *Jesus as God: The New Testament Use of Theos in Reference to Jesus.* Eugene, OR: Wipf & Stock, 2008.

———. *John.* Exegetical Guide to the Greek New Testament. Nashville, TN: B&H Academic, 2015.

Harris, W. Hall, and W. Hall Harris III. *1, 2, 3 John—Comfort and Counsel for a Church in Crisis.* Exegetical Commentary on the Letters of John. Dallas: Biblical Studies, 2003.

Harrison, John P., and James D. Dvorak, eds. *The New Testament Church: The Challenge of Developing Ecclesiologies.* McMaster Biblical Studies Series 1. Eugene, OR: Pickwick, 2012.

Hasel, Gerhard F. "The Sabbath in the Pentateuch." In *The Sabbath in Scripture and History,* edited by Kenneth A. Strand, 21–43. Washington, DC: Review and Herald, 1982.

Howard-Hassmann, Rhoda E. *Human Right in Commonwealth Africa*. Totowa, NJ: Rowman and Littlefield, 1986.
Ikuenobe, Polycarp. *Philosophical Perspectives on Communalism and Morality in African Traditions*. Lanham, MD: Lexington, 2006.
Jones, Larry P. *The Symbol of Water in the Gospel of John*. Journal for the Study of the New Testament Supplement Series 145. Sheffield: Sheffield Academic, 1997.
Jonge, Henk J. de. "The Jews in the Gospel of John." In *Anti-Judaism and the Fourth Gospel*, edited by Reimund Bieringer et al., 121–40. Louisville: Westminster John Knox, 2001.
Kanagaraj, Jey J. *John: A New Covenant Commentary*. New Covenant Commentary Series 4. Eugene, OR: Cascade, 2013.
———. *"Mysticism" in the Gospel of John: An Inquiry into its Background*. Journal for the Study of the New Testament Supplement Series 158. Sheffield: Sheffield Academic, 1998.
Kaunda, Kenneth. *Letter to My Children*. London: Longman, 1973.
Keenan James F. "Justice and Social Justice." In *Jesus and Virtue Ethics: Building Bridges Between New Testament Studies and Moral Theology*, edited by Daniel J. Harrington and James F. Keenan, 121–26. Chicago: Sheed and Ward, 2002.
Keener, Craig S. *The Gospel of John: A Commentary*. Vol. 1. Grand Rapids: Baker Academic, 2003.
———. "'We Beheld His Glory!' (John 1:14)." In vol. 2 of *John, Jesus, and History: Aspects of Historicity in the Fourth Gospel*, edited by Paul N. Anderson et al., 15–26. SBL Symposium Series 44. Atlanta: SBL, 2009.
Kissi, Seth. "Social Identity in Hebrews and the Akan Community of Ghana." PhD diss., University of Pretoria, 2017.
Klink, Edward W., III. *The Sheep of the Fold: The Audience and Origin of the Gospel of John*. Cambridge: Cambridge University Press, 2007.
Kobel, E. *Dining with John: Communal Meals and Identity Formation in the Fourth Gospel and its Historical and Cultural Contexts*. Biblical Interpretation Series 109. Leiden: Brill, 2011.
Koester, Craig R. *Symbolism in the Fourth Gospel: Meaning, Ministry, Community*. 2nd ed. Minneapolis: Fortress, 2003.
Kok, Jacobus. *New Perspectives on Healing, Restoration and Reconciliation in John's Gospel*. Biblical Interpretation Series 149. Leiden: Brill, 2017.
Köstenberger, Andreas J. *Encountering John: The Gospel in Historical, Literary, and Theological Perspective*. 2nd ed. Grand Rapids: Baker Academic, 2013.
———. *John*. Baker Exegetical Commentary on the New Testament. Grand Rapids: Baker Academic, 2004.
———. *The Missions of Jesus and the Disciples According to the Fourth Gospel: With Implications for the Fourth Gospel's Purpose and the Mission of the Contemporary Church*. Grand Rapids: Eerdmans, 1998.
Kruse, Colin G. *The Gospel According to John: An Introduction and Commentary*. Grand Rapids: Eerdmans, 2003.
Kunene, Musa Victor M. *Communal Holiness in the Gospel of John: The Vine Metaphor as a Test Case with Lessons from African Hospitality and Trinitarian Theology*. Carlisle: Langham Monographs, 2012.
Kysar, Robert. *John: The Naverick Gospel*. Rev. ed. Louisville: Westminster John Knox, 1993.

———. *Voyages with John: Charting the Fourth Gospel*. Waco, TX: Baylor University Press, 2005.
Labahn, Micheal. "Living Word(s) and the Bread of Life." In *What We Have Heard from the Beginning: The Past, Present and Future of Johannine Studies*, edited by Tom Thatcher, 59–62. Waco, TX: Baylor University Press, 2007.
Lacan, Marc-Fr. "Le Prologue de Saint Jean: Ses Thèmes, sa Structure, son Mouvement." *LumVie* 33 (1957) 91–110.
Lamarche, Pierre. "Le Prologue de Jean." *RSR* 52 (1964) 529–32.
La Potterie, Ignace de. "Structure du Prologue de Saint Jean." *NTS* 30 (1984) 354–81.
Lim, Sung U. *Otherness and Identity in the Gospel of John*. Cham: Springer, 2021.
Lindars, Barnabas. "The Persecution of Christians in John 15:18—16:4a." In *Suffering and Martyrdom in the New Testament*, edited by William Horbury and Brian McNeill, 48–69. Cambridge: Cambridge University Press, 1981.
Loader, William. *Jesus in John's Gospel: Structure and Issues in Johannine Christology*. Grand Rapids: Eerdmans, 2017.
Loba-Mkole, Jean C. "Rise of Intercultural Biblical Exegesis in Africa." *HvTSt* 64 (2008) 1348–64.
Lund, Nils W. "The Influence of Chiasmus upon the Structure of the Gospels." *ATR* 13 (1931) 42–46.
Malina, Bruce J. "Collectivism in Mediterranean Culture." In *Understanding the Social World of the New Testament*, edited by Richard E. DeMaris and Dietmar Neufeld, 17–28. London: Routledge, 2010.
———. "Love." In *Biblical Social Values and their Meaning: A Handbook*, edited by John J. Pilch and Bruce J. Malina, 110–14. Peabody, MA: Hendrickson, 1993.
———. *The New Testament World: Insights from Cultural Anthropology*. Rev. ed. Louisville: Westminster John Knox, 1993.
———. "Patronage." In *Biblical Social Values and their Meaning: A Handbook*, edited by John J. Pilch and Bruce J. Malina, 133–37. Peabody, MA: Hendrickson, 1993.
———. "Pity." In *Biblical Social Values and their Meaning: A Handbook*, edited by John J. Pilch and Bruce J. Malina, 139. Peabody, MA: Hendrickson, 1993.
———. "Who Are We? Who Are They? Who Am I? Who Are You (Sing.)? Explaining Identity, Social and Individual." *ASE* 24 (2007) 103–9.
Malina, Bruce J., and Richard L. Rohrbaugh. *Social Science Commentary on the Synoptic Gospels*. Minneapolis: Fortress, 2003.
Maluleke, Tinyiko S. "Identity and Integrity in African Theology: A Critical Analysis." *Religion and Theology* 8 (2001) 210–19.
Marguerat, Daniel, and Yvan Bourquin. *How to Read Bible Stories: An Introduction to Narrative Criticism*. Translated by John Bowden. London: SCM, 1999.
Martey, Emmanuel. *African Theology: Inculturation and Liberation*. Eugene, OR: Wipf & Stock, 2009.
Martyn, James L. *History and Theology in the Fourth Gospel*. 3rd ed. Louisville: Westminster John Knox, 2003.
Maxey, James A. *From Orality to Orality: A New Paradigm for Contextual Translation of the Bible*. Biblical Performance Criticism Series 2. Eugene, OR: Cascade, 2009.
Mbiti, John S. *African Religions and Philosophy*. 2nd ed. Oxford: Heinemann, 1989.
———. "The Bible in African Culture." In *Paths of African Theology*, edited by Rosino Gibellini, 27–39. Maryknoll: Orbis, 1994.

———. "Children Confer Glory on a Home." In *Hearing and Keeping: Akan Proverbs*, edited by John S. Mbiti, ix–xiv. Accra: Asempa, 1997.

———. *Introduction to African Religion*. Nairobi: Hennemann, 1977.

McGrath, Alister E. *Christian Theology: An Introduction*. 3rd ed. Oxford: Blackwell, 2001.

McHugh, John F. *A Critical and Exegetical Commentary on John 1—4*. Edited by Graham N. Stanton. International Critical Commentary. London: T&T Clark, 2009.

Menkiti, Ifeanyi A. "Person and Community in African Thought." in *African Philosophy: An Introduction*, edited by Richard A. Wright, 171–81. New York: University Press, 1984.

Metzger, Bruce M. *A Textual Commentary on the Greek New Testament: A Companion Volume to the United Bible Societies' Greek New Testament*. 3rd ed. London: United Bible Societies, 1971.

Moloney, Francis J. *Belief in the Word: Reading the Fourth Gospel: John 1—4*. Minneapolis: Fortress, 1993.

———. *Glory Not Dishonor: Reading John 13—21*. Minneapolis: Augsburg Fortress, 1998.

———. *The Gospel of John*. Sacra Pagina 4. Collegeville, MN: Liturgical, 1998.

———. *Signs and Shadows: Reading John 5—12*. Minneapolis: Fortress, 1996.

———. "The Structure and Message of John 15:1—16:3." *AusBR* 35 (1987) 35–49.

Moltmann, Jürgen. "God in the World—the World in God: Perichoresis in Trinity and Eschatology." In *The Gospel of John and Christian Theology*, edited by Richard Bauckham and Carl Mosser, 369–81. Grand Rapids: Eerdmans, 2008.

Morris, Leon. *The Gospel According to John*. Rev. ed. Grand Rapids: Eerdmans, 1995.

Mounce, William D. *Basics of Biblical Greek Grammar*. 2nd ed. Grand Rapids: Zondervan, 1993.

Moxnes, Halvor. *The Economy of the Kingdom: Social Conflict and Economic Relations in Luke's Gospel*. Philadelphia: Fortress, 1988.

Nasselqvist, Dan. "Style." In *How John Works: Storytelling in the Fourth Gospel*, edited by Douglas Estes and Ruth Sheridan, 23–40. Atlanta: SBL, 2016.

Neequaye, George K. "Personhood in Africa." In *The Palgrave Handbook of African Social Ethics*, edited by Nimi Wariboko and Toyin Falola, 103–27. London: Palgrave Macmillan, 2020.

Nelson, Richard D. *Deuteronomy: A Commentary*. Old Testament Library. Louisville: Westminster John Knox, 2004.

Newman, Barclay M., and Eugene A. Nida. *A Translator's Handbook on the Gospel of John*. New York: United Bible Societies, 1980.

Neyrey, Jerome H. "Dyadism." In *Biblical Social Values and their Meaning: A Handbook*, edited by John J. Pilch and Bruce J. Malina, 49–52. Peabody, MA: Hendrickson, 1993.

———. "Group Orientation." In *Biblical Social Values and their Meaning: A Handbook*, edited by John J. Pilch and Bruce J. Malina, 88–91. Peabody, MA: Hendrickson, 1993.

Ngewa, Samuel M. *The Gospel of John*. Nairobi: Evangel, 2003.

Nkansah-Kyerementeng, Kofi. *Akan Heritage*. Accra: Sebewie, 1999.

———. *The Akans of Ghana: Their Customs, History, and Institutions*. 2nd rev. ed. Kumasi: Sebewie, 2010.

Nukunya, Godwin K. *Tradition and Change in Ghana: An Introduction to Sociology.* Accra: Woeli, 2016.
O'Day, Gail R., and Susan E. Hylen. *John.* Westminster Bible Companion. Louisville: Westminster John Knox, 2006.
Odeberg, Hugo. *The Fourth Gospel Interpreted in its Relation to Contemporaneous Religious Currents in Palestine and the Hellenistic-Oriental World.* Uppsala: Almqvist and Wiksells, 1929.
Opoku, Kofi A. *Hearing and Keeping: Akan Proverbs.* Vol. 2. Accra: Asempa, 1997.
———. *West African Traditional Religion.* Accra: FEP, 1978.
Opokuwaa, Nana Akua K. *Akan Protocol: Remembering the Traditions of our Ancestors.* New York: Authors Choice, 2005.
Osborne, Grant R. *The Hermeneutical Spiral: A Comprehensive Introduction to Biblical Interpretation.* 2nd ed. Downers Grove, IL: InterVarsity, 2006.
Ossom-Batsa, George. "African Interpretation of the Bible in Communicative Perspective." *GBT* 2 (2007) 91–104.
———. "Biblical Exegesis in the African Context: A Communicative Approach." In *Unpacking the Sense of the Sacred: A Reader in the Study of Religions*, edited by Abamfo O. Atiemo et al., 128–34. Banbury: Ayebia Clarke, 2014.
Painter, R. Jackson. *The Gospel of John: A Thematic Approach.* Eugene, OR: Wipf & Stock, 2011.
———. "The Signs of the Messiah and the Quest for Eternal Life." In *What We Have Heard from the Beginning: The Past, Present and Future of Johannine Studies*, edited by Tom Thatcher, 233–56. Waco, TX: Baylor University Press, 2007.
Penwell, Stewart. *Jesus the Samaritan: Ethnic Labelling in the Gospel of John.* Biblical Interpretation Series 170. Leiden: Brill, 2019.
Pilch, John J. "Cooperativeness." In *Biblical Social Values and Their Meaning: A Handbook*, edited by John J. Pilch and Bruce J. Malina, 33–36. Peabody, MA: Hendrickson, 1993.
———. *Healing in the New Testament: Insights from Medical and Mediterranean Anthropology.* Minneapolis: Fortress, 2000.
Pilch, John J., and Bruce J. Malina. "Introduction." In *Biblical Social Values and their Meaning: A Handbook*, edited by John J. Pilch and Bruce J. Malina, xiii–xxxix. Peabody, MA: Hendrickson, 1993.
Plevnik, Joseph. "Honour or Shame." In *Biblical Social Values and their Meaning: A Handbook*, edited by John J. Pilch and Bruce J. Malina, 95–104. Peabody, MA: Hendrickson, 1993.
Porter, Stanley E. *John, His Gospel and Jesus: In Pursuit of the Johannine Voice.* Grand Rapids: Eerdmans, 2015.
Powell, Mark A. *What is Narrative Criticism?* New Testament Series. Minneapolis: Fortress, 1990.
Pryor, John W. "Covenant and Community in John's Gospel." *RTR* 47 (1988) 44–51.
———. *John, Evangelist of the Covenant People: The Narrative and Themes of the Fourth Gospel.* London: Longman and Todd, 1992.
Quast, Kevin. *Reading the Gospel of John: An Introduction.* New York: Paulist, 1991.
Rattray, Robert S. *Ashanti Proverbs.* Oxford: Clarendon, 1916.
Reinhartz, Adele. "Jews and Jews in the Fourth Gospel." In *Anti-Judaism and the Fourth Gospel*, edited by Reimund Bieringer et al., 213–30. Louisville: Westminster John Knox, 2001.

Ridderbos, Herman. *The Gospel of John*. Grand Rapids: Eerdmans, 1997.

———. "The Structure and Scope of the Prologue of the Gospel of John." *NovT* 8 (1966) 180–201.

Robinson, John A. T. "The Relation of the Prologue to the Gospel of St. John." *NTS* 9 (1963) 120–29.

Rohrbaugh, Richard L. "Ethnocentrism and Historical Questions about Jesus." In *The Social Setting of Jesus and the Gospels*, edited by Wolfgang Stegemann et al., 27–43. Minneapolis: Fortress, 2002.

———. "Honor: Core Value in the Biblical World." In *Understanding the Social World of the New Testament*, edited by Richard E. DeMaris and Dietmar Neufeld, 109–25. London: Routledge, 2010.

Salm, Steven J., and Toyin Falola. *Culture and Customs of Ghana*. Wesport, CT: Greenswood, 2002.

Schnackenburg, Rudolf. *The Gospel According to St. John*. Vol. 3. London: Burns & Oates, 1982.

Schubert, Judith. *The Gospel of John: Question by Question*. Mahwah: Paulist, 2008.

Segovia, Fernando F. "John 15:18—16:4a: A First Addition to the Original Farewell Discourse?" *CBQ* 45 (1983) 210–30.

———. "The Theology and Provenance of John 15:1–17." *JBL* 101 (1982) 115–28.

Servotte, Herman. *According to John: A Literary Reading of the Fourth Gospel*. London: Darton, Longman & Todd, 1994.

Shorter, Aylward. *Toward a Theology of Inculturation*. Eugene, OR: Wipf & Stock, 2006.

Siebald, Manfred. "Bethesda." In *A Dictionary of Biblical Tradition in English Literature*, edited by David L. Jeffrey, 84–85. Grand Rapids: Eerdmans, 1992.

Skinner, Christopher W. "Characterization." In *How John Works: Storytelling in the Fourth Gospel*, edited by Douglas Estes and Ruth Sheridan, 115–32. Atlanta: SBL, 2016.

———. *Reading John*, Eugene, OR: Wipf & Stock, 2015.

———. "Virtue in the New Testament: The Legacies of Paul and John in Comparative Perspective." In *Unity and Diversity in the Gospels and Paul: Essays in Honor of Frank J. Matera*, edited by Christopher W. Skinner and Kelly R. Iverson, 301–24. Early Christianity and its Literature 7. Atlanta: Society of Biblical Literature, 2012.

Smith, Daniel L. *Into the World of the New Testament: Greco-Roman and Jewish Texts and Context*. London: Bloomsbury, 2015.

Smith, Daniel J. "Burials and Belonging in Nigeria: Rural-Urban Relations and Social Inequality in a Contemporary African Ritual." *AA* 106 (2004) 569–79.

Smith, Dwight M. *John*. Nashville: Abingdon, 1999.

———. *The Theology of the Gospel of John*. Cambridge: Cambridge University Press, 1995.

Sogolo, Godwin. *Foundations of African Philosophy: A Definitive Analysis of Conceptual Issues in African Twilight*. Ibadan: Ibadan University Press, 1993.

Stibbe, Mark W. G. *John's Gospel*. New Testament Readings. Edited by John M. Court. London: Routledge, 1994.

Stovell, Beth M. *Mapping Metaphorical Discourse in the Fourth Gospel: John's Eternal King*. Linguistic Biblical Studies 5. Leiden: Brill, 2012.

Talbert, Charles H. *Reading John: A Literary and Theological Commentary on the Fourth Gospel and the Johannine Epistles*. Rev. ed. Macon: Smyth and Helwys, 2005.

Tanye, Gerald K. *The Church as a Family and Ethnocentrism in Sub-Saharan Africa.* Berlin: Lit Verlag, 2010.
Tenney, Merrill C. *John: The Gospel of Belief.* Grand Rapids: Eerdmans, 1997.
Thompson, Marianne M. *The God of the Gospel of John.* Grand Rapids: Eerdmans, 2001.
Ukpong, Justin S. "Christology and Inculturation: A New Testament Perspective." In *Parts of African Theology*, edited by Rosino Gibellini, 40–61. Maryknoll: Orbis, 1994.
———. "Development in Biblical Interpretation in Africa: Historical and Hermeneutical Directions." In *The Bible in Africa: Transactions, Trajectories, and Trend*, edited by Gerald O. West and Musa Dube, 11–28. Leiden: Brill, 2000.
———. "Rereading the Bible with African Eyes: Inculturation and Hermeneutics." *JTSA* 91 (1995) 3–14.
Van Eck, Ernest. "Inclusivity as the Essential Nature of the Gospels." In *Insiders versus Outsiders: Exploring the Dynamic Relationship between Mission and Ethos in the New Testament*, edited by Jacobus Kok and John A. Dunne, 49–83. New Jersey: Gorgias, 2014.
———. "When Neighbours Are Not Neighbours: A Social-Scientific Reading of the Parable of the Friend at Midnight (Luke 11:5–8)." *HvTSt* 67 (2011) 1–14.
Vincent, Marvin R. *Vincent's Word Studies in the New Testament.* Peabody, MA: Hendrickson, 2009.
Voorwinde, Stephen. "John's Prologue: Beyond Some Impasses of Twentieth-Century Scholarship." *WTJ* 63 (2002) 15–44.
Waetjen, Herman C. "Logos πρὸς τον θεόν and the Objectification of Truth in the Prologue of the Fourth Gospel." *CBQ* 63 (2001) 256–86.
Watt, Jan G. van der. *Family of the King: Dynamics of Metaphor in the Gospel According to John.* Biblical Interpretation Series 47. Leiden: Brill, 2000.
———. *An Introduction to the Johannine Gospel and Letters.* London: T&T Clark, 2007.
Webb, Robert L. *John the Baptizer and Prophet: A Sociohistorical Study.* Eugene, OR: Wipf & Stock, 1991.
Wenham, David. "Paradigms and Possibilities in the Study of John's Gospel." In *Challenging Perspectives on the Gospel of John*, edited by John Lierman, 1–13. Tübingen: Mohr Siebeck, 2006.
West, Gerald O. "African Biblical Scholarship as Post-Colonial, Tri-Polar, and a Site-of-Struggle." In *Present and Future Biblical Studies*, edited by Tat-Siong B. Liew, 240–76. Leiden: Brill, 2018.
Westcott, Brooke F. *The Gospel According to John: The Greek Text with Introduction and Notes.* Grand Rapids: Baker, 1980.
Wheaton, Gerry. *The Role of Jewish Feasts in John's Gospel.* Cambridge: Cambridge University Press, 2015.
Whitacre, Rodney A. *John.* Downers Grove, IL: InterVarsity, 1999.
Wiredu, Kwesi. "The Moral Foundations of an African Culture." In *Person and Community: Ghanaian Philosophical Studies I*, edited by Kwasi Wiredu and Kwame Gyekye, 193–206. Washington DC: Council for Research in Values and Philosophy, 2010.
Witherington, Ben, III. *John's Wisdom: A Commentary on the Fourth Gospel.* 3rd ed. Louisville: Westminster John Knox, 1995.
Wuest, Kenneth S. *The New Testament: An Expanded Translation.* Grand Rapids: Eerdmans, 1983.

———. *Wuest's Word Studies from the Greek New Testament.* Vol. 3. Grand Rapids: Eerdmans, 1973.

Yankah, Kwesi. *The Proverb in the Context of Akan Rhetoric: A Theory of Proverb Praxis.* New York: Peter Lang, 1989.

Yee, Gale A. *Jewish Feasts and the Gospel of John.* Eugene, OR: Wipf & Stock, 2007.

www.ingramcontent.com/pod-product-compliance
Lightning Source LLC
Chambersburg PA
CBHW050345230426
43663CB00010B/2001